Acting

Also by TOBY COLE (with HELEN KRICH CHINOY)

ACTORS ON ACTING
DIRECTING THE PLAY

Acting

A HANDBOOK OF THE

Stanislavski Method

Compiled by TOBY COLE
Introduction by LEE STRASBERG

Revised Edition

CROWN PUBLISHERS, INC.   NEW YORK

Published by Crown Publishers, Inc., 225 Park Avenue South, New York, New York 10003 and represented in Canada by the Canadian MANDA Group

CROWN is a trademark of Crown Publishers, Inc.

Manufactured in the United States of America

ISBN: 0-517-05035-8

15 14 13 12 11

CONTENTS

ILLUSTRATIONS

ACKNOWLEDGMENTS

This collection is primarily indebted to the New Theatre League, whose vigorous allegiance to the concept and craft of a socially responsible theatre in the decade spanning the Thirties has left a lasting heritage to the American stage. From its publication *Theatre Workshop* came the contributions to this handbook by Rapoport, Sudakov, Giatsintova and Zakhava, copyright 1936, 1937 by People's Theatre, Inc.

The excerpt from Stanislavski's *Production Plan for Othello* (Rezhisserskii Plan "Otello") and V. I. Pudovkin's *Film Acting* were made available by Helen Black.

Stanislavski's *Direction and Acting* is reprinted by permission from the Encyclopaedia Britannica (1947), article THEATRE, Volume 22, pp. 35–38.

I wish to express my thanks for generous permissions given by:

Lucie R. and Oliver Sayler for *Stanislavski To His Players;* Molly Day Thacher for *Stanislavski's Method of Acting* by Michael Chekhov; and Lee Strasberg for his many valuable suggestions on the selection and arrangement of material and for making available the Group Theatre's notes from the diary of Eugene Vakhtangov.

The photographs are from the archives of the Moscow Art Theatre Museum and Sovfoto.

TOBY COLE

INTRODUCTION

By LEE STRASBERG

A FEW YEARS AGO, a study was made of the opinions held by the dramatic
critics of various outstanding American actors. These were compared with
the opinions held within the profession. One of the illuminating results
was the discovery that the high critical evaluation of the performances of
one very respected actor was not shared by a good number of fellow
craftsmen.

The dissatisfaction of actors with their fellow craftsmen has a long and
honorable history. Shakespeare was outspoken about those "players that I
have seen play, and heard others praise, and that highly, not to speak it
profanely, that neither having the accent of Christian, nor the gait of
Christian, pagan, nor man, have so strutted and bellow'd, that I have
thought some of nature's journeymen had made men, and not made them
well, they imitated humanity so abominably."

Moliere in the "Impromptu at Versailles," wrote a devasting satire on
the rival company, a satire based not upon personal jealousy or envy, but
dissatisfaction with the principles exemplified in their art.

The modern theatre is in fact the creation of people who turned their
backs upon the outmoded acting traditions of their day and called for
the formation of a new theatre. Otto Brahm announced his intention with
an essay entitled "Old and New Acting." Andre Antoine, founder of the
"Theatre Libre," proclaimed the need for a new theatre by explaining that
though plays in a modern style were being written, they were being acted

in such outmoded fashion that the intention of the author was completely destroyed. Copeau, Craig, Meyerhold—all made the revision of the actor's training the basis of their concern with the modern theatre.

It is out of this concern that the Stanislavski system derives. It is no isolated or foreign phenomenon in the history of the theatre, but grows out of a deep, continuous desire to better the standards of the craft. What the great German critic and dramatist Lessing wrote in the eighteenth century still holds true today: "We have actors but no art of acting."

This situation is aggravated by a fact peculiar to the art of acting. In other arts, standards are formed and maintained by means of the creation of a reservoir of classic precept embodied in the works of the great masters. The 'masterworks' serve as a beacon to the young and old practitioner. It is not intended to be blindly imitated, but it serves as a constant reminder of what has already been accomplished. But in acting, the achievement dies with its creator. Each new generation must constantly rediscover for itself truths previously discovered but always lost. In this situation the teacher of acting and the text books utilized serve an unusual and important function. But if the body of masterworks which serves as a basis on which principles of any art are formed is in this case lacking, where do the teachers of acting and their text books derive the body of precept and advice they hand out? Despite the obvious importance of the subject, no one has ventured to examine the origin of their ideas and the derivation of their systems.

As we examine a variety of manuals from different periods, we become aware of a curious kinship—the same scheme of procedure, the same emphasis upon the bodily expression, and classification of the elements of physical expression, a kind of grammar of expression; and an analysis of the voice and its production, and the means by which it is suited to different ideas, characters, and moods. This has by now become such a generally recognized procedure that it seems to be accepted as the only possible one. A recent catalogue of a dramatic school states quite simply: Speech and body movement are the language of the acting art. Yet Aristotle said, "He who considers things in their first growth and origin will obtain the clearest view of them." An investigation of the rise and origin of manuals for actors may reveal some startling data.

The first modern text we are aware of derives not from theatrical experience, but from the efforts of the French academicians to create an all inclusive aesthetic theory. This book was published in 1657 under the aegis of Conrart, one of the leading lights of the French Academy. It is entitled "Traite de l'action de l'Orateur ou de la Prononciation et du Geste," and went into its third edition before it was followed by a work by Grimarest in 1707. Grimarest improves upon his predecessor who had already declared that it is by means of the voice that we express our inner actions. But Grimarest now succeeds to build the typical classification we still find in our contemporary text books, based upon vocal behavior. Hope, Joy, Grief, Fear, Jealousy, Compassion, Anger—all these are characterized by a vocal expression suitable to each emotion. He demonstrates these by examples from Corneille and Racine. But proper use of the voice is not enough, it is necessary to accompany it with gesture to give the proper semblance and vitality to the action. He does not go into detail but adds the important dictum that each passion has its facial expression. But whereas he lays down rules for the use of the voice, he is content with the remark that an actor who really feels will find the proper facial expression.

The first English handbook in 1710 takes advantage of the recent death of the great tragedian to call itself "The Life of Mr. Thomas Betterton, Wherein the Action and Utterance of the Stage, Bar, and Pulpit, are distinctly considered." While it pretends to give Mr. Betterton's ideas, it carries on where our French authors left off. The author acknowledges his indebtedness to the French but desires to improve upon them. He repeats the previous grammar of vocal expression wherein Love is expressed by a "gay, soft and charming voice; Hate by a sharp, sullen, and severe one; Grief by a sad, dull and languishing Tone; not without sometimes interrupting the Continuity of the Sound with a Sigh or Groan drawn from the very inmost of the Bosom. A tremulous and stammering voice will best express his Fear, inclining to Uncertainty and Apprehension. A loud and strong Voice, on the contrary, will most naturally show his Confidence, always supported with a decent Boldness, and daring Constancy. Nor can his auditors be more justly struck with a Sense of his Anger, than by a Voice or Tone, that is sharp, violent and impetuous, interrupted with a frequent taking of the Breath, and short Speaking" (pp. 113-114). Examples are given from Shakespeare. But our author now continues to build a pyramid of physical expression. Since "the Passions and Habits of the Mind discover themselves in our Looks, Actions and Gestures," he proceeds to describe the action of the eye, the action of the hands, the position of the head, the posture of the body, very much in the manner of most text-books today. Our author is quite aware that actors do not entirely follow this method. He cites a number of examples, amongst them Mrs. Bradshaw, who told a friend of his "that she endeavor'd first to make herself Mistress of her Part, and left the Figure and Action to Nature" (P. 41). But here we are confronted with an interesting problem. If these rules did not derive from the experience of the acting profession, where did they come from, who discovered them, who codified them, and what are they based on? Our author is clear upon this matter. "I have borrowed," says he, "from the French, but then the French drew most . . . from Quintillian and others" (p. ix).

The name Quintillian is well known as is the fact that he is the author of the classic "Institutes of Oratory" written two thousand years ago. But what is not so fully realized is that Quintillian is the direct source for the elaborate structure of vocal and physical expression taken over bodily and literally in the early manuals, and which have found their way down to the present day with slight modifications. But one may argue, does the fact that this author lived two thousand years ago make his conclusions incorrect? Human beings are universal, and the truths of human behavior may transcend the passage of time and space. Quite true! But the important point is that Quintillian's exposition never pretended and was never intended by him to apply to actors! It is a manual for speakers, public orators and lawyers—people who do not act or portray other characters, but must through speech and gesture suitable for platform behavior, convey their meaning to the audience. A good actor may be a good speaker, but the contrary is by no means true. Quintillian himself is never under the illusion that his precepts are intended for actors. Realizing that oratory can learn from acting he utilizes some examples from theatre practice and takes pains to point out on numerous occasions that the behavior of actors is different from that of the orator, and specifically warns that the latter should not try to imitate the former. "For what can be less becoming to an orator than modulations that recall the stage?" Quintillian therefore well knew what he was doing. His remarks are keen and observant. His description of certain details of behavior, for instance the use of the different fingers of the hand in creating emphasis, has never been bettered. But his book was never intended to be a guide for actors! It was mistakenly used as such by the early theoreticians and the Jesuit priests who were very influential in the training of amateur actors in the seventeenth century. And it has formed the basis of most of the current handbooks on acting, though their authors may never directly have read Quintillian. Much of the modern day training of actors is thus based on an error. The early manuals still show the traces of Quintillian's original intention in their subtitles; "Where the action and utterance of the Stage, Bar, and Pulpit, are distinctly considered." But that distinction, so clearly drawn by the Latin author and his master Cicero, has been completely obliterated.

The next important book on acting is an original work by a French journalist Remond de Sainte-Albine, published in 1747. Called "Le Comedien," it is the first to break completely with the previous oratorical school, and to address itself to a systematic discussion of the actor and his art. The work had a great influence and an odd success. Reprinted in a second edition two years later, it was translated into English as "The Actor" in 1750, and went into a second English edition in 1755. This was an enlarged version with many stories and examples from English actors added to the French author's theory. In this form it was then translated back into French in 1769 without any realization that it was based upon a French original. Utilizing Garrick's tremendous reputation it was called "Garrick ou les Acteurs Anglais" and was soon issued in a German version also available in the Scandinavian countries.

Instead of repeating the classic structure which stresses vocal and physical expresion, the author addresses himself to the central problem: What qualities are necessary to create an actor? Aware that great actors have often lacked physical or vocal means he builds a new triad. The first requisite is understanding, "for to that he is to owe the proper use of all the rest." The second is sensibility—"a disposition to be affected by the passions which plays are intended to excite." The third is spirit or fire which "consists in a daring spirit, a vivacity of imagination, and rapidity of thought" but has no connection with noise or blustering though they are too often mistaken for it by the common observer.

"It is to this spirit and fire, that the representation owes its great air of reality. Understanding will make a player perceive properly, and sensibility will make him do it feelingly. But all this may be done in reading the passage; it is this fire and spirit that produce the living character, and he who has judgment to regulate this, can never have too much of it." (The quotations are from the English edition "The Actor," 1755).

It can be seen that the author is struggling to describe in eighteenth century terms and on the basis of insufficient knowledge of psychology what we would today describe as the sensory receptivity and the emotional activity. The author is aware that he is using words to describe vague entities but his discussions are perceptive, observant and cogent. In reference to the question of the actor's intelligence, a matter still doubtfully argued today, he points out that many people hold that the actor need have no understanding. They confuse academic intellectual attainments with craft intelligence. "That kind of sense which gratifies the man of figure for shining in

14

conversation, is very different from that by which the trader amasses a fortune." As to the relation between sensibility and understanding; "People who feel the most from reading a passionate speech in a play, are not always those who understand it most perfectly; this being the effect of sensibility, a peculiar quality of the mind, not always, as already observed, proportioned to the understanding. Either of these alone therefore will not do for the player; and as it is plain he may possess one without the other. We are to acknowledge the pretensions of that actor great indeed, who has both in such a dgree that while the judgment regulates the sensibility, the sensibility animates, enlivens, and inspires the understanding." Here we have a parallel to our own Joseph Jefferson's "a warm heart and a cool mind," and Talma's "la sensibilite extreme et l'intelligence extraordinaire." Our author does not forget recitation, declamation, and how an actor should look. None of these are left out of account but they are given their proper place and proportion. Disregarding the old fashioned verbiage, and the inability to come to grips with certain concepts, due to the level of knowledge existent at that period, the argument of the book is sound and well reasoned. But dealing with imponderables (at least for that age) the book is unable to crystalize its deepening critical understanding into concrete training exercises for the actor. This inability hinders the full effectiveness of that approach. Thus while the understanding and formulation of the acting problem heightens until it reaches in the great French actor Talma's essay its best formulation—the text-books with the same stress on vocal and physical mechanics and exercises continue to deluge the market in ever increasing numbers.

Only one great effort is made to break through the morass. In the nineteenth century the Frenchman Delsarte becomes dissatisfied with the routine acting techniques taught in his time. Aware of its mechanical and stultifying character, he grows to realize that under the stress of natural instinct or emotion the body takes on the appropriate attitude or gesture, and this gesture was not at all what his teachers taught it was. But unable or unwilling to rely on what he had discovered he tried to create a new series of elaborate pictorial descriptions that ended by being just as mechanical as those he originally broke away from. The time was not ready. For the understanding of the conscious and unconscious, the functioning of the senses, the knowledge of the affective behavior, had simply not advanced far enough for it to be utilized in concrete practice.

This was the situation which Stanislavki found and tried to remedy. On the one hand a heightened critical understanding and sensitivity to the actor's problem plus the remarkable achievement of individual great actors who left no heritage but that of inspiration for their followers—on the other a remarkable mediocrity of sameness in the handbooks and textbooks of acting which have by now become legion. Stanislavski himself has stated his purpose well:

"We have retained random thoughts uttered by Shakespeare, Moliere, Ekhof, Schroeder, Goethe, Lessing, Riccoboni, the Devrients, Coquelin, Salvini, and other individual lawgivers in the realm of our art. But all these valuable opinions and advices are not systematized, and are not reduced to one common denominator, and therefore the fact remains that fundamentals which might guide the teachers of our art are missing. . . . Notwithstanding the mountains of written articles, books, lectures and theses on the art, notwithstanding the researches of the innovators . . . we had written nothing that might be of practical aid to the actor in the moment of the realization of his creativeness, or that might be of aid to the teacher at the moment he meets his pupil. All that has been written about the theatre is only philosophizing, very interesting, very deep, it is true, that speaks beautifully of the results desirable to reach in art, or criticism of the success or failure of results already reached. All these works are valuable and necessary, but not for the actual practical work in the theatre, for they are silent on how to reach certain results, on what is necessary to do firstly, secondly, thirdly, and so forth, with a beginner, or what is to be done with an experienced and spoiled actor.

"What exercises resembling solfeggi are needed by him? What scales, what arpeggi for the development of creative feeling and experience are required by the actor? They must be given numbers . . . for systematic exercises in the school and at home. All books and works of the theatre are silent on this score. There is no practical textbook." (*My Life in Art*, pp. 166-167)

The Stanislavski "system" is therefore no continuation of the textbooks of the past or present. It represents a sharp break with traditional teaching and a return to actual theatre experience. It tries to analyze why an actor is good one night and bad another, and therefore to understand what actually happens when an actor acts. His actual methods have more than vindicated themselves wherever they have been used. Theatres and actors of great variety and diversified form have created outstanding works on the basis of the training acquired by use of Stanislavski's principles. The works created are never copies or imitations of one another but are original creative achievements. That is the purpose of the Stanislavski idea. It teaches not how to play this or that part but how to create organically.

The material in this collection should therefore be extremely useful. It is written by people who have distinguished themselves in their own right. Vakhtangov was Stanislavski's greatest student, and one of the most original and striking theatre talents of our era. His early death was a great loss to the theatre of the entire world. Zakhava and Rapoport are members of the Vakhtangov Theatre, of which the former is the director. His productions are outstanding examples of the combination of the Stanislavski approach to the actor and a heightened theatric style. Sudakov has directed for the Moscow Art Theatre, and Michael Chekhov was one of its finest talents. Pudovkin is one of the great film pioneers whose remembered works are characterized by amazing reality, sweep, and vitality. What these people say is rich in theory and practical application and should help the actor enlarge his creative potentialities and realize his talent.

THE ACTOR'S RESPONSIBILITY

By CONSTANTIN STANISLAVSKI

BEFORE WE BEGIN TO STUDY, let us determine precisely what it is we want to learn. Otherwise misunderstandings may arise in the course of our studies.

Elements of that beautiful and lofty art toward which we aspire also existed in the theatre of the past.

We shall conscientiously and attentively study the old in order better to understand the new.

We shall not say that the theatre is a school. No, the theatre is entertainment.

It is not to our advantage to lose sight of this very important element. People should always go to the theatre to be entertained. Let us assume that they have come to the theatre and that we have closed the doors and turned out the lights. Now we may do whatever we want with them, instill them with whatever emotions we will.

But there are various forms of entertainment.

Let us assume that you have come to the theatre and taken a seat. Lovely stage settings sometimes a bit strident in color, sometimes more harmonious, depending on who designed them, splendid actors, marvellous g .stures, brilliant lighting effects that dazzle and overwhelm you, music— all these things arouse, agitate and stimulate your nerves more and more until at the end of the play you are applauding, shouting "Bravo!" and climbing up on the stage to thank one of the actors, embrace another, kiss a third, jostle a fourth. When you leave the theatre you feel so disturbed that you cannot sleep and so you go to a restaurant with a crowd of friends. There, at the supper table, you relive the play you have just seen, recalling the charm of a certain actress, etc., etc. . . .

But what remains of your impression after the sobering effect of a night's sleep? Practically nothing at all. And in a few days you will not even be able to recall at what theatre it was that you shouted and applauded so enthusiastically—was it at the Korsch, or the Nezlobin or the Zimin Opera House? Oh yes, you will decide it was probably at the Korsch.

I am very fond of such shows. I adore music halls and vaudeville as long as there is nothing smutty about them.

But there is another kind of theatre. You come in and take a seat as one of the audience. Without your being aware of it, the director transports you from the world of the audience to that of the stage where you become a participant in the life being depicted in the play. Something has happened to you. You no longer feel like one of the audience. When the curtain goes up you immediately say:

"I know that room. Here comes Ivan Ivanovich, and now Marie Petrovna. That man is a friend of mine . . . Yes, I know all this. But what will happen next?"

You are all attention. You look at the stage and say:

"I believe everything, everything, everything . . . There is my mother, I recognize her . . ."

The play is over, you are disturbed but in an entirely different way. Here you feel no desire to applaud.

"How can I applaud my own mother? It would seem strange, somehow . . ."

The elements contributing to your disturbed state of mind and emotions in this case are such that you are made to concentrate and think deeply. After the performance you feel no urge to go to a restaurant. You would like to sit around some happy family table with a steaming samovar on it. You feel the need for an intimate talk about life's problems, philosophical outlooks and social questions.

And this time your impression has quite a different effect after a night's sleep. In the first case you could not for the life of you remember what had made you climb up on the stage and kiss the tenor the night before. What a stupid thing to have done, was your thought the next morning. True, he had sung very well but why kiss him? How stupid!

In the second case your impressions have entered deep into your soul. Serious problems clamor for solution and you feel that something is lacking, that you have failed to understand something very important and that you must go to see the play a second time.

You feel that those people whom you saw on the stage last night have become near and dear to you. You want to share their sorrows and their joys. In them you see a part of your own soul. They have become your friends. I know people, many of them, who say:

"Let's go to the Prozorovs' tonight."

Or,

"Let's go to Uncle Vanya's."

For them it is not a matter of going to see a performance of *The Three Sisters* or of *Uncle Vanya*. They really go to see Uncle Vanya or the Prozorov sisters, as the case may be.

Old actors used to say that such intimate communion with an audience was impossible to achieve on the stage, that it could only be done in a small room. The Art Theatre, however, has found a way to accomplish this in the theatre. Perhaps this would be impossible in such a theatre as the Bolshoi or the Coliseum—there are certain limits and boundaries governing performances in such theatres—but during our tour abroad we played in the theatre at Wiesbaden which is almost as large as the Moscow Bolshoi Theatre. This proves that such art as ours can be conveyed to a large audience.

And so—

The first type of theatre is designed to entertain the eye and the ear. Therein lies its ultimate aim.

The second type of theatre uses visual and auditory impressions only as a means of penetrating deep into the heart of the audience.

In the first type it is necessary to please the eye or, perhaps, to shock it; no matter what the means, the predominating purpose is to get a strong reaction from the audience. The actor is aware of this and what doesn't he do to achieve this aim! If he lacks a sufficiently artistic temperament, he begins either to shout or to talk very quickly, or to clip his words, or to sing.

Consider for a moment how powerful the theatre is! In the theatre you can arouse an audience to ecstasy, drive it to distraction, make it tremble. Or, on the contrary, you can make the spectator sit quietly in his seat and obediently absorb whatever you wish to pour into him. You can arouse the herd instinct in the audience if you wish.

Painting, music and other arts, each of which exert a strong influence on the soul, are all brought together in the theatre, and their effect is therefore all the more powerful.

I remember meeting Leo Tolstoy for the first time at the home of Nikolai Davydov and his saying: "The theatre is the strongest pulpit for the modern man." And that is true. The theatre is more effective than the school or preaching could ever be. You must have a special desire to go to school, but people always want to go to the theatre because they always want to be entertained. At school you must be able to remember what you learn, but in the theatre you do not have to remember—everything you see and hear is so strongly impressed that the mind naturally retains the impressions.

The theatre is the strongest of weapons, but like all weapons it works both ways. It can bring the greatest good to people and it can also be the greatest of evils.

If we ask what our theatres offer the people, what will the answer be? I have in mind all our theatres, from Duse, Chaliapin and other great artists to Saburov and the Hermitage—in general, everything that can be classed under the term theatre.

The harm caused by a bad book cannot be compared with that caused by a bad theatre, either in the extent of the infection or the ease with which it spreads.

And yet, the theatre as an institution possesses elements making it an instrument of education and primarily, of course, of the aesthetic education of the masses.

Thus you see what a powerful force we are preparing ourselves to wield. You see how responsible we are to see that this force is used as it should be.

Speech made on March 10, 1911 at the first lesson for students and actors of the affiliated department of the Moscow Art Theatre.

DIRECTION
AND ACTING

By CONSTANTIN STANISLAVSKI

THEATRICAL ART HAS ALWAYS been collective, arising only where poetical-dramatic talent was actively combined with the actor's. The basis of a play is always a dramatic conception; a general artistic sense is imparted to the theatrical action by the unifying, creative genius of the actor. Thus the actor's dramatic activity begins at the foundation of the play. In the first place, each actor, either independently or through the theatre manager, must probe for the fundamental motive in the finished play—the creative idea that is characteristic of the author and that reveals itself as the germ from which his work grows organically. The motive of the play always keeps the character developing before the spectator; each personality in the work takes a part conforming to his own character; the work, then developing in the appointed direction, flows on to the final point conceived by the author. The first stage in the work of the actor and theatre manager is to probe for the germ of the play, investigating the fundamental line of action that traverses all of its episodes and is therefore called by the writer its transparent effect or action. In contrast to some theatrical directors, who consider every play only as material for theatrical repetition, the writer believes that in the production of every important drama the director and actor must go straight for the most exact and profound conception of the mind and ideal of the dramatist, and must not change that ideal for their own. The interpretation of the play and the character of its artistic incarna-

22

tion inevitably appear in a certain measure subjective, and bear the mark of the individual peculiarities of the manager and actors; but only by profound attention to the artistic individuality of the author and to his ideal and mentality, which have been disclosed as the creative germ of the play, can the theatre realize all its artistic depth and transmit, as in a poetical production, completeness and harmony of composition. Every part of the future spectacle is then unified in it by its own artistic work; each part, in the measure of its own genius, will flow on to the artistic realization aimed at by the dramatist.

The actor's task, then, begins with the search for the play's artistic seed. All artistic action—organic action, as in every constructive operation of nature—starts from this seed at the moment when it is conveyed to the mind. On reaching the actor's mind, the seed must wander around, germinate, put out roots, drinking in the juices of the soil in which it is planted, grow and eventually bring forth a lively flowering plant. Artistic process must in all cases flow very rapidly, but usually, in order that it may preserve the character of the true organic action and may lead to the creation of life, of a clear truly artistic theatrical image, and not of a trade substitute, it demands much more time than is allotted to it in the best European theatres. That is why in the writer's theatre every dramatization passes through eight to ten revisions, as is also done in Germany by the famous theatre manager and theorist, K. Hagemann. Sometimes even more than ten revisions are needed, occasionally extending over several months. But even under these conditions, the creative genius of the actor does not appear so freely as does, for instance, the creative genius of the dramatist. Bound by the strict obligations of his *collectif*, the actor must not postpone his work to the moment when his physical and psychic condition appears propitious for creative genius. Meanwhile, his exacting and capricious artistic nature is prompted by aspirations of his artistic intuition, and in the absence of creative genius is not reached by any effort of his will. He is not aided in that respect by outward technique—his skill in making use of his body, his vocal equipment and his powers of speech.

THE ARTISTIC CONDITION

But is it really impossible? Are there no means, no processes that sensibly would help us, and spontaneously lead to that artistic condition which is born of genius without any effort on its part? If that capacity is unattainable all at once, by some process or other, it may, perhaps, be acquired in parts, and through progressive stages may perfect those elements out of which the artistic condition is composed, and which are subject to our will. Of course the general run of acting does not come into being from this genius, but cannot such acting, in some measure, be brought by it near to what is evidence of genius? These are the problems which presented themselves to the writer about 20 years ago, when reflecting on the external obstacles that hamper actors' artistic genius, and partly compel substitution of the crude outward marks of the actor's profession for its results. They drove him to the rediscovery of processes of external technique, *i.e.*, methods proceeding from consciousness to sub-consciousness, in which domain flow nine-tenths of all real artistic processes. Observations both upon himself and other actors with whom he happened to rehearse, but chiefly upon growing theatrical skill in Russia and abroad, allowed him to do some generalizing, which thereupon he verified in practice.

The first is that, in an artistic condition, full freedom of body plays a principal rôle; *i.e.*, the freedom from that muscular strain which, without our knowing it, fetters us not only on the stage but also in ordinary life, hindering us from being obedient conductors of our psychic action. This muscular strain, reaching its maximum at those times when the actor is called upon to perform something especially difficult in his theatrical work, swallows up the bulk of this external energy, diverting him from activity of the higher centres. This teaches us the possibility of availing ourselves of the muscular energy of our limbs only as necessity demands, and in exact conformity with our creative efforts.

PUBLIC SOLITUDE

The second observation is that the flow of the actor's artistic force is considerably retarded by the visual auditorium and the public, whose presence may hamper his outward freedom of movement, and powerfully hinder his concentration on his own artistic taste. It is almost unnecessary to remark that the artistic achievement of great actors is always bound by the concentration of attention to the action of their own performance, and that when in that condition, *i.e.*, just when the actor's attention is taken away from the spectator, he gains a particular power over the audience, grips it, and compels it to take an active share in his artistic existence. This does not mean, of course, that the actor must altogether cease to feel the public; but the public is concerned only in so far as it neither exerts pressure on him nor diverts him unnecessarily from the artistic demands of the moment, which last might happen to him even while knowing how to regulate his attention. The actor suitably disciplined must automatically restrict the sphere of his attention, concentrating on what comes within this sphere, and only half consciously seizing on what comes within its aura. If need be, he must restrict that sphere to such an extent that it reaches a condition that may be called *public solitude*. But as a rule this sphere of attention is elastic, it expands or contracts for the actor, with regard to the course of his theatrical actions. Within the boundary of this sphere, as one of the actual aspects of the play, there is also the actor's immediate central *object of attention*, the object on which, somehow or other, his will is concentrated at the moment with which, in the course of the play, he is in inward communication. This theatrical sympathy with the object can only be complete when the actor has trained himself by long practice to surrender himself in his own impressions, and also in his reactions to those impressions, with maximum intensity: only so does theatrical action attain the necessary force, only so is created between the actual aspects of the play, *i.e.*, between the actors, that link, that living bond, which is essential for the carrying through of the play to its goal, with the general maintenance of the rhythm and time of each performance.

CONCENTRATION

But whatever may be the sphere of the actor's attention, whether it confines him at some moments to public solitude, or whether it grips the faces of all those before the stage, dramatic artistic genius, as in the preparation of the part so in its repeated performance, requires a full concentration of all the mental and physical talents of the actor, and the participation of the whole of his physical and psychic capacity. It takes hold of his sight and hearing, all his external senses; it draws out not only the periphery but also the essential depth of his existence, and it evokes to activity his memory, imagination, emotions, intelligence and will. The whole mental and physical being of the actor must be directed to that which is derived from his facial expression. At the moment of inspiration, of the involuntary use of all the actor's qualities, at that moment he actually exists. On the other hand, in the absence of this employment of his qualities, the actor is gradually led astray along the road leading to time-honored theatrical traditions; he begins to "produce" wherever he sees them, or, glancing at his own image, imitates the inward manifestations of his emotions, or tries to draw from himself the emotions of the perfected part, to "inspire" them within himself. But when forcing such an image by his own psychic equipment, with its unchanging organic laws, he by no means attains that desired result of artistic genius; he must present only the rough counterfeit of emotion, because emotions do not come to order. By no effort of conscious will can one awake them in oneself at a moment, nor can they ever be of use for creative genius striving to bring this about by searching the depths of its mind. A fundamental axiom, therefore, for the actor who wishes to be a real artist on the stage, may be stated thus: he must not play to produce emotions, and he must not involuntarily evoke them in himself.

ACTIVITY OF IMAGINATION

Considerations on the nature of artistically gifted people, however, inevitably open up the road to the possession of the emotion of the part. This road traverses activity of imagination, which in most of its stages is subject to the action of consciousness. One must not suddenly begin to operate on emotion; one must put oneself in motion in the direction of artistic imagination, but imagination—as is also shown by observations of scientific psychology—disturbs our aberrant memory, and, luring from the hidden recesses beyond the boundaries of its sense of harmony whatever elements there may be of proved emotions, organizes them afresh in sympathy with those that have arisen in our imagery. So surrounded within our figures of imagination, without effort on our part, the answer to our aberrant memory is found and the sounds of sympathetic emotion are called out from us. This is why the creative imagination presents itself afresh, the indispensable gift of the actor. Without a well developed, mobile imagination, creative faculty is by no means possible, not by instinct nor intuition nor the aid of external technique. In the acquiring of it, that which has lain dormant in the mind of the artist is, when immersed in his sphere of unconscious imagery and emotion, completely harmonized within him.

This practical method for the artistic education of the actor, directed by means of his imagination to the storing up of affective memory, is sufficiently enlarged upon; his individual emotional experience, by its limits, actually leads to the restriction of the sphere of his creative genius, and does not allow him to play parts dissimilar to those of his psychic harmony. This opinion is fundamental for the clearing away of misunderstandings of those elements of reality from which are produced fictitious creations of imagination; these are also derived from organic experience, but a wealth and variety of these creations are only obtained by combinations drawn from a trial of elements. The musical scale has only its basic notes, the solar spectrum its radical colors, but the combination of sounds in music and of colors in painting are infinite. One can in the same way speak of radical emotions preserved in imaginative memory, just as the reception in imagination of outward harmony remains in the intellectual memory; the sum of these radical emotions in the inner experience of each person is limited, but the shades and combinations are as infinite as the combinations that create activity of imagination out of the elements of inward experience.

Certainly, but the actor's outward experience—*i.e.*, his sphere of vital sensations and reflections—must always be elastic, for only in that condition can the actor enlarge the sphere of his creative faculty. On the other hand, he must judiciously develop his imagination, harnessing it again and again to new propositions. But, in order that that imaginary union which is the actor's very foundation, produced by the creative genius of the dramatist, should take hold of him emotionally and lead him on to theatrical action, it is necessary that the actor should "swing toward" that union, as toward something as real as the union of reality surrounding him.

THE EMOTION OF TRUTH

This does not mean that the actor must surrender himself on the stage to some such hallucination as that when playing he should lose the sense of reality around him, to take scenery for real trees, etc. On the contrary, some part of his senses must remain free from the grip of the play to control everything that he attempts and achieves as the performer of his part. He does not forget that surrounding him on the stage are decorations, scenery, etc., but they have no meaning for him. He says to himself, as it were: "I know that all around me on the stage is a rough counterfeit of reality. It is false. But if all should be real, see how I might be carried away to some such scene; then I would act." And at that instant, when there arises in his mind that artistic "suppose," encircling his real life, he loses interest in it, and is transported to another plane, created for him, of imaginary life. Restored to real life again, the actor must perforce modify the truth, as in the actual construction of his invention, so also in the survivals connected to it. His invention can be shown to be illogical, wide of the truth—and then he ceases to believe it. Emotion rises in him with invention; *i.e.*, his outward regard for imagined circumstances may be shown as "determined" without relation to the individual nature of a given emotion. Finally, in the expression of the outward life of his part, the actor, as a living complex emotion, never making use of sufficient perfection of all his bodily equipment, may give an untrue intonation, may not keep the artistic mean in gesticulation and may through the temptation of cheap effect drift into mannerism or awkwardness.

Only by a strongly developed sense of truth may he achieve a single inward beauty in which, unlike the conventional theatrical gestures and poses, the true condition of the character is expressed in every one of his attitudes and outward gestures.

INTERNAL TECHNIQUE

The combination of all the above-named procedure and habits also composes the actor's external technique. Parallel with its development must go also the development of internal technique—the perfecting of that bodily equipment which serves for the incarnation of the theatrical image created by the actor, and the exact, clear expression of his external consciousness. With this aim in view the actor must work out within himself not only the ordinary flexibility and mobility of action, but also the particular consciousness that directs all his groups of muscles, and the ability to feel the energy transfused within him, which, arising from his highest creative centres, forms in a definite manner his mimicry and gestures, and, radiating from him, brings into the circle of its influence his partners on the stage and in the auditorium. The same growth of consciousness and fineness of internal feelings must be worked out by the actor in relation to his vocal equipment. Ordinary speech—as in life, so on the stage—is prosaic and monotonous; in it words sound disjointed, without any harmonious stringing together in a vocal melody as continuous as that of a violin, which by the hand of a master violinist can become fuller, deeper, finer and more transparent, and can without difficulty run from the higher to the lower notes and vice versa, and can alternate from pianissimo to forte. To counteract the wearisome monotony of reading, actors often elaborate, especially when declaiming poetry, with those artificial vocal *fioritures*, cadences and sudden raising and lowering of the voice, which are so characteristic of the conventional, pompous declamation, and which are not influenced by the corresponding emotion of the part, and therefore impress the more sensitive auditors with a feeling of unreality.

But there exists another natural musical sonorousness of speech, which we may see in great actors at the moment of their own true artistic elation, and which is closely knit to the internal sonorousness of their rôle. The actor must develop within himself this natural musical speech by practising his voice with due regard to his sense of reality, almost as much as a singer. At the same time he must perfect his elocution. It is possible to have a strong, flexible, impressive voice, and still distort speech, on the one hand by incorrect pronunciation, on the other by neglect of those almost imperceptible pauses and emphasis through which are attained the exact transmission of the sense of the sentence, and also its particular emotional coloring. In the perfect production of the dramatist, every word, every letter, every punctuation mark has its part in transmitting his inward reality; the actor in his interpretation of the play, according to his intelligence, introduces into each sentence his individual nuances, which must be transmitted not only by the motions of his body, but also by artistically developed speech. He must bear this in mind, that every sound which goes to make a word appears as a separate note, which has its part in the harmonious sound of the word, and which is the expression of one or other particle of the soul drawn out through the word. The perfecting, therefore, of the phonetics of speech cannot be limited to mechanical exercise of the vocal equipment, but must also be directed in such a way that the actor learns to feel each separate sound in a word as an instrument of artistic expression. But in regard to the musical tone of the voice, freedom, elasticity, rhythm of movement and generally all external technique of dramatic art, to say nothing of internal technique, the present day actor is still on a low rung of the ladder of artistic culture, still far behind in this respect, from many causes, the masters of music, poetry and painting, with an almost infinite road of development to travel.

It is evident that under these conditions, the staging of a play, which will satisfy highly artistic demands, cannot be achieved at the speed that economic factors unfortunately make necessary in most theatres. This creative process, which every actor must go through, from his conception of the part to its artistic incarnation, is essentially very complicated, and is hampered by lack of perfection of outward and inward technique. It is also much hindered by the necessity of fitting in the actors one with another—the adjustment of their artistic individualities into an artistic whole.

PRODUCTION

Responsibility for bringing about this accord, and the artistic integrity and expression of the performance rests with the theatre manager. During the period when the manager exercised a despotic rule in the theatre, a period starting with the Meiningen players and still in force even in many of the foremost theatres, the manager worked out in advance all the plans for staging a play, and, while certainly having regard to the existing cast, indicated to the actors the general outlines of the scenic effects, and the *mise-en-scène*. The writer also adhered to this system, but now he has come to the conclusion that the creative work of the manager must be done in collaboration with the actor's work, neither ignoring nor confirming it. To encourage the actor's creative genius, to control and adjust it, ensuring that this creative genius grows out of the unique artistic germ of the drama, as much as the external building up of the performance—that in the opinion of the writer is the problem of the theatre director to-day.

The joint work of the director and actor begins with the analysis of the drama and the discovery of its artistic germ, and with the investigation of its *transparent effect*. The next step is the discovery of the transparent effect of individual parts—of that fundamental will direction of each individual actor, which, organically derived from his character, determines his place in the general action of the play. If the actor cannot at once secure this transparent effect, then it must be traced bit by bit with the manager's aid—by dividing the part into sections corresponding to the separate stages of the life of the particular actor—from the separate problems developing before him in his struggle for the attainment of his goal. Each such section of a part or each problem, can, if necessary, be subjected to further psychological analysis, and sub-divided into problems even more detailed, corresponding to those separate mind actions of the performer out of which stage life is summed up. The actor must catch the *mind axes* of the emotions and temperaments, but not the emotions and temperaments that give color to these sections of the part. In other words, when studying each portion of his part, he must ask himself what he wants, what he requires as a performer of the play and which definite partial problem he is putting before himself at a given moment. The answer to this question should not be in the form of a noun, but rather of a verb: "I wish to obtain possession of the heart of this lady"—"I wish to enter her house"—"I wish to push aside the servants who are protecting her," etc. Formulated in this manner, the mind problem, of which the object and setting, thanks to the working of his creative imagination, are forming a brighter and clearer picture for the actor, begins to grip him and to excite him, extracting from the recesses of his working memory the combinations of emotions necessary to the part, of emotions that have an active character and mould themselves into dramatic action. In this way the different sections of the actor's part grow more lively and richer by degrees, owing to the involuntary play of the complicated organic survivals. By joining together and grafting these sections, the *score of the part* is formed; the scores of the separate parts, after the continual joint work of the actors during rehearsals and by the necessary adjustment of them one with another, are summed up in a single *score of the performance.*

THE SCORE CONDENSED

Nevertheless, the work of the actors and manager is still unfinished. The actor is studying and living in the part and the play deeper and deeper still, finding their deeper artistic motives; so he lives in the score of his part still more profoundly. But the score of the part itself and of the play are actually subject by degrees during the work to further alterations. As in a perfect poetical production there are no superfluous words but only those necessary to the poet's artistic scheme, so in a score of the part there must not be a single superfluous emotion but only emotions necessary for the *transparent effect.* The score of each part must be condensed, as also the form of its transmitting, and bright, simple and compelling forms of its incarnation must be found. Only then, when in each actor every part not only organically ripens and comes to life but also all emotions are stripped of the superfluous, when they all crystallize and sum up into a live contact, when they harmonize amongst themselves in the general tune, rhythm and time of the performance, then the play may be presented to the public.

During repeated presentations the theatrical score of the play and each part remains in general unaltered. But that does not mean that from the moment the performance is shown to the public the actor's creative process is to be considered ended, and that there remains for im only the mechanical repetition of his achievement at the first presentation. On the contrary, every performance imposes on him creative conditions; all his psychical forces must take part in it, because only in these conditions can they creatively adapt the score of the part to those capricious changes which may develop in them from hour to hour, as in all living nervous creatures influencing one another by their emotions, and only then can they transmit to the spectator that invisible something, inexpressible in words, which forms the spiritual content of the play. And that is the whole origin of the substance of dramatic art.

As regards the outward arrangements of the play—scenery, theatrical properties, etc.—all are of value in so far as they correspond to the expression of dramatic action, *i.e.*, to the actors' talents; in no case may they claim to have an independent artistic importance in the theatre, although up to now they have been so considered by many great scene painters. The art of scene painting, as well as the music included in the play, is on the stage only an auxiliary art, and the manager's duty is to get from each what is necessary for the illumination of the play performed before an audience, while subordinating each to the problems of the actors.

THE WORK OF
THE ACTOR

By I. RAPOPORT

THE BEST WAY to understand how the actor must rehearse his part, is to call to mind and carefully consider all those performances which we have either seen, or taken part in. Let us check back on what specific features of the acting we either liked or disliked.

When we see a wooden-faced actor who is fussed, who does not know what to do with his hands and feet, and tries in fact to hide them—or who, as a result of his confusion, makes faces, holds himself too loosely and waves his hands aimlessly, when such an actor speaks in an unnatural voice, rattling off his part, without hearing the other actors, or in general behaves unnaturally and inappropriately, not as a person in real life would behave under similar circumstances, it is safe to say that the actor's performance will not find favour with the audience. He is either a poor actor, or else has failed properly to prepare himself for the role.

Let us now recall the actor whom we liked. It is safe to say that his behaviour was the direct opposite of that of the poor actor. His hands and feet did not get in his way, he did not make foolish faces, he regarded the surrounding objects and the other people on the stage in a simple and plain fashion; he listened to what his partner said to him, and answered naturally, delivering his part as though it were his own words and not lines that he had memorized. The actor we liked laughed frankly, naturally, genuinely, and did not make faces in order to amuse us, and he cried from fright as though he had actually been frightened. In short, on examining the performance of such an actor, we reach the conclusion that we liked him because as we watched him and listened to him, we felt that everything that happened to him on the stage could also have happened in real life.

The enumerated shortcomings—tenseness or unnecessary slackness of the body, strained voice, lack of attention to what the other players are saying, mechanical memorization of the part, and so on, do not necessarily prove that the performer is bad and cannot do otherwise. Often it is a sign of the fact that he failed to prepare himself for the part, that he either imitated poor actors or unconsciously and unintentionally went about preparing his part the wrong way.

After analysing the matter and discovering the proper approach, the same performer can play better and more correctly.

Now let us try to understand how we can rid ourselves of everything that interferes .with correct work on the stage, everything that leads to a bad performance of a part.

ORGANIC ATTENTION

When we observe a person in life, we see that he acts plainly, freely and naturally. If we examine the behaviour of the given person, or for that matter our own behaviour, we will see that *at any given moment our attention is sure to be focused on something.* When we work, our attention is centered on our work; if our work is habitual and we do it mechanically we may think of something else and then our attention will be focused on our thoughts. When we rest, our mind is apparently idle and it seems to us that our attention is not focused on anything, but it only *seems* that way; actually various thoughts course through our minds in succession. We think about the weather, of the past summer, of books we have read, or of yesterday's newspaper which we did not finish reading—and remembering this newspaper, we get up in order to find it and read it. (Notice, incidentally, and we shall return to this later, that everyone of our actions in life—this law is also applied to the stage—invariably has a motive, that it is prompted by some cause, for example: in the example cited, we remembered the newspaper and went to find it.)

Hence the attention of every person is always to some degree or another focused on some object, and this vital law is also obligatory for the stage.

ORGANS OF ATTENTION AND THE OBJECT

Our attention is conveyed by 1) *Sight* (we look at something) ; 2) *Hearing* (we hear something) ; 3) *Touch* (mainly of the hands or fingers: we hold, touch something) ; 4) *Smell* (we smell something) ; 5) *Taste* (we eat or drink something).

That object, person or thought *to which our attention is directed,* we shall term *the object of attention.* On the stage, as in life, our attention must always be organically focused on some object or another.

The difference between attention in life and on the stage consists of the following: in life our attention is either *voluntary* (when we compel ourselves to concentrate on some object—we work, we read, etc.) ; or else *involuntary,* when our attention is occupied by this or that object as if independent of our will. On the stage we must, voluntarily, by using our will, direct our organs of attention towards those objects which we ourselves have selected while playing the part.

The first prerequisite of stage presence is the ability to control our own attention, to use our will-power to focus our attention on the object we have selected.

MUSCULAR STRAIN

We said that in watching a person in life, we note that his actions are motivated and purposeful, that they arise from this or the other cause and are directed to the attainment of a given end.

But now suppose that the person sees that he is being watched, or that we ourselves feel we are being carefully observed. Under such circumstances a person's behaviour will change: he begins to feel embarrassed; he is no longer "himself"; he becomes awkward. When a person is watched, and especially when he is watched by many spectators, he is cramped by their attention. Anyone who has had to make a speech before a meeting or has watched an inexperienced speaker on a platform knows that the sight of the audience almost invariably tends to rattle the person appearing before it; his voice does not obey him; his movements become forced, he cannot find the right words, etc. But the more the speaker becomes engrossed in the object of his speech, the more he focuses his attention on the content of his speech, the stronger will be his desire to convince his audience, and the sooner will he overcome his initial stage-fright. You undoubtedly have noticed that the time comes when the orator has mastered himself and loses his embarrassment and awkwardness. His movements acquire assurance, his voice grows stronger, he has found "himself" and has become convincing. It is this feeling of stage-fright before an audience which makes the actor awkward in his movements and produces that bodily stiffness or slackness which we spoke of at the beginning.

ATTENTION AND MUSCLES

As in the case of the developed orator, the actor too can free himself of the strain of body, face and voice—from muscular strain, as we shall term it—only by learning consciously to direct his attention to a definite object.

Before going on further to examine the part, to ascertain the character which is to be played, the actor must go through a series of exercises, which will enable him to master in practice the thing discussed above.

He must know how to prepare the basic material from which he shall construct the part. And this material consists of the actor himself—his face, body, voice, thoughts and feelings, in a word, his entire organism.

The actor's performance will only carry conviction provided the actor himself actually experiences all the feelings and emotions which the character in the play, as drawn by the author, undergoes.

Preparatory to mastering this scenic life, the actor must begin to learn consciously to direct his attention, starting with the simplest exercises.

All the students of the dramatic group should sit together in the theatre or in the rehearsal hall. One of the group goes on the stage, picks some object—*the object of attention*—and looks at it. The director of the group watches him as do the rest. The actor must examine the object, but must not do so casually, merely trying to *look* as if he is examining it; he must try to become interested in the object so that his attention becomes *organic* and is thus real attention,

36

so that he actually sees all the detail of the object (and afterwards can easily recall them), and must not merely pretend to be looking.

When his attention is actually focused on the object, the pupil will notice that the physical strain, the embarrassment, he experienced when he first stepped on to the stage, has vanished or has considerably diminished.

It should not be supposed that this exercise is far removed from the actual rehearsing of a part. After all, in any part there are likely to be places where the actor is called to examine something: read a book, look into the face of the person playing opposite him, etc. If he learns to look at things on the stage simply and naturally, this will help him tremendously in practising his next part.

The same exercise should be repeated with each of the various faculties.

Take *hearing*. The person performing the exercise begins to listen, standing or sitting before the group—just as previously with *sight*; he does not make a pretense of listening but listens intently. He does not simply listen to noise in general but directs his attention towards something specific, for instance he listens to what is going on beyond the wall in the street, striving to catch everything down to the tiniest sound. And once he actually becomes really interested and centers his hearing on the given object, the others will see, and he himself will feel, that he has become muscularly (physically) free, and his attention will have become organic.

The actor must learn to listen on the stage and this exercise has an immediate practical significance. On the stage it is absolutely essential that he hear and understand what he listens to.

By learning to listen on the stage he learns at the same time to play any part, because catching the words of the person playing opposite is as important as delivering the words of his own part. There are varying degrees of attention, beginning with light interest and going as far as complete absorption.

In order to train himself how thus to control his attention the actor should bring into the exercise obstacles which must be overcome in order to achieve concentration on the required object. For instance, if he is reading a book, let those present interrupt him with conversation, make jokes at his expense, noises, etc. The actor must compel himself to be so absorbed in his book that he does not notice what goes on around him and is completely buried in the contents of the page he is reading.

The next exercise consists of remembering in detail how one spent the day, what one did, with whom one spoke, and about what, etc.; meanwhile let the others interrupt, talk, but the actor must continue to think only his own thoughts, and in this way train his attention.

Repeat such exercises with each of your perceptive faculties separately. *Look* at different objects. *Listen. Touch* an object so that all your attention is concentrated in your finger tips (remember how developed this sense is in the blind, where it takes the place of sight). *Smell*—center all attention in your nose—try to detect this or that smell (remember how developed this sense is in animals: dogs trailing a scent, etc.). And, finally, *taste*—strive to concentrate on this or that kind of food or drink. Do all these exercises in turn. Let the rest of the group and its director determine how successful you were in focusing your attention in the course of the exercises.

In working directly on a part you will find opportunities to practise all these exercises. For example, the dominance of this or that perceptive faculty over the others is an important factor in creating a character. The glutton prefers the sense of taste to all the rest; he will focus his attention on a dinner table, or a locked cupboard full of food, with particular intensity. The sly, curious, cunning fellow—who reminds one of a fox—may have smell as a dominant sense. His nose then would play an exceptional role in his behaviour (note the saying, "poking his nose into other people's business").

It is likewise necessary to practise a series of simple exercises which develop observation, attention and keenness of perception.

An example of such exercises is the so-called "mirror" exercise. The two people doing the exercise stand opposite each other; one makes a movement, the other copies him exactly, as though in a mirror. The director of the group looks on and points out any errors.

The second exercise might be called "Director and Actor." One person, the "director," gets up on the stage and goes through a series of fairly simple movements which the other person, the "actor," must remember and copy exactly. The "director" goes off stage and watches in turn how the "actor" repeats his movements. The "actor" must reproduce as closely as possible the facial expression, the gait, and all the actions of the "director."

When the "actor" has finished the "director" must show and explain exactly what mistakes were made and why. Then the two trade places—the "actor" becomes the "director" and vice-versa, and they repeat the exercise. This exercise develops the powers of observation and teaches how, in his future work on a part, the actor can grasp the essence of the part as the director demonstrates it.

The following exercises are very useful in developing memory and attention. The entire group sits in a row; the first person says a word (anything that comes into his head, e.g. "table"), the second repeats the first word and adds one of his own (e.g. "book"), the third repeats the first two words and adds a third, and so on. If ten are taking part, the tenth one must repeat the nine preceding words and add a tenth; then the first one repeats these ten and adds another, and so on.

In conclusion remember that these exercises are not only necessary in preparing for work on a part; they can be directly applied to current work on the stage. Let us suppose in one place in your part your entire attention is directed to the words of the player opposite. You will either listen to him; or else to some noise off-stage (someone has arrived); or in another place you yourself are speaking, and at the same time your attention is directed to some object you are holding in your hand, etc.

Examine the role you may now be working on from the standpoint of how to direct the attention. Analyse to what degree your attention is focused and on what (object, thing) at every given moment. This will aid you in your work on the part from the very beginning.

On the stage the objects of attention are the things around us, the events of the play that involve us, the other members of the cast, i.e., those characters whom we come in contact with in the play.

We reached the conclusion that when we focus our attention on an object in earnest in a living organic manner (look at something, listen, etc.) simultaneously muscular strain begins to diminish. We stated that the actor on the stage must be muscularly free.

MUSCULAR FREEDOM

What is muscular freedom?

The whole time we are on the stage we perform certain motions. Our consciousness, as it were, gives commands; our body, obeying, fulfills these commands: we speak, walk, sit, gesticulate (that is, strive to express our thoughts or emphasize them by means of our motions), etc. We perform these various motions with our muscles; we speak with our throat and mouth muscles, walk with our leg muscles, etc. Any act we perform demands the expenditure of a certain amount of energy.

By reference to life, the source from which we obtain all our knowledge for the stage, we can easily discover that we normally expend as much muscular energy as is required for a given operation and not one iota more. Thus, if we have to lift an object that weighs a pound, we expend energy, we exert ourselves to the extent of one pound, so to speak. When we stand, the muscles of our legs are exerted only to the extent required to support the weight of our body. And in life this happens instinctively, we don't think about it. In life we are always muscularly free.

This vital law is mandatory for the actor on the stage: *it is necessary to expend precisely the amount of energy required by every given operation of the action—no more and no less.* The actor's movements must never be performed either with an over-expenditure or an under-expenditure of muscular energy. If he lifts an object which is in reality light, but which must appear heavy to the audience, he must expend more energy than the actual weight of the object requires. Otherwise, if he lifts this "heavy" object with excessive ease, with under-expenditure of muscular energy the result will be an unconvincing performance. He must accordingly take cognizance of the things which he does instinctively in real life, learning to subordinate them to his will and thus transfer them convincingly to the stage.

Let us proceed to check up on our muscular system and learn to control it. Let us again remember, to start with, that freedom from muscular strain is only possible with the aid of organic attention, focused on some object, for under such circumstances we forget about our muscles. Physical awkwardness, stiffness and strain disappear only when we compel ourselves to regard the chosen object with genuine interest.

The awkwardness a person experiences when he appears before the public is due to that over-expenditure of muscular energy that comes from being rattled by the fact that people are looking at him. See how much strength (muscular energy) it takes to move a chair from place to place in your room, and how much surplus energy you expend on the same operation on the stage when you are being watched.

See whether your other hand (which is idle) is needlessly tense or not, whether your neck and shoulders are free.

Do the following exercise: sit on a chair with your muscles perfectly free making only the effort necessary to sit upright in the chair. See for yourself (and let the person directing the exercise also see) whether your arms, neck, shoulders face and leg muscles are perfectly free. Completely relax your muscles. Next tauten the muscles of one hand (let everything else remain as it was), then the other hand, then the muscles of your feet, shoulders, neck (in any order) till your whole body is tense.

Learn to master different degrees of muscular tension and transfer muscular energy from one part of the body to another. For example, relax the whole body, hold your feet extremely taut, hold your right hand and foot taut, sit and walk in such a state. Check up on yourself and on one another—see to what degree your are successful.

Control of your body directly assists your work on a part, as when you are practising the gait of a given character, his manner of expression, etc., etc. Walk freely with only your neck stretched out and taut like the neck of a goose. Let us assume you are billed to play the part of a drunkard, of a person whose muscles will not obey him; he wants to go straight, but his legs carry him to one side, he wants to speak clearly, but his tongue gets twisted, etc.

Thus on many occasions in the course of rehearsing a part exercise of the conscious control of your muscles will prove useful in working out the movements of the stage character. Now we come to the practice of such exercises as—including and growing out of our previous exercises—will prepare us for the next section of our work.

JUSTIFICATION

At a given signal (hand-clap) every member of the study-group strikes some pose, quite spontaneously and without premeditation, be it the most unexpected, even foolish pose. Next, without changing your pose, observe yourself: relax your muscles, exerting only the effort required to retain the pose.

Finally, attempt to "justify" the pose. We are now coming to the central question of our system, the very essence of our work on the stage. For the basis of everything that takes place on the stage—as we shall see later—is *justification*.

Going back to the pose that was struck at the given signal, let us assume that you raised both hands above your head. You made this movement accidentally, without preconception. Now try to imagine under what circumstances you might make such a movement in real life. Say you raised your hands in order to reach wash hanging on the line, or that you wanted to keep a basket from falling off a shelf. And when your imagination has supplied you with a meaning for the given pose, that *pose* is said to have been *justified*.

By now you are no longer simply standing with lifted hands; this position is required for a definite purpose, e.g. to catch the imaginary basket. Having found the justification you yourself will feel the difference between the pose that has a reason behind it and one without a reason.

In the one instance it will appear meaningless; in the other instance (after finding the justification) it will become reasonable, understandable. Let each student find justification for the pose he has struck and repeat the pose, keeping in mind the justification.

Now do the following exercise—the director instructs you to perform three or four movements which you must do in succession without considering them before-hand or connecting them up with each other. For instance: 1) raise your right hand; 2) put it to your forehead; 3) put your left hand in your pocket. Try to find justification for each movement separately and at the same time link all of them up in one general justification, e.g. 1) you hush the audience—raise your hand to attract attention, 2) you try to recall the opening of your speech—put your hand to your forehead, 3) you search for your notes —put your hand in your pocket. In this manner a purpose has been found for each of the movements separately and general justification has been provided.

Many more justifications could be found for the same set of movements. Now let us go further. We said, "Think of a justification, or find one." How is this justification to be found? By means of *imagination*, or as we shall call it in the future, by means of our *creative fantasy*.

CREATIVE FANTASY

Man is endowed with the faculty of creative fantasy: the ability to combine, unite different phenomena from life into special new phenomena. It is impossible for man to imagine something non-existent, but to unite different parts of the existing into a new whole—creating thereby a new "artistic image"—can be done with the help of the imagination or creative fantasy.

This faculty of creative fantasy is a necessary quality for an artist—you, as well as every artist, must develop it in yourself in every possible way.

And the easier it becomes for you to use this faculty (creative fantasy) the richer your characterizations will be. You will become more qualified to select appropriate and expressive elements necessary for creating the character, and the more true and convincing will be your interpretation of the part.

Develop your fantasy beginning with the justification of poses and the separate exercises which we have already mentioned. The more detailed the justification your fantasy suggests, the more profitable will be the exercises. Find a motive, explain each movement to yourself as precisely as possible; the pose itself may be slightly altered to fit the justification (provided it remains basically the same).

Let us return to the pose with the raised hands. As you remember, one of the proposed justifications (and there can be any number) was the desire to keep a basket from falling off of the top shelf in a railroad car. Develop this justification further: what kind of basket is it, how heavy is it, what is inside it, whose is it, why on that shelf, why does it fall, what happened before and after, etc? In a word, let your imagination create a story round the theme of this exercise. This will be justification of the given pose by means of your creative fantasy. Only try to keep your fantasy within the bounds of plausibility (making sure that the forms of everything you recount to be are found in actual life), directing your fantasy to the particular basket or to the given incident, which may be imaginary and interesting yet at the same time must be plausible.

Otherwise, by going outside the bounds of the possible, the true-to-life, creating an abstract fantasy (purposeless, so to speak) you run the risk of replacing genuine creative fantasy by idle fancy unnecessary to the actor in creating a role. An actor must have at his command a creative fantasy that is easily aroused yet at the same time he must be able to supply the creations of his fantasy with meaning. It is necessary to direct fantasy toward a definite goal, to have purposive fantasy.

Thus, we *justify* with the help of *fantasy*. Everything on the stage must be justified—every action, movement, thought, every glance must have a reason and a goal.

STAGE ATTITUDE

On the stage the actor is surrounded entirely by fictions; this applies to the settings, costumes, props, to the other actors, and even to himself in make-up.

The actor must be able to regard all this as though it were true, as though he were convinced that all that surrounds him on the stage is a living reality and, along with himself, he must convince the audience as well. This is the central feature of our method of work on the part.

To acquire a serious attitude to the surrounding make-believe of the stage, you must justify this attitude; and you must find the justification by using your creative fantasy. In other words, creative fantasy is the way to justification, justification is the way to a correct attitude, and on the stage, attitude counts for everything.

The various attitudes which the actor acquires in order to render his part (attitudes to the other characters, to events, to things) go to constitute the stage character. The work of the actor on his part consists fundamentally in choosing and adopting these attitudes and justifying them with the help of his creative fantasy. We shall speak of this later; meanwhile let us practise some elementary exercises in attitudes.

Take any object, a cap for example, lay it on the table or on the floor and try to regard it as though it were a rat; make believe that it is a rat, and not a cap; try to justify this attitude with your creative fantasy: picture what sort of a rat it is, what size, colour? Here you must be sure to understand and to remember one thing: you must see the actual object, i.e. the cap; but you must regard all its attributes, colour, shape, etc., as though it were not a cap but a rat; as though these attributes were those of a rat.

Pretend that the cap is an attractive puppy and acquire a corresponding attitude towards it. The more detailed you make your justification of the imaginary puppy—determining where its head, its tail, paws, and ears are—the easier will it be to establish the correct attitude. Try sitting in a row and have each actor play with the "puppy" in turn, carefully (or otherwise, according to the attitude agreed upon) passing it from hand to hand. As he passes it to his neighbour each

44

person must try to define his attitude to it as to a puppy. If you carefully justify this attitude (i.e. the peak is its muzzle, the opposite end is its tail, the top of the cap is its back, etc.) then you will sense that an attitude has been established appropriate to a puppy, even though you see that the object is only a cap. Those who like puppies will under such conditions enjoy playing with the cap, and will be angry if someone takes it by the "tail" and roughly throws it around.

That is one example (further on there will be more, meanwhile imagine others yourselves) of regarding make-believe (we know and see that this is a cap, and not a puppy) as though it were real (as though the cap actually were a puppy). We thus compel ourselves to believe quite naively that the object before us is something other than it is and at the same time we learn to compel the audience to believe it.

Remember how naively and seriously children play? How convinced they are that the stick they straddle is a horse? The child sees a stick (otherwise he would be psychologically abnormal) but regards it as though it were a horse. Ask him what he is riding on, he will become embarrassed and say that it is a stick, but when he is playing by himself, he is convinced he is riding on a fine horse. This "seriousness," naivete natural to children's play, must become natural to the actor also in his work on the stage.

The "stage attitude" is the most important section of our work; it coordinates into a single whole all the former separate parts of our method.

After all everything around us on the stage—the scenic atmosphere, the events that involve us, the words we utter or hear, the other characters with whom we come in contact—is fiction, make-believe, rigged together and placed on the stage for the sake of the particular production, for presentation to the audience. And like the audience, we actors know that everything taking place on the stage is "not really so," that actors "play," that the play is "play."

We also know that the more we are able to make the spectators feel that what is taking place on the stage is real, the more we shall be able to compel them to believe in the scenic life we are creating, the better will be our acting and the better our performance.

How can we achieve this effect on the spectator? We must regard the fiction and make-believe that surrounds us on the stage as though it were real.

By means of stage-belief, as serious an attitude towards the fictitious as towards the real, the actor can carry the audience with him, and by living and feeling his part he can compel the spectators to be moved by these emotions along with himself.

How do we achieve this attitude?

By means of justification.

Without their being justified our actions and words on the stage will not ring true, they will be nonsensical and consequently unconvincing to the spectators.

If I. say to you or to a member of the cast that "I went along the Arbat" (the street in Moscow where the Vakhtangov Theatre is situated) for me the statement will be charged with a living content. The name "Arbat" will conjure up a mass of familiar impressions . . . The street itself, the side streets going left and right, the automobiles and trucks, the white-gloved traffic cop, the richly-trimmed shop-windows, etc. Then the word "Arbat" will be *justified,* it will ring true, and be convincing and will prove I know what I am talking about. Similarly everything that I say and do on the stage must have a specific content, must be justified.

I must know myself in my part and likewise those around me in their parts, just as I know my real self and those around me in life. Justification provides a foundation of truth in the creation of the part and on this foundation the structure of the part and of the performance as a whole will be firm and secure.

We justify the stage situation by studying the reality which we are to reproduce on the stage, and by using our creative fantasy, which selects from the material we have studied and from our observations the features required in the given instance. The consequent unification of these features constitutes the justification of the part as a whole.

Why do we consider "attitude" the central point of our work?

Because every stage part is essentially made up of various attitudes. Every part is, as it were, woven from these attitudes. The ability to gauge these attitudes correctly and master them means to play the part correctly.

Any number of exercises on "attitudes" can be thought up. Begin with the simplest ones, such as were proposed in the preceding section. For example take a stool and establish an attitude to it, 1) as though it were a beehive, 2) a dog-kennel where there is a fierce dog in front of which you have to pass, 3) a basket of good things to eat, etc. Let the director watch and see whether your behaviour with reference to the given object is correct, and when you yourself feel that you are really acting towards the stool as though it were, for example, a basket of things to eat (when you feel that you have justified the attitude) pass on to the next exercise.

PUBLIC SOLITUDE

You must further widen the range of objects to which you acquire a stage attitude. Take such an exercise as: go on the stage (in the presence of the group) having agreed in advance that it is your own room. Establish an attitude towards the surrounding objects as though they were your own, and "in your own room" do what you wish: read, rehearse your part, sew, write, go through all the actions you might go through if you were alone in your own room. We shall call this exercise *public solitude*. Next, suppose that you are alone in a forest. Your attitude to the objects around you must change, and be appropriately justified. You will regard the chairs as though they were bushes, stumps and trees, the stage-floor as though it were the earth strewn with pine-needles, etc. Your actions can be of any kind: you may be going for a walk, lying down, thinking of something, etc. Strive to confine your attention to the range of objects appropriate to the place which the stage is now supposed to represent, and make yourself feel in complete solitude (in front of the audience).

If you pretend that the stage is a forest, and you acquire a serious attitude toward it, then gradually your thoughts and feelings will become what they actually would be if you were really in a forest. You will walk round the chair and look for mushrooms, you will see a nail and be surprised at finding it in the middle of a forest, etc. As a result of such a series of justifications you will acquire a correct attitude toward your predicated surroundings; you will believe that you are in a forest, your behaviour will be correct, corresponding to the atmosphere of the forest, and you will also compel the audience to regard the stage as though it were a forest.

Let each student practise such an exercise in "public solitude" ("in the forest," "in the fields," "in a boat on the river," "at home," etc.) and afterwards discuss who was most convincing, and why he achieved such a realistic effect.

Along with this exercise, continue to do the exercises in attitude towards things, facts, and people. For example you come home and find a letter with good news or bad news, etc. Acquire an attitude toward a stick as though it were 1) a gun, 2) a snake, 3) a musical instrument, etc. Go on the stage by two's and acquire various attitudes toward each other (in pantomime): 1) be afraid of each other, 2) like each other, 3) hate each other, etc. Remember, the more detailed the justification, the more convincing will be your attitude. For example in the exercise with the letter, know what is in it, from whom, from where, etc.; in a "quarrel"—why it arose, where you have come from, etc.

RECOLLECTION OF PHYSICAL ACTIONS

Let us now pass on to the next, more complex, exercise in attitudes: try to reproduce exactly some physical action, e.g., light a lamp, but without any lamp and without matches; with *imaginary objects*.

Remember how to strike a match, how to remove the lamp chimney, remember the size of the objects, their shape, weight, texture. Bear all this in mind and go through the movements as faithfully as possible. Sew—put an imaginary thread through the eye of an imaginary needle and sew on an imaginary button. Choose the most simple and ordinary actions: chop wood, put the kettle on, catch fish.

Let each pupil select some action not too complex at first and go through the exercise at home and afterwards repeat it during the lesson. Let those present correct him, in order to achieve the most exact, realistic and expressive "recollection of physical actions."

Here, as it were, you review all the former exercises:—your attention must be organically focused on this or that object, you must be muscularly free. Using your creative fantasy you must justify as serious an attitude to a non-existent object as to an existing one. In a word, all the separate parts of our system of acting become interwoven here into a single whole; and from the results of this particular exercise you can judge with certainty how successful you have been in mastering the former exercises.

In the next section we begin an important new subject: *stage action,* but meanwhile, let us interrupt the continuity of the system in order to examine what possibilities there are for applying all that we have learned to your current work on a play.

By studying the material of the play and using your creative fantasy try to picture the entire life of the character: his childhood, how he grew up, how his character was formed, how he spends the day, his likes and dislikes, what he wants, what he looks for in life, etc. In your imagination place the character you are playing in the most varied situations and during your lessons and rehearsals try to act in keeping with these circumstances and continue to do so until you feel, and others watching see, that you have adapted yourself to the circumstances, and behave just as the character you are playing would.

Repeat all the previous exercises in any sequence—exercises on attention; on muscular freedom; on justification of pose; physical actions; development of creative fantasy; on attitudes and the change of attitudes towards things, facts, fellow players; on the recollection of physical actions; on "public solitude." All this will supply you with material for your current work, and, most important, it will prepare you for serious consecutive work on the part, on the text, and on the character of the role which you are to play.

STAGE ACTION

When we read any play be it drama, comedy, vaudeville, or any form of literary work intended for production on the stage, we at once encounter the words "in so-many acts." The very word actor obviously means "he who acts." The task of the actor is the creation of a stage character by reproducing the actions of a human being.

Consider the behaviour of man in life, and you will see that he is constantly acting. But one must have a correct understanding of the word. Action is not only external, i.e., connected with motion in the course of which man changes his position in space, but also internal (psychological) taking place in the consciousness of man and causing a change of his mental condition.

Suppose you contemplate some action, reach a decision, and carry out the action you contemplated. Can you determine when you "acted" most: in contemplating, in deciding, or in carrying out the action? No, it is impossible to do so, for without the decision (internal action) there would have been no deed (external action).

Our environment acts on us through our senses (sight, hearing, etc.) and reflects itself in our consciousness (thoughts, feelings); these

49

thoughts and feelings which are formed within us call forth this or that action as a response, which in its turn acts on the environment. The whole of life is made up of these actions and interactions.

External action is indissolubly linked up with internal action, and is a result of it.

In these interactions with our environment not one moment of our behaviour is lost, it is inevitably reflected externally, even in those moments which are habitually termed "inactive" (we place the word in quotation marks because such inactivity is only *apparent* inactivity: when a person's condition is not expressed in external action). Imagine, for example, that an "inactive" signalman caused a railway wreck, that public property was stolen from an "inactive" watchman. "Inactivity" serves as the cause of sequence of involved events.

What distinguishes stage action from action in real life? First, in life *actual* objects act on our sense organs and call forth corresponding thoughts, feelings and actions; on the stage such objects do not exist or they are only fictions. Consequently in order to evoke a corresponding reaction, the stage objects must, as it were, be brought to life by means of our imagination. That is why the actor must command an easily aroused imagination, a rich creative fantasy (remember the sections on justification and stage attitude). Second, in life we often act unconsciously, unaware of the causes that determine our behaviour, and the aims which our actions pursue—but on the stage we must always know what we are doing and why.

THE STAGE TASK

Follow the links of the character's relations with the external world. Show the causes that prompted this or that action, and the aims to which the actions are directed. This is the way to create a character. It should be understood that the actor must not only carry out the action and deliver the words of his part (external action), but most important of all, he must compel himself *to have the same objectives as the character he is playing* (internal action). He sets himself his stage task by determining what aim he is pursuing, what his wishes are at any given moment of his presence on the stage. The fulfilling of his task will be stage action.

We said that the actor must make himself share the objectives of the character he is playing. He must fulfill the task by using his will-power. This means that *the will lies at the root of stage action.*

We have already compared play on the stage with the play of a child. Resorting once more to this comparison the child at play must first of all want to play. If this desire disappears he stops playing. We must consciously direct our desire and deliberately involve ourselves in stage action the entire time we are on the stage.

Note that when we compare the play of children with that of an actor, we do not regard them as one and the same, or consider them equivalent. We only make this comparison to clarify the nature of acting, to bring out something which is present in the unconscious play of the child and which in a conscious form, on a much higher level and with a new quality, is present in the playing of the actor.

THE THREE ELEMENTS OF THE STAGE TASK

The three main elements of the stage task are: 1) *Action—What I am doing*, 2) *Volition—Why I am doing it*, 3) *Adjustment—How I am doing it* (form, character of action).

The first two elements—*action* and *volition* are consciously determined by the actor and as a result of their performance the third element, *adjustment,* arises involuntarily. For example: 1) You bang your fist on the table, 2) In order to quiet the meeting, 3) The corresponding adjustment arises (the form, character of the blow). Let the action remain, but change the desire, 1) Bang the table, 2) In order to test the firmness of table (appraise it). As a result of the change of the second element of the task (volition) a new adjustment appears— the bang will be unlike the one in the first case. Let us again change the volition element in the same action: 1) Bang the table, 2) In order to play a joke on a friend who is dozing at the table (to frighten him) —again the bang will be different—the volition has changed and likewise the adjustment changes.

Do several exercises of this sort, and remember: never anticipate how you will act, nor plan the adjustment beforehand (e.g., *how* you will bang on the table), but always strive to concentrate on *why* you are acting (why you are banging), then, quite independently, the proper adaptation will appear.

Perform the following exercise. Call on a friend in order to tell him some bad news, or to please him (bring him a present), or to scold him for something. In doing these exercises remember all that we have previously studied, i.e., the attitude to environment, and consequently justification by the creative fantasy. You must know in each case: 1) Who the news is for, and from whom it comes, etc. 2) What the present is and in connection with what (birthday, winning of a lottery prize, etc.). 3) Why you are angry, why you came to scold him, etc.

Practise a number of exercises, beginning with simple ones, without a partner; or, if you have a partner, find a form of justification that will enable you to communicate entirely without words. For example: you call on a friend, but he is not in the room, he has either gone out or is asleep—thus you put yourself in circumstances where you will be able to act for some time without speaking and your silence will be natural, organic. Here are some examples: 1) You live in one room with a friend but you do not speak to each other, as you have recently quarreled; you feel yourself in the wrong and want to make up with him. 2) Tidy the room preparatory to studying (know who your neighbours are, perhaps they are making a noise, which prevents you from studying; or, more complex: tidy the room because you expect company, wait, dress; then you receive a letter with unpleasant news, and you have to leave at once. 3) Come home with the published results of the lottery and find your number listed; you have a record of your number in a notebook but you cannot find the ticket itself; then you remember where you hid it, look for it, find it and go out to claim your winnings.

From among your surroundings on the stage try to pick out obstacles which interfere with your task, e.g., in the above exercise you want to study, but the neighbours are noisy or flies in the room annoy you, etc. The more obstacles—the more energetically you will bring yourself to fulfilling the task, the more expressive your stage action will be, and the more correctly you will carry out the exercise. Stage feeling will arise as a very result of the clash of your action with the obstacle, with the interference. Never play feeling or strive to squeeze it out of yourself—thus you need to study, someone prevents you, and as a result of your struggle with this obstacle the feeling of anger, excitement, etc., will arise. Test yourself, and let the director see how convincingly and correctly you have done it.

What we shall call the sense of truth must come to your aid. Do not "portray" anything for the effect that you want it to have on the spectator; do not concoct adjustments but actively fulfill your task because you believe in the given circumstances. You must experience an organic necessity for achieving the aim you have set yourself on the stage. Under such conditions true stage feelings will be engendered: gladness, sorrow, anger, shame, etc., depending on the task and its justification. Stage action is indissolubly linked up with, and invariably accompanied by, a certain internal feeling, which we call *the sense of truth*. This sense of truth, which constantly keeps check on stage action, will tell you where you are acting right (justifiedly), where you have slipped up, "overacted," as we say.

It is necessary to develop your sense of truth both in your own work and by carefully observing the work of others. Note where the person doing the exercise has violated the feeling of truth, where he has "over-acted"; and why you did not believe in his sincerity, in the authenticity of his stage feelings. Point out these places, discuss them, strive to correct them, do them in some other way. Let several students in turn practice the same exercise, but each in his own way, and then decide who did it best. Many exercises similar to the ones we discussed can be thought up. Take any theme (for the time being without a partner or under such circumstances that conversation with your partner is not necessary; if as a result of the action the necessity to speak organically arises, halt the exercise) and determine the first two elements of the task, "*what* I shall do" (action), and "*why*" (volition). As a result of the fulfillment of these tasks the proper adjustment will arise involuntarily. Let the director observe how well justified and convincing your stage action is.

STAGE ACTION AND COUNTER-ACTION

The proper performance of the stage task is possible only when it is directed toward overcoming the obstacles in its way. The stage task grows, develops and is accomplished in the struggle with such obstacles. As a result of this struggle and of overcoming of the obstacles, stage feeling is generated. By obstacles we mean not only external but also internal circumstances which counteract our task.

For example, I am in a hurry to catch a train, my things are in my room, packed and ready; I come for them, but the door is locked and I cannot find the key. In this case a purely physical obstacle confronts me—a locked door, which I have to open to get my things.

The more difficult it is to overcome the obstacle, the more actively the task will develop and the feelings which result from fulfillment of the task will become deeper and more expressive. I shall be upset, angry, annoyed at my absent-mindedness (as I mislaid or lost the key), etc.; in a word, I shall experience the same sequence of feelings as would have been aroused if such an accident had happened in real life.

STAGE FEELINGS: RESULT OF FULFILLING THE TASK

All these feelings will be a *result* of the conflict of my task with the counter-acting circumstances, and must never be evoked or "wrung out," must never appear independently of the circumstances in which we have placed ourselves in the given exercise.

Never seek a mood of feeling merely in the abstract, never do such exercises as "fear in general," "sorrow in general," etc.

A search for a so-called "condition" on the stage will always lead to a poor result: either to "over-acting" (or to nervousness and hysteria—which on the stage is the most harmful of all phenomena).

The only correct course is *justification* (detailed circumstances), then on the basis of *stage attitude* (an attitude to a fiction as though it were real), and finally *action* (as we have just treated it). Only by this course will we arrive at true stage feeling.

Take, for example, fear. What is fear in general? It is a feeling which arises in a person as a result of some external phenomena threatening danger. Something which seems inexplicable also evokes fear, as we do not know what it portends. Thus primitive peoples out of a sense of fear deified inexplicable natural phenomena.

But this explanation is insufficient for the stage, for this is a definition of the *concept* of "fear," i.e., that which is general and present in all cases of fear. In life, and consequently on the stage (which must be a true reflection of life) there is no "fear in general" or any other feelings "in general."

There are as many individual instances of fear as there are people.

It is one thing to be frightened by a frog which jumps up before one's foot, and quite another thing to be frightened by an explosion. A young girl's fright differs from that of a healthy lad. Every person has his own individual expression of this or that feeling under any given set of circumstances.

It is *therefore impossible to act feelings "in general." One must perform the task which will evoke the specific feeling.*

Justify the circumstances in which you find yourself; define the object which threatens danger, and seek to avoid this danger; only then will a genuine stage feeling of fear arise appropriate to the given situation.

Take another feeling—sorrow, for example. There can be no "sorrow in general." Every person will have *his* own variety of sorrow, peculiar to himself. In every given instance we must find the particular circumstances and the task which lies at the root of the given feeling, so that it will be plausible and convincing to the audience.

Let us take the following exercise: someone you are fond of is seriously ill. You want to help him, ease his suffering, but you are unable to do so. Here is your task, fulfill it, fight for the person's health, do this in all sincerity—and you will evoke the authentic stage feeling which corresponds to the feeling we call sorrow.

Let us now return to the question of obstacles to the stage task.

The first exercise with the locked door was used to illustrate *external* (physical) obstacles.

In the last example of the sick person we meet with another kind of task and counter-action. Imagine that you are sitting close to the sleeping patient; you are waiting for the doctor. You look at the patient, there is no outward action, but inwardly you are very active indeed. Internally, you are fighting with the sickness; with all your heart and soul you want to help your friend get well. But the disease is making inroads as you can see by the face and the movements of the patient and as you can judge by his breathing. In this case too there is conflict, struggle, action and counter-action, but they are *internal* and are reflected in your eyes, in your entire appearance and in your behaviour, although outwardly you are practically motionless and silent.

Thus, in the concept of the stage task (remember the basic parts: action, volition and adjustment) we include as a necessary condition—counter-action.

You will recall our saying that practically the whole of life is made up of our *inter-actions* with the surrounding world. These inter-actions act upon our consciousness through our sense organs, and our consciousness in its turn then influences external reality.

The source of the counter-action, the obstacle, may be any object

—a physical impediment (locked door) an external circumstance (sickness) or else an internal circumstance.

The source of *such counter-action* may also be another character in the play.

STAGE INTER-INFLUENCE

We now come to a new section of our system, a section which we shall call *stage inter-influence*—the influence of the players upon one another.

Let us return to our previous method of studying living reality, to an attentive observation of the facts of life.

Only by understanding and grasping the laws of human behaviour can we establish the laws of stage behaviour, and then according to these laws reconstruct the stage life of the character we are playing, i.e., create a character.

Stage inter-influence we can define as the influence of the players on one another under the conditions of an indissoluble inner relationship between them when the least change in the behaviour of one inevitably brings with it a corresponding change in the behavior of the other, and vice, versa.

How do these changes appear, how do they correspond, can we draft a ready-made plan of inter-influence beforehand?

When we direct an exercise in which two actors are participating, can we instruct one to look to the side, and the second straight ahead, and then tell the first to shout, which is to evoke a quiet answer from the second, etc.? Can we work with actors on the basis of such a scheme of movements, intonations, etc.? That would obviously be impossible. It would take all the life from the role, and deprive the actor of what is most important in him—*authenticity of feeling.*

After all, can we in life foresee what will be done, with what expression something will be said by the man we are talking to, and consequently what reaction his behaviour will cause in us? We cannot, of course. Any particular meeting with another person, even with someone we meet frequently and habitually, can never be repeated exactly in later meetings.

In life we influence each other not only by listening to or looking at each other, but also directly by the mere fact of our presence. Suppose for example that two people love each other, or hate each other.

Imagine that they are sitting silently in different corners of the same room, aware of each other's presence. Inevitably inter-influence will develop between them.

For the moment it is unimportant for our purposes how this intercourse is manifested; on the contrary we want to emphasize the fact that people may directly influence each other almost imperceptibly to the eye. *This vital law of inter-influence, inner relations and their mutual influence on each other between people must be understood and transferred to the stage.*

We approached the question of organic attention, muscular freedom, etc., the same way, but it is necessary to point out that stage inter-influence, which we also learn from life, is a much more complex problem.

Here it is important to understand, that we must talk to each other, look at each other, make demands on each other, as required by the play, *not in a formal fashion, not by means of memorized external movements, but organically, on the basis of living relationships between people.* Then our inter-actions will appear life-like and convincing to the audience. We must learn to listen and watch on the stage, not in a formal way, not by just *pretending* that we are listening or watching the movements of our partner, but by grasping the substance of his words and actions, striving to apprehend not only the action, but what is behind it.

For these reasons we begin our first exercise in stage inter-influence without words.

We justify this by such a situation as: *when people who are in a definite relationship with each other are forced to refrain from talking.* Under these conditions we can easily learn stage inter-influence. For example, you are sitting in a room by the window, studying; your father, mother, or eldest brother are also there. Through the closed window you see your friend who wants you to come for a walk. You are constrained by the other people in the room and try unobserved to let your friend know that you cannot go with him.

Or another exercise: in the room, behind a curtain, your father lies very ill. You are taking care of him. Your brother and sister are on the stage, you are waiting for the doctor, any conversation or noise is harmful to the patient. You carry water, medicine, etc., behind the curtain. Between the three characters on the stage must arise a silent stage inter-influence. You are united by a common love for your father, a common sorrow caused by his sickness, and a common attitude to the expected doctor who must diagnose the illness.

Your *sense of truth* and that of the onlookers will help you determine whether the stage inter-influence arose organically, and consequently, whether you compelled the audience to believe in the act.

After doing a series of such exercises on stage inter-influence without words, pass on to stage inter-influence *with words*.

Determine your relations and the circumstances beforehand. Justify them, as you did in the former exercises. Decide on the given task (*what* and *why* you are acting); and the task your partner is to counter-act you with.

This brings us back to the leading question of our lesson, to action that encounters obstacles. Here the obstacles must be the stage task of your partner (just as your task is to counter-act him).

For instance, you come to borrow a text book from your friend, but he needs the book himself and refuses to let you have it. As a result you begin to quarrel. You start reproaching each other, bring up old scores, etc. If a living inter-relation arises between you—(inter-influence)—then you do not have to think of *what* you must say, and *how* you say it. This inter-influence will itself determine the entire course of your behaviour and its verbal expression. Remember the tasks ("I need the book," "I won't give it to you"); try to influence your partner, overcome his task, and pay no attention to the means of expression, let the words come naturally. For in life we do not stop to wonder whether our words are beautiful, coherent, and literary. We know what we need and we express our thoughts simply, often awkwardly, just as they come. Therefore, in this exercise in intercourse with words, your thoughts must be couched in simple, sincere, unpremeditated language.

We now pass on to the spoken exercises:—*the indissoluble interconnection of all elements of the system.*

The spoken exercises in inter-influence mark the culmination of everything you should have learned in the course of your lessons. Your attention must be organic. You must be muscularly free; by means of the appropriate justifications you must acquire a stage attitude (to things, facts, partners). You must act on the stage in conformity with a task which you have consciously set yourself and finally in the conflict with your partner you must become inwardly connected with him; you mutually influence each other: you establish stage inter-influence.

Remember that it is not enough to master the elements of a system separately. One must be able to combine them into a single whole (they must be indissolubly connected with one another) and as a result produce authentic stage behaviour—a reflection of behaviour in life.

If a single element is missing, then everything collapses and there is no stage life.

Look for sincere, convincing inter-relations. All must be simple and natural. Observe and study life, the simplicity of words, actions, and feelings of living people and try not to *"portray" everything on the stage, but to bring with you on to the stage that inner impulse which prompts people to act this way or that.*

And always remember that the best test of the correctness of your stage behaviour will be that feeling of truth inherent in everyone of us. For we ourselves in our capacity as spectators notice that the only good actor is the one who is simple and who convinces us by his performance, while a poor actor acts ostentatiously; he is untrue to life and therefore we do not believe him.

When thinking about subjects for spoken exercises on stage inter-influence you can place your partner and yourself in different circumstances with different degrees of dependence upon one another, while at the same time you retain your own personality, your own voice, and the expression and mannerisms natural to you in life. For instance one of you can be a watch-maker, the other—a person who has had his watch repaired and is dissatisfied with the result. The task of the second is to make the watch-maker take back the watch. The task of the first—to prove that the watch worked all right after it was repaired and to refuse to repair it a second time free-of-charge. The scene will be the watch-maker's workshop. Second example—you are urging a boatman to row you across the river but he refuses because a storm is brewing. The scene will be the river landing.

In both cases you will see that the inter-relationships are unusual —you must regard each other as strangers. You will justify the surroundings in all detail: the watch-maker should prepare the necessary instruments, watch, etc. (not real ones, of course, but articles that will serve the purpose). In the second case the passenger can be wearing an overcoat and carrying a brief-case.

In these inter-relations and surroundings you must carry out your task just as though you yourself were the watch-maker, or the passenger or the boatman. Behave as though you were a boatman and someone tried to induce you to row through a storm. As though you were a watch-maker and someone tried to induce you to repair a second time a watch you had just repaired, etc.

You must justify your behaviour to such an extent that the spectator will believe you are a watch-maker. You must handle the watch (or rather the object that represents a watch) so deftly that no one doubts you are a genuine watch-maker, although your appearance, voice, and manner have not changed.

Search for different subjects, different circumstances, different inter-relations, conflicts, and tasks, i.e., with someone you know, with someone you do not know, someone you love, father and son, brother and sister, husband, wife and mother-in-law and so on. Circumstances: a party at home, at the station, etc. You may also use the themes of separate scenes from a play for which you are rehearsing.

Each exercise should be carried on as long as possible. Try to understand and feel practically everything we have studied and in particular understand and master stage inter-influence without which all the skill of the actor, even the cleverest, will be lifeless and unconvincing.

WORK ON THE PART

In order that the spectator shall be convinced by the acting, the actor must himself be absorbed by the role, he must be moved by the feelings of the character he is playing. Accordingly we must determine the best way to work on the part. Let us assume we have a part in a particular play. We realize that in order to play the part, it is not enough just to memorise what we ourselves are to say and the cues of the other actors. We must know how to apply everything we have learned of how the actor should train himself to our work on the text and on the action that the part involves.

In considering and studying the text of the play and of your part, first determine the following points: what the play is about, what events occur in it, and what are the actions of the character you are to play. At the same time it is necessary to distinguish the main events and actions from those which are of secondary importance.

The more faithful and convincing the *action* of the role is reproduced on the stage the better will be the execution of the role. It has already been stated that the external reproduction of a person's actions is insufficient for external action is integrally connected with internal action. You must also reproduce internal action (thoughts and feelings) if your behaviour is to be lifelike, convincing, and organic. Therefore, when studying the role we must determine what were the immediate causes that evoke this or that action on the part of the character, i.e., *what desire* prompts him to the given action.

We also know that internal action (thoughts, feelings) arise in our consciousness as a result of the action of external reality. So in order to find the immediate reasons for the character's actions (his desire) we must also seek their deeper causes. We must ascertain under the influence of what other characters and events the given character acts thus and not otherwise. In other words, we must ascertain *the character's relations with the outside world.*

From this follows the third basic point to be determined: what is the particular character's attitude toward each of the remaining characters, to the events of the play, and to the outside world in general? As we shall see later this is the most complex part of our work and this is the way of establishing the *personality* of the part.

Thus the actor, in playing this or that part, must perform definite actions. In order that the words and actions of the actor shall be convincing, he must be able to delineate his character's inner makeup and pursue the same ends as are desired by the given character.

In order to assimilate this inner world, the actor must define his attitude toward, and inter-actions, with the outer world as given within the limits of the play. As a result, the thoughts and feelings of the role become clear to the actor. By sympathising with the part and living the part he will experience its emotions and thereby carry the audience along with him.

DIVISION INTO SECTIONS

The text and the respective parts are first divided according to acts, then according to scenes; either an encounter with a new character or the exit of some character, etc. Finally a sudden turn in the course of events may mark the end of one and the beginning of another section (of a scene).

Find the chief task—the prevailing action. By dividing the role into sections, ascertaining the basic task of each section and discarding all that is of secondary importance, we arrive at a definite series *of tasks, actions and desires.* There begins to appear before us the central, leading action of the character and the *goal which he aims at throughout the play. We shall term this the prevailing action of the role.*

TEXT AND SUB-TEXT

You should go about learning the text of the part the same way that you did the exercises on fulfilling the scenic task.

You must make the words of the role your own words. And this will only be accomplished once it is clear to you not only *what* the person says but *why* he says it. Only then will you acquire lifelike expression (adjustment).

The written words of the role constitute the text. But *the purpose for which the words are spoken, their inner meaning, we call the "sub-text."* The sound of the phrase, the expression, will be lifelike and plausible provided the words are said with the intention of influencing your partner through their meaning (sub-text). This also is one of the means of stage inter-influence which we discussed previously.

PRINCIPAL FEATURES OF CHARACTERIZATION

While analysing and determining the sections, tasks and prevailing action of the role the work done on ascertaining the inter-relations with other characters in the play proceeds. This work proceeds on the basis of *careful and thoughtful study of the play. And as well as careful study of the reality which the play portrays.*

The manners and customs of the time in their turn reflect the social relations. The writings of contemporaries, newspapers, journals, photographs, pictures, works of art, fashions, etc., should all furnish material for our *creative fantasy* which selects the most characteristic, expressive traits, and these when combined result in our interpretation of the role. *For the selecting and uniting of these traits we shall be influenced by the thoughts, feelings, and attitudes that the given epoch and given characters arouse in us.*

The character's personality, his inner world, finds its expression in his actions and words, as well as in the actions and opinions of those around him. The better the author—the clearer and more vivid are his word pictures, and the more expressive and distinct the form of the character appears before us. Naturally the external appearance of the actor must be in accordance with the characteristics of the role.

IMPORTANCE OF THE VARIOUS SECTIONS

In dividing the role into sections, determining their content, noting the task in each section, and the main line of the role present in every section (*the prevailing action*), we determine the degree of importance of each section. The closer the task of the section conforms to the prevailing action of the role, the more important the section is. This does not mean, of course, that there are sections of a role where the acting is of no importance. Every section, even the most insignificant, helps in the creation of the role as a whole. There must be no dissonance; each section must organically follow from the one before. To strike a false note in any one section means to spoil the role as a whole. It is however necessary to determine what is more important, what less important (transitory) in the role, to understand what is essential, to appraise the various sections of the role, and to distribute the "emphasis."

If you want to build a house, you plan the most important features—the living room, kitchen, etc.; the remainder—the attic, the roof, the window frames, etc., are all quite necessary, but less important to the building as a whole. We know that to the size of the house all its parts must correspond. To violate this proportion—to make a small section bigger than the more important parts—means to create an ungainly building. One could, of course, build without a foundation or with only an attic, but that would alter the character of the structure; it would no longer be a house but, say, a dovecot. Thus the proportion between the sections of the role must be observed. Otherwise it is impossible to understand the role, and make it understandable to the audience.

To make this or that part of the role more or less important, to bring to the foreground or gloss over this or that characteristic trait is the work of the actor and the director on their attitude to the role. This is called the interpretation of the role.

We shall now attempt to explain the technique of work on the character, the process of delineating the external characteristics, etc.

Let us once more remind ourselves to observe life and study life. On the stage we must reproduce the actions contained in the role, making them as true to life as we can. Having memorized the words we must strive to deliver them simply, making them comprehensible to our partner, and in order to do this we must listen to and catch the meaning of what our partner says.

All our work on the role must be guided by our *sense of truth*.

DESIGN OF THE ROLE (INTERNAL AND EXTERNAL)

We already said that in our work on the role we must assimilate the words of our part thoroughly. To this end we try to understand them, master their inner meaning so that we may determine at any given moment why the words are being said.

In this way we establish a sub-text in accordance with which this or that quality of expression is generated in the delivery.

In defining the main elements of the stage task we pointed out that the third element—adjustment (nature and form of action)—appears as the result of the first two elements—the action (*what* I do) and the purpose behind it (*why* I do it). We also said that it never does to invent adjustments, i.e., *how* to carry out an action. In performing the action it is necessary to concentrate on "*why* I am doing it,"—the corresponding form, the character of the action (adjustment) will then follow of itself.

The meaning of a phrase is brought out by the same process. We must not predetermine our expression. We must not seek the proper expression, the tone of the phrase, so to speak, "by ear." On the contrary, in pronouncing the phrase we must concentrate on *why* we are saying it, we must attempt to influence our partner by its meaning (stage inter-influence). Only then will we achieve the proper expression. It is the task of the director and the actor himself, guided by his sense of truth, to catch the most correct expression, make sure of it, and remember it. Indeed it is not so much the given expression that should be remembered as the inner feeling which evoked it.

In this way, during the process of rehearsing, various adjustments accumulate and the expression of the text is established.

From the selection and combination of the most convincing stage actions, corresponding to our interpretation of the role, arises the basic pattern of the role. We accomplish this selection by constant application of our sense of truth and sense of stage expressiveness in the course of our work. We then perfect and memorize the design we have decided upon.

We don't use the word "memorize" in the sense of something merely learned by rote. The actor must memorize the pattern of the role organically with his whole being. He must impress upon his mind the entire continuity of thoughts and feelings and corresponding external actions which was established in the course of the rehearsals, during the creative work on the mastery of the role.

THE ATTITUDE TO THE CHARACTER

Thus we master the character's words and actions. We master his thoughts and feelings, and try to put ourselves in his place, reproducing his behaviour. We create a stage character and attempt to evoke in the audience this or that attitude to the character. If we sympathise with the character, if we approve of the character's actions, then our aim will be to arouse a similar attitude to the character on the part of the audience. We shall be satisfied with our performance if we feel on the stage that our sorrow as acted in the given role has brought tears of sympathy to the eyes of the spectators or that our happiness makes them happy. And vice versa, if our attitude to our character is a negative one, if we want, say, to make fun of the character, our aim will be achieved when we evoke a corresponding response from the audience, when they laugh at the character we have created. In one instance the laughter will be ironical, in another well-meant, and the very nature of the laughter evoked in the audience will depend on the actor's attitude to the character. And in this case, as in every case, we must live and feel the emotions of the character. But when we have established the design of the role, chosen the adjustments—the so-called 'colors" of the role—we must be guided by our attitude to it and this will constitute our concept, our interpretation of the role.

Our attitude to the role we are playing is formed as a result of studying the material of the play and the reality which it reflects. In many instances our attitude to the character may coincide with the author's attitude. The conception presented by the author in the given role is one that is familiar to us—and therefore we need only go into the role thoroughly and fully, and present the author's conception. But it may happen that in studying the epoch, the reality portrayed by

65

the author, our attitude may be other than that of the author, and then will arise a new conception of the character, our own conception, correcting and supplementing the author's.

It is perfectly obvious that the nearer the author's material and the roles are to the reality we ourselves are familiar with the easier it will be for us to master the treatment of this material and supply our own corrections in its interpretation.

CHARACTERIZATION: INNER AND OUTER FEATURES

Let us once again repeat what you must do in order to achieve the above. Study the material of the role, analyse what the given character does in the play, the aims and desires that prompt his actions. Through the sequence of stage tasks, determined by you in the different sections of the role, the main action and the main end to which it is directed, the prevailing action of the role runs like a red thread. This prevailing action to a large extent determines the main traits of the character of the given role.

But the determination of the prevailing action alone does not provide a sufficient basis on which to establish our attitude to the given role, or consequently to choose the corresponding character traits, by means of which we are to build up the role. We must also understand the relation of the given character to the surrounding reality. We must study this reality and thereby determine what causes determine his behaviour and what ends he pursues. In this way we make a social analysis of the play and of the role and at this point only can we finally determine the attitude on the basis of which we shall seek to create the character.

Different social circumstances call for different attitudes. We feel sorry for a poor farm-hand who steals because he is starving. We do not laugh at him. We laugh, however, at a rich banker who cheats his depositors and who then walks into a trap himself. And there will be malice in our laughter; we shall in no way feel sorry for him.

Hence the determination of the prevailing action and simultaneously the social evaluation of the character are the foundation upon which we build the given character.

After this we must clothe this frame in its external attributes.

In studying the play and the part we ascertain the age, the physical constitution and the profession of the given character, his principal traits, his relations with the other characters. We attempt to picture him to ourselves as fully and clearly as possible. Using our creative fantasy, we try to *justify everything* pertaining to the role, to imagine how he should walk, talk and gesticulate, how his character was formed, how he spends his time. We must picture his past and future in our fantasy, his behaviour in circumstances not in the play. We must live with him, mentally, through his entire life, so that the action reproduced in the play will be for us the portrayal of a life almost as familiar as our own. In this way, using our fantasy, we picture the inner and outer characteristics of the part, and strive to render them as convincingly and sincerely as possible.

The role of a heavy, corpulent, headstrong banker requires considerable physical adaptation. Learn to walk the way fat people walk. It is hard for a fat man to turn his neck; how does he do it? It is hard for him to sit down or stand up; how does he do that? How does he eat and drink? Reproduce the physical behaviour of a fat man in such a way that no one will doubt you are really fat. But do not pretend, do not over-act—"as if you were fat." Observe fat men in life and try as correctly as possible to reproduce them on the stage. The same applies in other cases, as in mastering the external characteristics of the part. If you are to play an old man, acquire the appropriate gait so that from the back everyone will take you for an old man. The sound of your voice and your diction should be so modified that if you were to speak from behind a curtain, everyone would take you for an old man. Choose the proper make-up which will blend with your own face to give the impression of old age. It is necessary that the characteristics appear natural and not artificial. They should be so combined with your own given characteristics that the result will provide the required impression.

But remember that the most important thing of all is stage attitude, which is the foundation on which the role is built up. And above all do not forget that the essence of the role appears in the actor's eyes.

Let us suppose you are to play a jolly character: everything makes him happy, everything he looks at is pleasant. His eyes will have a merry twinkle in them. Try to regard the surrounding world the way such an exhuberant fellow would, and your eyes will also acquire a twinkle. That will be the inner essence of the role. Or, on the contrary, you are to play an irritable fellow, a grouch. Seek to express his attitude to the world. *Look at the world through the eyes of your character.* This is the most important requisite for the actor in his work on the role. Everything that has been said above about external characteristics (gait, voice) is partly a consequence of and partly a supplement to the inner characteristics which are primarily expressed in the actor's eyes.

In accumulating the many attributes and features that go to constitute the character and trying to reproduce them at rehearsals, you will reach a certain point where you will feel that you have found the essence, that you have mastered the role. You feel at home in it. The character has taken definite shape; it has become organic. You have acquired a complete understanding and feeling of the role from all angles, you have grasped its rhythm; it has come to life.

The word "rhythm" which is hard to define is in practice very familiar to the actor. The actor knows that every role, properly played, has its own distinguishing rhythm. A person's manner of thinking and feeling and his own way of expressing his feelings, his manner of moving, looking, speaking, in a word, his entire behaviour, finds expression in a definite rhythm peculiar to the given person.

We shall illustrate this concept with the following example: a cat can run, arch its back, raise its tail, move either swiftly or slowly but it does all this with an inherent feline rhythm. Or take an elephant, for example; it can move slowly or run, dance or flap its ears—all with the rhythm natural to an elephant.

In the work on the role the time will arrive for combining the separate parts of behaviour into a single whole. The ends of the circle of action meet. The role will then be complete, its rhythm established.

It is, of course, difficult within the limits of this article to say everything regarding work on the role and the requisite preparation for this work. Our task in this respect is further complicated by the fact that in no other sphere does the transmission of experience depend to such a large extent on direct contact with the student, on the possibility of showing and checking up on what is shown as it does in the theatre. It is exceedingly difficult to use the so-called correspondence-course method. But if the present article does not explain the question of the actor's technique to the full, we can at least hope it will arouse a measure of interest and make for a serious approach to the art of the stage in general and to the work of the actor in particular.

THE CREATIVE
PROCESS

By I. SUDAKOV

THESE LECTURES WHICH I PRESENTED TO THE YOUNG STUDENTS of the
theatrical schools and young actors do not pretend to expound the system
of Constantin Stanislavski or V. Nemirovitch-Dantchenko. They are a
part of the studies which I conducted for two years at the Department of
Directing of the Moscow Theatrical University. The ideas contained
in these lectures doubtless took shape under the influence of the knowledge obtained from the leading figures of the Moscow Art Theatre, but
these lectures are only a modest interpretation of their doctrines and, I
wish to emphasize, they do not pretend to be a presentation of the
complete system of these great master of the dramatic arts.

INTRODUCTION

When viewed from the angle of our study course an actor performing upon the stage can be considered an apparatus set up for certain
functions; an apparatus, similar, let us say, to a rifle which exists for
the purpose of shooting. Sometimes the latter is taken apart and its
parts are analyzed, (as is done in military schools). This is somewhat
the way we must study the elements which enter into the creative work
of the actor. For, in the light of accumulated experience, it becomes

clear that the creative process has definite conscious mainsprings (the intuitive subconscious or superconscious creativeness—"proceeding from the visceral self"—even when we grant its existence, is of little interest to us since we cannot study it.) Former theatre schools confined themselves to teaching diction, plastique, fencing, recitation; but that which is essentially the function of the actor, *his real work,* was not analyzed by those schools which had but fragmentary, meagre understanding of this activity. This was due to the lack of an accumulated, consciously analyzed experience.

Today such experience already exists; and it is possible to speak of the science of art, of the assimilation of some of the laws of creative work, the ignorance of which revenge themselves upon the creator in the form of bitter failures and pangs of discontent. In order to study those laws and to train one's artistic nature in subjection to them, one must be organically predisposed to the work—one must possess the ability to sense and release into action the elements that must necessarily participate in the process of creative work. These elements must, under favorable circumstances, be released into action with more or less spontaneity. This means that the person in question must possess the abilities and a specific predilection for such work. Later on this predilection and these abilities which, I repeat, must be there originally, will be worked over and will become subject to a process of training and cultivation. This means that upon comparing the working apparatus of the actor with that of a rifle we find that the difference lies in the ability of the former to improve itself. The elements that go to make up this apparatus may rise to a higher quality when used correctly, cautiously, and with a certain degree of thoughtful attentiveness. Such are the remarkable qualities possessed by this living apparatus when used in such a manner as to have them brought out in their true light.

I shall therefore insist somewhat arbitrarily upon approaching the creative nature of the actor as an expeditious apparatus. This is of importance from the view-point of methodology and basic principles; for the essence of the study of the complex psychic nature of the creative process consists in reducing its complexity to the simple and most primary elements; and of reducing complex psychology to elementary physical acts, to the simplicity of concrete physical behavior.

I shall now try to list in a cursory manner the elements of the creative process, name them, analyze their nature, show their interaction and also point out the maladies to which these things may become subjected. Then I will point out the remedies to be applied.

The creative work of the artist is participated in by elements of a twofold nature: namely, those relating to the so-called *inner technique* and those relating to the *outer technique*. Both are subject to the working of certain laws and this obliges us to study the nature of these laws. Let us first analyze the inner technique.

What is the essence of the actor's work and of the theatre itself, inasmuch as the actor constitutes the essential part of the latter? The basis of everything is *action*. This may sound like a truism and it is possible there will be many a truism in my lectures for such truths now seem to be in the very air. However, the very fact that these truths enter our consciousness does not assure their proper assimilation. Years are required to understand them properly. A purely intellectual mastery of these ideas does not add anything to the actor. It does not signify that he really understands the nature of a given work: he will not be able to understand it unless he makes this knowledge a part of his organism, unless he comes to feel it in "his hide"; for the acting apparatus is the living actor himself and all acting elements are the elements of a given individual. In order to sense the inter-action of those elements it is necessary to bring them into *action*; only thus shall we be able to understand those truisms which now seem to pervade the consciousness of the entire theatrical world. All home-spun theories and current opinions and thoughts on the nature of theatrical creativeness must inevitably give place to a system of knowledge, some notion of which I shall now try to impart to you.

The actor must first of all *act*. But the actor's actions are very complex and often the actor takes for action something which is not so.

Take an elementary example. Those things which can be done by anyone and which we perform mechanically almost every day. Let us, for instance, ask every one that comes to these lectures what he is interested in? He comes in, looks around, wants to listen to a lecture, looks for an empty seat. This can be performed by anyone because it is by its very nature a very simple operation. I could ask you, "Please latch the door so that no one can enter the room." You can also do that mechanically. As you see, at the basis of every elementary act is appetency, desire, want. And in the last analysis, all human life is resolved into such simple actions. Imagine that you experience some unusually strong emotion: you may suffer from jealousy or from some similar emotion, but in the long run, all your actions can be resolved into a series of elementary acts. I shall never forget the instance related to us by Nemirovitch-Dantchenko. During the rehearsal of one of the scenes of *The Brothers Karamazov* in which Mitya—L. M. Leonidov—rushes into Grushenka's apartment looking for her and suspecting that she went to Feodor Karamazov, L. M. Leonidov frantically broke into the apartment and rushed along the room from one end to the other, but neither he nor the director nor anyone else present at the rehearsal had that feeling of satisfaction which comes when actual truth is achieved. Wanting to find the cause, Nemirovitch-Dantchenko went up on the stage and began to experiment with himself in the role of Mitya. All of a sudden everyone felt—there it was—the real truth. What had happened? "I just began", Nemirovitch-Dantchenko told us, "to look for a comb which I felt I had lost in that room". And so it turned out that he had to strike upon an elementary act, to be actually looking for something, in order that all could come to believe in the genuine truth of the painful frenzy of jealousy on the part of Mitya breaking into Grushenka's apartment.

No sooner does the actor come out upon the stage to enact a part that is packed with intense feeling than he seizes upon those feelings, trying to act them out, and thus foredooms himself to clichés which inevitably distort the nature of his acting. Feelings should never be forced. One should ask himself: what would one do, what simple action would he perform if he found himself in despair; if, for example, he were rejected by the girl whom he loved or if he were to vacate an apartment for failure to pay his rent. In such cases he would start doing something or at least he would begin thinking about some plan of action. This observation is of the utmost importance to us because actions and thoughts are subject to our will. I can give myself an account of what I might possibly think. Yes, I might think this or do that. "But what might *I* think"? Just ask yourself that question and you will see how inappropriate that question is, say, at the moment one is being ordered out of his apartment. The question does not give one a program of action; it is a question of the nature of one's mood. Of greater interest are other questions: how to arrange one's affairs, what to do about one's debts, where to put up one's family. What I might feel—this should not even be answered. To think of what I might have thought, said or done in such a case—that is the best way of making oneself have that inner experience. To think of how I might feel in any given situation is the surest way of falling into the beaten track of affected acting. Try to act, to meet obstacles and to overcome them and you will come to feel as you should in the given case.

What does it mean to act artificially? It is the direct opposite of *scenic action*. One can, for instance, rant or, as they say, "tear a passion to tatters". This means to inflate a passion—rapture, anger, fright—without concretely executing the actions which accompany those emotions. Likewise one can give a stereotyped impersonation of a character, that is, portray all the habits, manners, and ways of the given character without the logic and consistency of action which find their external expressions in these habits and manners. One can act a phrase; that is, portray and stress a certain passion in the intonation of a phrase, thus acquiring a stereotyped manner of pronouncing the phrase. Crude examples of this were given by the ranting of provincial tragedians in former times. In milder forms the same can be found upon any stage now when the actor, for instance, puts a sentimental quiver into his voice, or injects a throbbing saccharine note into some emotional phrase.

The line of affected acting is opposed to the true line of life, that is, to stage acting. And all the perversions and failings of the elements of scenic actions which we shall analyze mark the downward trend toward the path of stenciled acting.

If you analyze human life, you will see that it can be resolved into a series of actions which are simple and can be easily executed. An elementary action is remarkable because of the very fact that it is convenient and does not arouse any doubts as to the manner of its execution. It is reflex action—you just do it on the spur of the moment. This is what takes place in life. But no sooner do you ask someone to perform the same acts upon the stage than you begin to get a number of surprises, and a complex series of misunderstandings begin to pile up. Why? It is simply because everyone is likely to get lost when facing an audience. Right now I am speaking to you and I seem to be quite serene, but that is only apparently so. Should I stand in my room in the same manner, I should probably be calmer. But still my present calmness is undeniable; only it is of a factitious nature. And that is why it has to be learned. One who appears before a mass of people is apt to lose self-possession, and once this takes place he becomes irresponsible. He is liable to keep pouring his drinking water outside his glass or anything else equally as absurd. And that is the danger that faces any actor when he appears upon the stage.

ATTENTION AND OBJECT

How can self-possession be made secure? To answer this question we shall analyze the nature of a simple act. Just as infinitely complex organisms are made out of elementary cells so the complex patterns of behavior are made out of elementary acts. Every elementary act demands for its emergence the presence of two elements: *attention* and an *object*. When for some reason the actor loses the ability to act, then we have diffused attention. Suppose I lose control of myself and cannot see clearly where the decanter and glass are, I find it difficult to fill the glass because of my wandering attention. I come out upon the stage, see the audience and become confused; I cannot detach my attention and thoughts from the teeming auditorium. I speak and do not hear my own voice. I am at a loss what to do with my hands. A tense state on the part of the actor is, in the above case, a result of the loss of attention and object. *Scenic action demands the deepest concentration of attention.*

Attention is divided into two kinds—*directed and spontaneous.* Chelpanov (the author of a popular textbook on psychology) maintains that women and children have a more highly-developed spontaneous attention (that is, that they are greatly subject to the power of external impression and that they are more easily swayed by any external stimulus and are apt to lose control over their psychic processes), while men, on the other hand, possess a more concentrated attention. We shall soon refute the validity of this contention in regard to women but we must admit that the attention of children is more spontaneous, non-directed. When a child cries, he can be easily placated and will soon forget all about his tears. But anything that may come up is liable to precipitate a new fit of crying. The child is entirely swayed by external stimuli; his attention is of the spontaneous, non-directed kind.

The ability to concentrate differs with people. Some can attend to their work although everything around them may be turned upside down. Let us suppose that someone plays the piano and keeps on making

74

all sorts of noises in an adjoining room and notwithstanding all this we can continue to pursue our scientific or artistic work. But the more such obstacles arise, the greater the will power necessary for concentration upon one's work. Thus attention is a mobile, changing faculty which can and should be developed. This trivial truth is of special significance to us right now. Bear in mind that the training of the will—the ability to get hold of one's attention and direct it upon the required object—is very important. We need exercises for the concrete execution of separate tasks.

It sometimes happens that the actor has a full grasp of the action assigned to him. He begins to act but then something happens to his will; it cracks and he loses his power of attention. As a result, he becomes incapable of performing even the most elementary act which the given moment demands of him. He makes unnecessary, superfluous, non-functional movements; he begins to act in an ostentatious manner violating the nature of simple actions. The ability to master one's attention in full, regardless of any circumstances, and always to cleave to the necessary object is a fundamental rule for the actor. Once such mastery has been obtained the action is then executed as a reflex, a motor-discharge without any halts. But if the attention is distracted, the will gives way. Then we say, "I cannot rehearse in the presence of others", or, "I find it very hard to do it now, I'd rather do it alone". And then intimate rehearsals are arranged.

Let a young, inexperienced actor begin to execute simple actions before a large audience and let him begin to regulate his attention. He may immediately think, "I cannot rid myself of the idea that someone is looking at me, that someone is present right near me, and that is why I cannot direct my attention upon the right object". A muscular tension arises: "Something is bothering me, I feel that my muscles have become tense. I don't feel myself free any longer. I am paralyzed". But as soon as he obtains mastery of his attention, as soon as he succeeds in directing it expeditiously upon the object, everything becomes simple.

All of you have had more or less schooling in elementary theatre practise, and so you are acquainted with this kind of feeling. The nature of the difficulty lies in the fact that the attention is scattered, not focused, and that you cannot grasp the immediate object. Hence follows the conclusion made above—the attention must be exercised.

Let us begin with the most simple exercises. Look over the walls of this room very carefully and try to see whether they contain any spotty, uneven places. I will say, "Keep your attention riveted on those walls for about half an hour trying, of course, to constantly feed your attention with new material". Incidentally, this is an exercise for the fantasy. Imagine that you would have to sit in this very same room for about ten years. Then would you have studied it well indeed!

To exercise one's attention is to exercise one's will. Thus you exercise your will and after a certain time after studying a wall for one minute you will be able to mark all its peculiarities—an act which formerly required half an hour of concentration. Then you can train yourself to do this in half a minute, or possibly less.

But here difficulties begin. When the very same process has to be run over more quickly than usual, one sometimes loses the power of controlling attention; one ceases to see anything, and merely darts his eyes about. Attention has to be trained to notice things rapidly and to seize upon many objects at once. Alert minds can do this. In both literature and history such qualities are attributes of men of strong will, of vigorous and robust thought.

And now about the objective—that upon which your attention is centered. Here, for instance, is a decanter. It can be regarded from the point of view of form—whether it is beautiful or not; or from the point of view of convenience—whether, let us say, it should be used as a container for water or whiskey? In every given case the objective changes; that is, every decanter may serve hundreds of such objectives. A person may become one thing to me if I ask him for money, and another if I suspect him, or want to congratulate him about something and happen to meet with his indifference. It is to be noted in this connection that the nature of the action varies with the change of objective. Do you see now how significant the objective becomes?

Let us take, for instance, the phrase delivered by Natasha, the ten year old little girl from Afinogenov's play, *Fear*. Natasha comes to the apartment of Professor Borodin for the first time and, seeing dolls on the desk exclaims: "Auntie Clara, see how many dolls there are!" How should such a phrase be uttered? What kind of inner action should it be linked up with? The immediate suggestion is that of the resounding phrase, "Auntie C-L-A-R-A see how m-a-n-y do-o-lls there are!" We are trying to impersonate a little girl who sees ravishing dolls before her. Hence, the exclamation. Then follows "And to whom do these dolls belong? To—to your little girl"? This may be delivered in a sonorous manner, as is proper for a ten-year old girl.

And so everything falls directly into the groove of the stereotype—a theatrical "little-girl-in-general", who rejoices at and admires the dolls in a general way. Natasha does not frequent professiorial apartments— in fact, she sees such an apartment for the first time. Now, let us ask ourselves: what does it mean to enter a house for the first time and especially a house that would appear so unusual for Natasha? Large shelves filled with books, the austerity and even the stiffness of the setting, the strange arrangement of the vast rooms, the towering statue overhung with canvas—Natasha's attention is wholly occupied by these strange new things. And then all of a sudden, she sees dolls right here in this austere environment. Their presence cannot be taken in without intimate association with the environment. Although the dolls, being closest to the child, rivet her attention, they are an indissoluble part of a larger context—of an austere and strange apartment. And then the phrase: "See how many dolls there are"! will sound like an exclamation of amazement and perplexity carrying the unuttered thought. Who could possibly play dolls in this learned apartment? The child will not utter this in her loudest voice; the feeling of wonder will express itself in a different manner. The object in this case will be the sudden appearance of dolls in such a setting. The more the attention is fixed on this object, the more urgent becomes Natasha's question, "And to whom do these dolls belong—to your little girl"? Try to work all that out and you will see that in the second interpretation we fall into the line of action and not into just acting out the character. The false note arose because the actress in the first interpretation did not direct her attention upon a precise object. The organic intimate feeling of the object, the fullest concentration upon it— this is what the actor needs. A blurred object tends to undermine action.

Thus *attention* and *object* are the elements and conditions of the emergence of elementary action.

In actual life this apparatus works well. But as soon as the actor comes upon the stage, we observe that his attention weakens and that his objective loses its firm outlines or may vanish altogether. He listens, but we feel that he does not hear. That is, he does not realize what is taking place around him; he does not perceive the object to which his attention should be directed.

If you say something insulting to me, I will know how to respond. At first perhaps, I shall be surprised; then I shall try to find the cause of your behavior and finally, I will react in some manner. If I deserved the insult, I will try to apologize. If not, if I remain misunderstood, I shall be forced to take some proper action. But, let us say, such an insult is presented on the stage and the effect of it seems to be lost. And so we have an altogether incomprehensible and unwarranted sort of thing; but that is only apparently so, for in reality this all becomes quite easily understood when we come to see that the actor does not know, does not feel the object to which his attention should have been directed —and that is the reason why he did not *act*. That is, he let the insult pass by, he did not fix his attention upon it. He missed the malicious eye of the partner, the rhythm of the movements of his rancor, etc. (depending upon the form in which the wrath of the partner would have found its expression). For if he had come to feel the object, he would have begun to act immediately. That he could do *only* if his attention and the object were in close contact. That is, the attention would have been directed expeditiously upon the object necessary for the given action, each and every object demanding a different attention.

Such is the organic relation of the basic parts of human behavior. *Object and attention*—these are the component elements and conditions of the emergence of what we call elementary action.

I explain all this in a general way because I cannot convey to you all the necessary information in my brief talks. Two years of joint work would improve your acting. Four years of it would improve it more. Additional years—still more. I am saying this on the basis of the experience I and those who have been working with me or with the other directors of the Moscow Art Theatre or its school have had.

A long time is required before one begins to grasp the elementary truths to which I am now referring. And the more mutual understanding there is, the more interesting these talks will be, as a common language will evolve in time. Such a common language must be created upon every stage by the actors and director. Without it art as a culture can have no existence of its own, since it demands a definite atmosphere for its development. Only Motchalov could act without such a culture, or a common language, or a painstaking training in the basic elements of acting. But it sufficed to tell him, "Look here, today the Grand Duke is going to be present at your performance. You will have to make a good showing", and he would inevitably fail, simply because the Grand Duke was lodged in his brain, dispersing his attention. He could not release action and without that he was a mere zero on the stage. He failed because less than anyone else was he the actor of technique. With him, everything proceeded from intuition. And he paid dearly for that. This teaches us why we have to count upon an exact knowledge of our physical and mental apparatus—not upon intuition.

Let us go back to the problem of exercising one's attention. Take a mental trip to our Far Eastern territory. Then try to think what it would mean to pay a visit to Hitler. Picture to yourself the details of such a visit; try to find some warrant for it. How did you happen to go? Perhaps you were admitted into the place where he was delivering a speech. Run over in your mind the various objects conceived; do this within a given time. In all scenic work, wherever you begin to perform the most simple action, you necessarily have to train your attention. This reduces the necessary amount of special training in exercising the attention.

THE FEELING OF TRUTH

And so we break up man's behavior into separate, simple, physical actions. But parallel to those there is another process which differentiates the life upon the stage from man's ordinary life. When we perform ordinary acts in daily life, we do not think of how to do them. But upon the stage a certain modification is taking place which requires special attention in virtue of the fact that there emerges the new element of the actor's creativeness. This is the *feeling of truth* or *control*. Whenever I do something on the stage, I inevitably take cognizance of a sixth sense —I have to see to it that I perform my task correctly. I cannot rid myself of that feeling of *shadowing myself* (this shadowing is very beneficial, since it enables me to see whether I act correctly). Like the fabled Roman geese it raises an alarm whenever a catastrophe impends.

When one has to dissemble in life, he keeps an eye upon himself to see whether or not his dissembling is good enough, since any failure in this respect may lead to undesired results. In ordinary life, this feeling of falsity comes only when one has to enact something. But upon the stage it must always be present. An actor who loses his feeling of truth is like a blind man.

In Stanislavski's book, *My Life in Art,* you will find a somewhat different and broader definition of the term, *the feeling of truth.* I want to emphasize that I am deliberately using this term here in the sense of *ordinary control exercised upon the execution of an act.*

The more the actor cultivates his behavior, the less direct is his acting and the more is it done chiefly for the audience's sake. This leads to the transfer of the center of attention to the audience which thus becomes the object and distorts the nature of simple action. Nevertheless the underlying basis of the control of the actor's behavior will *always* be the eyes of the audience. No "fourth wall" will ever eradicate this feeling. Consequently, we should advise the actor not to watch the vibrations of the audience (the awareness of it being there just the same) but see that he has the right object upon which to fasten his attention in working out a scenic task and that truthful stage actions be executed with the utmost economy of means.

How can this be attained? Ask yourself, "What would I do if I found myself under such and such circumstances?" At this moment the imagination begins to operate and impels one toward concrete action. This renders possible the fixing of attention upon the right object and the emergence of truthful action, and immediately brings into life the instrument of control.

Thus an excessive awareness of the audience while exercising control leads to a breakdown—to the cessation of action. And, on the other hand, the necessary feeling of truth can be developed to the extent of hysteria.

There are actors who no sooner try to do something than they are immediately checked by the inner fear of a false tone. Such excessive feeling of truth may paralyze the will, and should be treated by exercising the will and the attention. While the objective is attained by concentrating with the intention of obtaining it, the feeling of truth cannot be intimidated.

There is another malady incidental to control and that is the underdevelopment of the feeling of truth. What are the methods of development and of strengthening of this feeling of truth? These are the so-called exercises of sense-memory, that is, actions lacking any object.

Let us, for instance, undertake systematic exercises of this sort: to wash without water or soap, or to dry one's self without a towel. To comb one's hair without a comb, to shave without a razor, to make tea without a samovar, to work on a sewing machine without the machine and material, etc. While you do these exercises try to recollect, to go through in your mind, the minutest details and particulars of executing these actions in such a manner as if they were being performed in real life. See that the smallest details correspond to actuality; try to take notice of everything that is unfinished, incorrect, untrue.

These exercises strengthen the feeling of truth. Here the control will assert its effectiveness, the action lacking a real object. Imagination will suggest in this case, "If I had a real object, I would do this and that", and the feeling of truth adds thereto, "I would do it in such and such a manner".

Sense-memory exercises develop the feeling of truth and also train the actor in the proper scenic awareness. The truthfulness of scenic behavior is dependent upon his physical self-awareness; upon the set of circumstances in which the actor finds himself at the given moment— whether he is hungry or satisfied, sleepy or rested, relaxed in the open air after work or sitting in a smoky room with a splitting headache; whether he is tired, ill, etc. Added to that is the concentration of attention upon the necessary object—the elementary action with which the actor is concerned at this given moment. Physical self-awareness and concentration of attention—these are the conditions necessary for release from the spell of the auditorium, for achieving the state wherein the actor may go on doing his work in public without being at all self-conscious. This gives him the maximum of freedom for the execution of scenic tasks. Such a state is the creative "I am". Otherwise, one may raise a cup and drink the wine in such a manner that not only will it be spilled, but also all one's neighbors will be splashed with it. One falsehood leads to another. If I swing out too far, this means that I have become self-conscious, perplexed and hence, in turn, I become inso-lent. I let myself go. Perplexity turns into brazenness and impudence. This is quite logical since the actor, when he comes out upon the stage, does not yet know the nature of his concrete tasks. That is why he is afraid, trying very often to suppress this feeling of fear by being over self-confident. He assumes an easy and happy-go-lucky manner (the outward show of impudence) in order to camouflage the feeling of fear.

Afterwards this becomes a habit with him. His fear is gone but the impudence remains, becoming a part of the assumed nature of the actor's "I am".

And so it is necessary to work upon this "I am", to find for it a simple, convenient form from which fear and timidity are absent. And for that one has to work upon the object and attention. Since there still remains the possibility of this "I am" becoming unbalanced, it would be well to learn the nature of the most elementary action, not only in a purely intellectual manner, *but also with one's whole being,* by working upon a great mass of experiments and exercises. This is especially important with a young actor. Then it is necessary, by proceeding from one's own inner self (and not from a character), to substitute all kinds of "ifs", to ask oneself for instance, what would I do *if* I had to wait a long time for the train? Or *if* I found out that I lost my last bit of money, or *if* I were told that people are waiting for me at the place where I work and I am still at home, still in bed, etc.? This means one must retain the feeling of truth, that voice of control which keeps on signaling all the time: all right! good! I believe . . . or else: not so, I don't believe it, you lied—just as soon as you begin to get out of tune. It is very important for the actor himself to be on good terms with his inner censor.

Let us assume we have a young actor before us. He has his book, the role, the play. He begins to read and immediately his voice becomes unnatural. I have had the opportunity to observe shop-workers. A man comes from the workers' club, begins to read not simply, but with a cheap kind of pathos. He visualizes himself as a peculiar sort of person and he reads in a peculiar voice, without realizing that this is altogether unnecessary and is taken from a very bad theatre that should have been laughed out of existence long ago. How can this be knocked out of him? The only way to do it is to train him with the "if" method. He has to be asked, "Well, what would you do *if* you were imparted such and such kind of news; how would you behave under those circumstances"? He will then start thinking how he would act, what he would say and think. This alone will enable him to find his own road.

To learn to execute simple actions upon the stage expeditiously means to work in harmony with one's histrionic apparatus; it means to discover one's ground and to plant oneself firmly upon it. In this lies the guarantee of a truthful behavior upon the stage. Such a neces-

sary ideal situation can be obtained by strengthening our feeling of
truth with the help of exercises built upon sense-memory and by re-
fining the power of inner control.

And so upon the basis of a great mass of exercises, it is necessary
to master the nature of the most simple action which is fully revealed
and exhausted by three elements: *a) Attention, b) the object, and
c) the feeling of truth*. This is necessary in view of the fact that in life
we achieve these things splendidly although we lose such ability upon the
stage. You see then how much of that knowledge is ingrained in those
habits which we have to acquire in order to safeguard this primary cell—
the simple action upon which all the rest depends. This cell is subject
to maladies. We already have seen that this is true of the faculty of
attention, and of the object and the feeling of truth.

In this connection it is to be noted that the presence of the audience
and the hypertrophied awareness of the audience beget certain distor-
tions and shortcomings in the nature of the communion. The triangle—
1) the actor, 2) partner, and 3) the audience—is transposed: 1) the
actor, 3) audience, 2) the partner. This comes from a hypertrophied
awareness of the audience, sometimes from fear of not being able to
reach the audience, and at times is the result of the subconscious, deeply-
ingrained desire to "show off". The direct appeal to the audience, and
through the latter to the partner, reduces the entire performance to
the plane of showmanship. Such a performance must necessarily be
distinguished by a certain chilliness that does not, at times, lack some
sort of craftsmanship—for after all, the audience must be held firmly in
hand. At any rate, the spontaneous ardor of an authentic and sincere
way of affecting the partner vanishes here. Likewise the inter-action of
the two partners, which is liable to stir up the third person (the audience) much more emphatically, also vanishes.

ADAPTATION

The element of the actor's creative work that comes next in order
and which arises mostly from the realm of subconsciousness is the
element of adaptation. Suppose I execute a certain action. Let us say
I am asking for a loan. This I can do in various ways: I can do it
humorously or in an embarrassed, humiliated tone. There are many
ways and manners in which one can ask for a loan, and this variety

of behavior we classify as *adaptation,* a very important element in the actor's work. Not vainly is the actor's talent said to be measured by the quickness of his adaptations. Formal uniformity can be repeated from performance to performance but a live, resourceful actor will always have new adaptations or new shadings. But at the same time what is to be done if adaptation arises in a subconscious manner? Is this domain beyond our control? Though we shall not reconcile ourselves to it, the subconsciousness cannot be relied upon to a very great extent; it may sometimes surprise us by simply refusing to work! Hence the tendency on the part of the actor to have fixed adaptations, leading to the emergence of stereotypes.

For some reason love scenes have a bungling kind of sentimentality deeply imbedded in them, a syrupy sweetness, although in life no one tells of his love in such a manner. The same distortion holds true whenever something frightful is being portrayed upon the stage: the actor's adaptations immediately take on the tenebrous colors of deep terror. "How terrible", the actor exclaims, and his face bespeaks his te-r-r-or. But in real life the same phrase is spoken with a smile, with loud laughter very often, or in tones of surprise. It is not the adaptations that are to be fixed, but the atmosphere in which the adaptations are to take place. For instance, one can evoke the incident of borrowing, and build it upon suavity and witticisms; and in a like manner create a love scene—with irony, impudence or even roughness, or just the reverse —upon embarrassment, bewilderment, etc. In such cases, the element of surprise and the contrast of adaptations become especially pleasant and suitable. For instance, it would be interesting to express rapture by loud laughter or some sort of terror. It also would be of interest to express joy not by a sugary smile, but by irony. A quiet, insignificant man is generally enacted upon the stage in too literal a manner as a shrinking, subdued sort of personality. It would be interesting to render this character in sonorous, major tones; but this should find its expression in a major love of the petty and trivial. The more emphatic his overwhelming love of the trivial, the more vividly will his quietness and insignificance be expressed.

Hence it follows that the function of a subconscious adaptation can also be exercised and that it can consciously be made to order. A certain action, for instance, can be ordered in the key of gloominess, irony, malice, pleasure, rapture, apathy, despair, etc.

I. SUDAKOV

When we prepare a role, the selection of the elemental setting (of the "color" for the container of the adaptations necessary for the execution of the action that goes to make up a part of the role), is determined by our feeling of the character of the person. Here we approach the generalization of the above; the thing we call character or the inner, distinctive features of the character that we create. The groping for the line of inner constitutive characteristic brings us up to the awesome term—re-incarnation. It should hold out no fears. To be sure, until recently the whole thing was conceived in the following manner: one keeps on thinking of the role, one keeps on seeking and plaguing himself, and finally something gets hold of him—he becomes re-incarnated. The afflatus rushes upon him—and he is already a different man. An intuitive penetration, a subconscious re-incarnation—such conceptions once had wide currency among people interested in art until the time these conceptions began to be seriously analyzed. But our contention now is that the process of re-incarnation begins with the choice of the very first action—when the actor starts to work on his role. What is he guided by when picking out a simple action of a definite nature? His guide is objective reality, the life from which the play springs. He is guided by the play itself as a piece of objective reality that is transmitted from within the author's consciousness. He is guided by his perception of the material in the role to be studied. And then he is also guided by his own life experience, by comparing people, by measuring things he has seen with that which is brought out by the author. All this gives him the feeling of the character which in turn serves as a compass in the selection of a simple action. It is very important to give a rational warrant to each and every simple action. If I am a coward and I am told that someone is beaten up in the neighboring room, how will I behave? I will choose acts conforming to the line of behavior of a coward. If I myself am somewhat of a scrapper then another line of behavior will emerge. Consequently, a line of conduct springs from the way of thinking and acting of a given person.

To analyze a role, to reveal one section * after the other, is to strive to discover an action that is contained in every little section of the role from the angle of the character himself.

*For explanation of the division of a role into *sections* see I. Rapoport, *The Work of the Actor.*

The selection of an exact object for each section and each series of consecutive sections of the part begets a series of actions—a line of conduct, which as a result lead us up to the character—that is, it will be very representative of the character of the little girl. The close study of every task will reveal what one must do at each and every given moment. It may happen, of course, that the immediate finding of a simple, exact action is not always within our power; very often we may lack the necessary intelligence, experience, intuition. Incidentally, intuition, is the ability to divine things. Intuitive guessing is an hypothesis which may arise on the basis of the experience in my possession. If I lack actual experience in a certain role, my intuition will be silent for the want of material for its construction.

Thus intuition is the searching quality, divination, which strives, on the basis of the material of experience, to reveal that which has not yet become a part of knowledge. It can do harm if it is not sufficiently equipped with knowledge. It is more valuable when backed up by such experience. If I found such experience, and it is typical for the character, then the intuition is planted upon a firm basis. Thus the work of intuition is not in the nature of a sudden illumination or the work of the "Holy Ghost"—it is the function of consciousness operating with the help of knowledge.

Just so, the choice of a concrete simple action is dictated by the perception one has of the character. And conversely, a logical series of simple actions gives us the embodiment of the conduct, of the typical behavior of the character, which we call "the line of inner typicality of the character".

In scanning the work of the actor's apparatus from the point of view of the result, that is the reaction of the inner typicality, we may arrange the elements of inner technique and their inter-action in the following manner. Here we have the living man—the actor who has the gifts of imagination, who can create mentally the condition suggested by circumstances and impel himself toward the conscious and deliberate execution of simple actions. (The apparatus of such actions has already been analyzed by us.) Furthermore, assisted by the same faculty of imagination and fantasy portraying for us new circumstances that may be suggested, a process takes place of modification of simple actions by way of changing their rhythmic pattern. That is how the function of evaluation arises. In addition, the nature of the simple action in various rhythms obtains a new quality in the process of social communion. And so the function of communion emerges.

All these functions—simple actions, evaluation, communion—can be placed in a specific element—color, lighting, which changes for each and every case the method of production of such functions. Hence the variety of colors, devices and shadings. Hence, as in the case in chess playing, the innumerable quantity of combinations, and upon the stage, the vast number of adaptations.

And again, the definite selections of simple actions accompanied by evaluations and moments of communion, taking the form of such and such adaptations gives us the result sought for—the line of inner character, that is the inner aspect of the life of the character.

And as a result of all this, we find out the way of thinking and acting of a given personage. In the light of these considerations, the problem of the interrelation of the actor and character becomes easily solved. The actor, proceeding from his own self and not from some other person, should project himself fully into the execution of simple actions laid down by the analysis of the role. The very variety of their combination, their inner logic, gives as a result a specific character differing from the manner of thinking and acting of the actor himself— that is, we have before us another person, a character. And the more sincerely an actor experiences his own feelings (that is, *acts*) the more vividly the life of the character will be revealed. We may be asked, "How is it possible that an actor can experience the life of a murderer if he has never killed anyone?" Our reply is that it is not necessary to commit murder in order to experience the feeling of a murderer. We are already being trained in the technique of murder when we are seized, very often for trivial reasons, with the impulse to drown our neighbor in a glass of water. In reading a book, or in listening to a story, we subconsciously train our organism to act out the things that we assimilate. That is why we can enact murder, and much else, things which we have never done in actual life. If we had to enact something which we had never experienced in life and of which we had not the slightest conception we would scarcely be able to act at all. We can enact whatever is rooted in our psychic life; it is within our subconsciousness that the possibilities of various performances reside. That is why we can do things upon the stage which we have never done in actual life.

Every man contains all the properties of human nature in their embryonic state within himself; conditions of life cultivate this or that or any other of them. Also, the actor carries within himself all these necessary properties, cultivating some of them in every given role. The selection of these properties to be used in a given role is dictated by the author, but it is the actor who has to work them out, and this has to be done with full sincerity and integrity. I can find the proper action for the character only when I ask myself—what would I do in his place if *I* had to do such and such a thing? And then I select out of all suggested actions the one that is typical for the character.

This means that this "if I" is a necessary condition, although by far not the only one, in creating the character. It is the actor's weapon, the gate through which he passes into the world of creative work guided by the compass of the author's ideas. The latter takes him, so to speak, through various chambers, but the actor always keeps his own mind, being aware at the same time of the fact that he is not himself, that he is going through chambers he has never seen before. In actual life he did not murder anyone, nor is he jealous. If he had been jealous that might have been a long time ago and as to murder, he probably never went beyond killing a chicken. But he is now going through the enaction of jealousy and that of murder. This is not a combination that is natural to him, but he has to perform it as if it had a personal bearing.

To lose oneself and to find the character can be achieved only by finding oneself. And when one finds oneself, one also finds the character. If one loses oneself, one cannot create anything for there is nothing to create with, and the character in such a case will of necessity be stilted. But if I am active and have succeeded in holding on to myself, the character will be a living one. Hence the need of training and cultivating the creative individuality. One thing is certain—the actor performs actions. He acts in various directions and perspectives. As a result the characters vary. If he ceases to execute actions he begins to affect passion or character. Here begins the domain of stock methods, of trade work, and not of art.

This is the brief resume of what I can tell you about the elements of the actor's inner technique. You see how much exercising one has to go through, how many maladies one has to be aware of and be able to cure in order to be a good actor in the sense of inner technique. That is why when we speak of technique, we speak in the first place of the inner technique, of the ability to act, to possess the feeling of truth, to grasp and change rhythms correctly, to treat all the injuries and maladies to which those abilities may become subject. This constitutes an integral part of the actor's training.

Whatever I said above is, properly speaking, but an outline of a part of a studio program. This is to be taught in schools. This must be the purpose of years of training. Only then shall we have literate actors developing in proportion to their gifts.

PART II

THE EXTERNAL TECHNIQUE OF ACTING

In my previous lecture I spoke of the elements of the inner technique of creative acting. Now I shall deal with the elements of external technique. The latter are the sole elements which were taught in the theatrical schools of former times. By external technique one meant: voice placement, diction, speech, plastique, gesture, and various forms of plastique such as dance, ballet, fencing. Diction contained two divisions: graphic reading (recitation, diction in the proper sense) and the placing of sound. In conclusion the school term was wound up with the presentation of the so-called "fragments"—bits of plays which the actor was supposed to master blindly, following the directions of the teacher, and the performance of which were entirely based upon methods of recitation.

I have already spoken of the vast knowledge required for the actor's creative work, a knowledge which has been entirely ignored up to the present time, and the ignorance of which is being paid for by the pro ductions, the theatre, and above all by the actor himself.

What do we mean by external technique? First comes *muscular freedom*. Not dance, plastique, fencing, but freedom of muscular movements. Any one who has had anything to do with the stage, or who has ever come out before an audience, knows that the execution of some actions in public view by untrained persons is very often accompanied by what is called a state of perplexity, which means a state of *muscular tension*. And vice versa, muscular freedom is typical and characteristic for a genuine creative state. Let us try to analyze the nature of muscular freedom and tension in the same manner as we did that of simple action, evaluation, communion, etc.

First of all, we recognize that a certain kind of muscular tension is always with us, regardless of whether we are upon the stage or in the auditorium. There is always a certain tension which keeps the muscles in a given position. The muscles are kept in a state so that they can perform expeditious and necessary work. Tension then is inevitable. If we remove this tension, we would take our body out of that functional state (if we are sitting, our body may become lax to the extreme; if we are standing, we may fall). There must always be a certain expeditious tension. But all of us are men of the twentieth century, of definite burdens, cares, anxieties—we are all city people. And as such we possess a number of superfluous tensions of a definite and specific kind (related to the specific nature of our occupations). These unnecessary, inexpeditious, superfluous tensions of the muscles shape those physical deformities which every one of us inevitably acquires. Every one is deformed to some extent because of these unnecessary, inexpeditious "constrictions" in his various muscles. It happens that one man raises his shoulders when walking; when he stops he lets them drop; and when he starts again he raises them. Why does he do it? A habit has come into existence. Others have similar "constrictions" in the back, in the thigh, etc. At times these manifest themselves in nervous ticking, in stammering, in speaking rapidly, in neurasthenia, all of which are the result of an inexpeditious, superfluous work of some of the muscles.

The nature of an excessive physical tension is in the non-functional heightened excitability of the nerve centers which release unnecessary muscular actions which tend to take part in tasks that do not require their activity. It is to be noted that this phenomenon inevitably arises in those cases in which the task with which the organism is charged proves to be difficult and beyond its power. When does this danger make itself felt concretely? In the moments of the so-called evaluations of which we have already spoken.

We have seen that human activity can be resolved into a series of simple actions. When the actor knows what action he is to execute at a certain moment he does it expeditiously and in an undeterred manner. With a given amount of practice he can do it quite easily with the minimum expenditure of energy and with a characteristic feeling of physical ease and freedom.

But here the moment of evaluation comes in—one that requires the passage from one rhythm into another and the functioning of the organism within this second rhythm. For instance, you may be sitting in a room when you are suddenly told that your close friend has been run over by an automobile. Immediately there is a change of rhythm. "Impossible! How could it be?" A definite physical activity begins. It may be discharged in certain actions—going out to find one's friends, rushing to render help, etc. We know very well what we should do in life but things are different on stage: the actor often does not know exactly what he should do.

Iago tells Othello about his wife and Cassio:

> *I speak not yet of proof.*
> *Look to your wife: Observe her well with Cassio;*
> *Wear your eye thus, not jealous nor secure.*
>   (Act III, Sc. iii)

Here the difficulty begins. How should this innuendo be evaluated; how shall the action be transferred into another rhythm, how shall an action be found that may be a key toward opening up the psychologica maze contained in this fragment. Let us take another fragment from the same tragedy:

> *If thou doest slander her, and torture me,*
> *Never pray more; abandon all remorse:*
> *On horror's head horrors accumulate;*
> *Do deeds to make heaven weep, all earth amazed;*
> *For nothing canst thou to damnation add*
> *Greater than that.*
>   (Act III, Sc. iii)

91

How can this frenzied demand of Othello, who wants to know the truth but who is poisoned by the venom of doubt, be translated into simple language. What simple physical task must the actor set before himself in order to lead himself up to the rhythm contained within the given fragment of life and in order to have his feeling of truth prompt him, "that's right; you are acting right"?

When an actor recites such a passage he feels that it contains a great deal and that "something" should be "stressed". It is clear to him that the passage weighs tons and not mere pounds, and that it demands a tremendous application of his powers. He sees that his entire organism must be put in order and on the alert; something out of the ordinary must be done just at this moment! Just *what* is to be done the actor does not know; he does not understand the simplest actions required by the given fragment and still he tries to act it out. Then the straining begins: all the muscles go into work. Let us imagine that a factory has just obtained some foreign equipment, that it lacks skilled workers to assemble the new machinery and start it working. In such a case an attempt might be made to assemble the new machinery with the aid of the unskilled workers, each of whom would begin guessing, "I think this should go here and that should be fitted in there" What a terrible confusion would result from this general incompetence!

A similar situation can occur with the actor if, realizing the importance of the task assigned to him, he attempts to solve this task without understanding it. All his muscles will attempt to work at once and the result may also be a complete breakdown.

Muscular tension is widespread among actors. What people call an histrionic emotion is very often nothing more than muscular tension which the actor himself mistakes for passion. He is agitated; he experiences something, for he realizes that here, at this particular moment of the role, some passionate but at the same time simple action should be executed. He does not know the nature of this action and so he substitutes for it a general histrionic agitation which manifests itself in gesture, phrasing, and in the voice—all of which give him some sort of satisfaction. He labors under the impression that he has been acting, but in reality he is like the woman who, during a fire, seized a samovar and ran around shouting, "Fire! Fire!", thinking that she was helping to move her furniture to safety by this action.

This sort of muscular tension arises most frequently in forceful, stirring, and dramatic passages. But it may arise on every occasion if the actor does not know definitely what he should do, nor what the nature of the thought to be expressed is. If he is ignorant of these things then muscular tension is inevitable for the actor tends instinctively to fill up such a vacuity as best he can. The lack of functional action is compensated for by uncontrolled actions which give him the satisfaction of having worked, of having accomplished something.

When such histrionic emotional agitation taking the place of simple actions recurs often, then we witness the formation of the habit of substituting general excitement for the proper stage action. This habit may become incurable and we know actors who were totally ruined by this malady and who cannot act at all unless they bring themselves to a state of terrific tension without which they cannot pronounce a single phrase. This is to be explained by the fact that such an actor failed to understand anything in the role or that he only seized upon the external, mechanical typicality. A talented man will always realize when he has admitted some mistake into his acting; he will seek out the roots of his misconception; he will try to free himself from tension, from excessive loadings; and in the long run, he will seize upon the missing characteristic feature. Less sensitive people will get stuck with their error and retain this muscular tension not only in the given role but in all future roles. This frequently happens to young actors who take parts unsuitable to their individual characters. They begin to over-act, and having done this several times, they become afflicted with a certain proclivity for chronic tension. It is a contagious disease and requires treatment. This "constriction" is caused by the performance of over-strenuous work, and as soon as the actor finds himself suffering from the latter he inevitably develops this muscular tension.

BODY WORK AND SPEECH

At our previous lectures we pointed out how the actor begins to affect passion and make a show of character when he does not understand the performance of simple action. That is true from the viewpoint of inner technique. Now we also see that, from the viewpoint of external technique, the very same result of ham acting occurs with the presence of muscular tension. One is parallel to the other; in the realm of inner technique—a twist, affectation, showmanship but not life, or genuine experience, occur; in the field of external technique, a muscular tension. Thus we arrive at a complete description of the stock actor. And vice versa, the execution of the most simple action is bound up with an unusual physical lightness, with genuine muscular freedom. The actor rejoices, "How good, how pleasant! There is no longer any trace of the weight, discomfort, and sweating exertion which I endured when I felt that 'something' must be done but did not know concretely what that task was".

Hence the course of struggle with this tension should be clear; it should proceed in two methods. The first—the simplest—consists in giving the actor a well-understood physical task which is to be executed in simple actions. The other method of struggle is the one of frequent exercises directed toward the relaxation of the muscles. Perform the following: lie down on your back and relax all the muscles on your right side for a while and give them a chance to rest; watch yourself for about ten minutes taking care that the muscles do not become tense again. If you carefully watch yourself you will notice that even in this state of rest you are not altogether free. During all this time uncalled-for flare-ups of nervous energy occur here and there and your muscular system becomes subject to unnecessary tensions. Frequent exercises in the nature of constant watching of oneself may help to remedy these flare-ups.

Do another exercise—not in the relaxation of muscles but in the development of fantasy. Strike a pose arbitrarily and try to *justify* it. The exercise falls into three periods. In the first—strike any pose at will. In the second—relax your muscles leaving tense only those that are necessary to sustain the pose. And in the third—ask yourself when, how and why you might find yourself in such a pose; that is, try to justify it.

Formed into habit, such exercises will prove of great use. They develop the need of an abiding sense of physical ease, a wonted attendance to the slightest tensions that arise here and there in various muscles. But the surest remedy, I repeat, is a simple, expeditious, physical task, and the centering of the actor's attention upon the execution of this task. If he is taken up with a definite, simple task which he is accustomed to in his daily life, he will find himself free to the utmost from any tensions, and he will do this task with a minimum expenditure of energy.

The cultivation of muscular freedom and the struggle against muscular tension are very important. Stanislavski and all the great masters of the earlier period always pointed out that muscular freedom is the first condition of a creative state. No creative work is possible when there is a muscular tension or "constriction". To work out within oneself this creative freedom—is the basic task upon which the actor must work. Davidov and all the best actors of the present day are at their peak upon the stage when they work simply and freely. They give the impression of working at ease because they do it with the minimum expenditure of energy. Every uncalled-for load makes the actor perform unnecessary work. If the spectator says, "But he does not seem to perform it, it is so simple", this means that the actor is playing well.

The simple is always the most difficult, for simplicity can be attained only after having mastered inner and external technique.

I am not going to expatiate on the necessity of studying plastique, dancing, fencing. This is desirable and even necessary. I only wish to say that ballet plastique does not guarantee litheness and plasticity for the dramatic actor for it is only the sum of devices connected with definite muscular tensions which are specific and typical for the ballet, but not for the ordinary behavior of the actor upon the stage. The plastique of the dramatic actor is muscular freedom, which means that dancing, gymnastics, ballet, when applied to the realm of stage acting, demand some supplementary correctives, just as the wig brought by the hairdresser has to be somewhat improved upon. The hairdresser brings in the wig, combs it, and we suggest to the actor: take the wig, tousle it somewhat, then bring it into order and put it on. That wig was excellent from the point of view of the hairdresser, but a more subtle artistic taste demanded a certain disorder. Only then will it be acceptable unless the actor wishes to portray a person permeated with the culture of a tonsorial parlor. The same is true about ballet bearing. It may be all right if we walk upon the stage like a ballet star but that would hardly be proper. It may be necessary in one out of a hundred cases, and perhaps even less often than that.

That kind of plastique and training is of value to the actor which does away with the muscular constrictions, personal deformities, and which helps him to take at will any of those constrictions and use them to illustrate characteristic behavior upon the stage.

A subtly developed perception of muscular energy, and the "transfusion" of this energy, connected with the awareness of muscular freedom —such is the basis of graceful plastique as well as of a clear-cut, completed gesture. Raise your hand horizontally, extend your forefinger and you will have a slight trembling at the end of it. Remove all the superfluous tensions, transfer all the attention upon the tip of your forefinger directed upon a distant object. Now hold this posture. You will then obtain a complete pose and gesture.

This awareness of physical energy can be consciously transferred from the tip of the finger and centered upon another part of one's body. It can be made to serve another pose and another gesture. Thus we approach the creation of natural, graceful plastique and finished gesture linked up with a feeling of muscular freedom and with the feeling of a minimum of necessary muscular tension.

The development of the ability to subtly feel this "transfusion" of muscular energy, of building up the harmony of bodily movement, of getting rid of any superfluous movement, and of cultivating the feeling of muscular freedom, is the basis of our plastique and of a clear-cut complete gesture.

We must especially point out the importance of the actor's wrist which is the mirror of his body. The elasticity and flexibility of the wrist is the necessary condition towards expressing, in the gamut of the hardly perceptible movements of the fingers, the most subtle shades of inner line and rhythm. Those who have seen Moissi will recall how fully expressive his wrist was.

The second all-important factor is human speech and, most of all, human sound.* A whole system of knowledge on placing sound and on training and bringing out sound exists. We shall touch upon this technique in a cursory manner only, this field, as well as that of dancing and fencing, not being our special line. A voice that is not placed breaks down, especially with young actors. This occurs when the acting is false. Then we hear hoarse voices like those of drunkards. In order to avoid this, the voice has to be placed; it has to rest upon breathing and upon the diaphragm.

To place the voice means to give it a support and impart musicality to it. A musical sound is not a knock; it does not consist of percussion

---

*The reader should take care to remember that in the following pages the author is referring to Russian speech and, while his general statements are valid and extremely useful to us, some of his specific references are applicable primarily to his native tongue.

notes, monotonous like autumnal rain or like the tapping of a stick; its nature is that of the sound of a violin—drawn-out, singing notes, out of which a musical phrase can be built. Every actor must strive to master the secret of the drawn-out, singing, violin sound. He can be helped in this by exercises in breathing and in building up a support for breathing and sound in the diaphragm. Then a good study should be made of the role of various resonators in the formation of the character of the sound. A musically drawn-out sound necessary for the actor can be obtained if the resonators of the chest work well. Voice teachers very often drive the sound into the back palate or into the neck resonator, thus imparting a foreign character to the speech. Russian speech, especially that of women, demands a clear, open phrase. Sound and phrasing must be at the tip of the lips, at the teeth. Watch yourself when doing this. The vowels and consonants, driven inside, alter the sounding of the speech sharply. Good diction and a voice placed correctly are the basic conditions for the actor and especially for the actress. In the latter, the charm of diction depends greatly upon the timbre of her voice. A speech sounding like the ripple of a brook is half the secret of success for the actress. Sound that is driven inside narrows the sphere of the actor's potentialities. Musicality, the drawn-out quality of a violin sound—this is the essential condition for the performance of such roles as Tchatzky (*Woe from Reason*), Ferdinand (Schiller's *Love and Intrigue*) and altogether so in roles where the actor speaks in verse.

Although there is a difference between voice placing for the opera and for drama, we are always transported by Chaliapin's art. Why so? Because his voice possesses exceptional shadings and colors. This in turn is due to the fact that in Chaliapin the sound is concentrated near the lips and the teeth. He makes excellent use of the other resonators and that is why he chisels out the vowel and the consonant sounds so excellently. When the chest and then the teeth resonator prevails one must be able to make as much use (Chaliapin does this to perfection) of the palate, nose and neck resonators as of separate colors.

These considerations are valid in the problem of placing the voice of the dramatic actor. It is very important for him to have frontal resonators; a voice driven into the back palate is of great danger to him.

The art of speech is the most essential and exacting problem for us. An actor should speak in such a manner that those people who do not even know the language he is using will understand him nevertheless. He has to develop a technique of speech which in itself should be a source of enjoyment to such listeners. There are a number of laws which should not be ignored by the actor, the knowledge of which imparts color to the actor's speech and takes off the depressing edge of monotony.

An actor should speak for the eye of the partner, and not for the ear. When you recall what we had to say about the inner technique of the actor, you will come to understand what we mean by this. Deacons in churches intone their psalms for the ear. Indictments and minutes of the court are read for the ear. And very often actors also speak for the ear, thus putting the audience to sleep by their monotonous recitation. Speech upon the stage suffers very often from a monotony and poverty of colors. This is due to the fact that the actor has not learned to speak for the eye. In order to speak for the eye, one has to visualize the things spoken upon the stage and become caught up by it in order to be able to produce the same effect upon the audience. It is really important to actually see, and to evaluate, in order to convey the same convincingly. The essential nature of such an active perception consists in the right performance of the functions of evaluation and in the ability to become permeated with the life of the rhythm of one's attitude to an event, and in the ability to affect the audience with the very same rhythm.

Suppose someone is telling you how the infantry marched to music at a parade on Red Square. He will tell you of their marching and he will convey the stateliness, the clear-cut effect of their marching, the quality of the spectacle, the rhythm of this given section of the parade. When the same man describes the marching of the cavalry, his voice and intonations will contain something new. He will spontaneously picture the impetuous rush of the horses, the flash of the bared swords at the moment of saluting. Why does he change his manner of narration? Because he *visualizes* the parade as he tells about it and he wants the listener to *see* it too, and to be affected by the same rhythm which he is re-experiencing in his imagination.

I will cite another instance. In Kirshon's drama, *Bread,* Rayevsky tells Michailov about Germany: "When you fly out of Königsberg in the morning you see Germany beneath you like the mechanism of an open clock. The humming of the motors, the earth vibrating with the clatter of dozens of subways—that's something to hear and to see!" Rayevsky says all that as though he were still seeing and hearing it, aiming to have his listener—Michailov—see the same thing he had seen from the aeroplane.

This law—*to speak for the eye*—is effective in all cases of human communion, in every case where the audience has to be drawn into the rhythm of one's experience. The actor must cultivate this faculty without fearing to be compared with naive and uncultured people with whom cultured people differ in the reserved manner of expressing their feeling in intonations and gesture. The actor needs a speech that is full of passion and full of the rhythm living within the one who speaks.

It is nice to listen to a child telling of an event that had attracted his attention. The variety, freshness, originality of his intonations help you to envisage the event so well! And the same alternation of one vivid phrase by another must also characterize the actor's speech.

But how can speech be made rich and colorful, how can one learn to speak for the eye and not for the ear?

People in their daily life either ask, affirm or exclaim. Let us analyze the nature of the sound of these three functions. If we ask, for instance, "Have you eaten already?" the sound-pattern of this question can be portrayed in the form of a dropping curve. When indignantly aroused by someone's desire to eat up someone else's breakfast, we exclaim: "But you have already dined!"—then the sound-pattern of this exclamation can be portrayed in the form of a curve shooting upwards.

Upon the stage it is of importance that a question be a question and not an exclamation or an affirmation or something in-between. One has to be able to say a real "yes" upon the stage. This "yes" being connected with concrete physical action can only be done by a very experienced actor.

By the nature of speech "yes" is an affirmation, a descending curve. An exclamation is by its nature an upward thrust, and one has to learn to love the nature of exclamation. Many a beginning actor can be distinguished by this inability either to speak a real affirmation which would sink to the bottom or a real exclamation shooting upwards or a real question going up and then dropping down. Out of these three basic "colors" a great number of shadings will arise if questions, affirmations and exclamations will be given in the ten rhythms established by us.*

Suppose I want to ask a question, "Are you going to the country today?" If I respond in the second or third rhythms the question posed will start with the premise that you go to the country almost every day. I shall be dealing with an ordinary occurrence and I shall be asking the question only in order to say something, or to remind you that it is time to leave if your presence is a burden to me, etc. The question proceeds from the premise which grows naturally out of living tones now being determined by rhythm 2. If we translate the sound curve of our question into the language of musical intervals the diagram of this curve will equal the major second, or, at the most, the major third. If I am playing in the rhythm 4, for instance (I am cheerful, the weather is nice; I envy you your luck in being able to go to the country; or, if I am going to the country myself and I want to know whether you are going also), then the sound curve of my question, when translated into the language of musical intervals, will be expressed in fourths or fifths. If I am playing in rhythm 6 (I am dashing off to the station just in time to make the train. There is an outing today in the country with interesting people, amusements, etc.; it is a rare opportunity to get away from town; I am going to meet my friends who are rushing to make the same train and this is all a pleasant surprise to me), then the sound curve will be expressed in an octave.

The diagram of musical rhythms will change in accordance with the rhythm number. This also holds true about affirmations and exclamations; their intervals change in accordance with the change in rhythms.

People speak in musical seconds and thirds about indifferent, habitual, generally accepted things. If the inner balance is undermined

*". . . rhythms must be based on the various 'offered circumstances'. Stanislavski used to use ten rhythms in a fractional arrangement. In rehearsing, every movement was marked. The normal rhythm was 5. Rhythm *1* was that of a man almost dead, 2 that of a man weak with illness, and so on progressively to rhythm 9 which might be that of a person seeing a burning house, and to 10 when he is on the point of jumping out of the window. Tempo and rhythm must not be confused, for tempo comes from outside whereas rhythm comes from within. There may be one general rhythm of the whole stage while individual rhythms differ.. The practical system is no longer in use (at the Moscow Art Theatre), but the principles of rhythm and the actor's understanding of their use are still a fundamental part of the system." Norris Houghton, *Moscow Rehearsals,* P. 61: "Actors at Work."

by a situation containing elements that shake one to the very roots of his existence (extreme joy or sorrow) then he will speak in fourths, fifths, sixths, or octaves depending upon the circumstances and the diapason of his voice. The wider the diapason the richer the power of expression. The reminiscences of contemporaries testify that the great Feodozova could give a very subtle shading to her emotional experiences. Obviously she possessed a full mastery of the secret amplitude of human speech from seconds, to thirds, to fourths, fifths, sixths, sevenths, and octaves. She had an acute sensibility of the nature of musically expressive speech.

If musical expressiveness of speech (that is, the variety of musical intervals) arises because of the change in psychological premises and the change in rhythm then the converse must also hold true; one should be able to proceed from the sound pattern of the intonation to its inner justification. One can, for instance, ask the question, "Have you dined today?" in thirds, and then ask oneself: under what circumstances would one ask such a question in thirds? This is an important problem. The possibility of a mechanical change of intervals, that is, the diapason of intonation, to evoke such or another psychological justification places a good weapon in the hands of the director and actor. It happens that the actor very often fails when having to express some great emotion; he understands the task but he cannot execute it. A muscular tension arises, his throat tightens, and his voice sounds in thirds whereas an octave is needed. The actor does not notice the false tone and in such cases he must be told, "Justify the intonation, give it a good high and a good low". Then everything will assume its proper place, for the hindrance will be removed—the third which was replaced by the organically necessary octave.

Thus the right sound coloring, the right intonation, the precise intervals in questions, affirmations and exclamations all have a direct bearing upon the correct and organic nature of the execution of a simple physical action. The reverse is equally true: an inexact intonation leads to a muscular tension and the disturbance of the inner creative state.

Stanislavski once asked Salvini, "What does the actor need in order to act in tragedy?" Salvini replied, "Three things are needed: first—voice, second—voice, and third—voice!" This meant that the tragic actor must have musically sounding notes within the diapason of one and a half or two octaves at his command, for high rhythms are natural to tragedy and imply the widest possible intervals in the sound curve of the intonation. The substitution of a third or a fifth for an octave will inevitably lead to disaster; it will conceal such psychological depths as would be unlocked by the explosion of intonations. And how useful is the description of Salvini's performance of the role of Othello which tells of voice colors that revealed to the audience the abyss of agony through which the Moor is dragged. In that performance were groans, whispers, roars, mighty outcries and pitiful babblings.

The actor's voice must have a musical gamut. Nothing can be acted out in two or three notes. Colorfulness of intonation is necessary in order to have the actor direct his speech to his partner's eye and not to his ear. We have already analyzed the role of sound colors in the enunciation of questions, affirmation and exclamations. Now we shall dwell upon the role of the right sound colors in comparisons and contrapositions. In such instances it is important to adhere to the following condition: everyone of the compared or contraposed elements should be placed in various voice registers; that is, if one of the compared or contraposed elements is placed in the lower register the second should be placed in the upper.

In Gogol's play, *Marriage*, Kotcharev speaks to Podkolesin, "Well, and what if you are single! Look at your room—what have you got in there? There is an unpolished boot in the corner, tobacco piled up on the table and you wallow around all day. But get a wife and everything will change so that you won't recognize yourself. You will have your couch here and your little dog, some embroidery, and a canary in a cage. And just think of it: you are sitting on the couch and the pretty, little dame comes over to you and her hand. . . ."

If we arrange the first phrases in the lower registers (ending with the words, "you wallow around all day", then beginning with the following words, "But get yourself a wife") the rest should be pictured in the upper registers. If, for the sake of greater persuasiveness, we try to draw the portrait of family happiness in the same sound colors as the portrait of bachelor life we shall never achieve the necessary contraposition and comparison. And so we achieve comparison and contraposition in utilizing different layers and planes, of the voice. We shall acquire the necessary powers of expression only when this is accomplished.

We shall point to another condition of correction—arrangement of color in human speech. Whatever bespeaks life is impelled towards it and is expressed by an ascending line of sound waves; whatever has death as its subject points downward in its voice expression. Let us cite two illustrations, "Imagine—spring, morning, sun, mountains and a splendid breeze!" and "The cemetery—graves, waste, silence and death". In the first illustration your voice will rise spontaneously upwards; in the second it will drop lower and lower. Whatever is connected with the upward flow of life, with energy, with amazement, rapture, wrath, or fright will go up. And whatever is bound up with the ebbing of energy, with apathy, disillusionment will sink down along the scale of sound.

Now let us dwell somewhat on the role of the psychological accent. In our school days we became familiar with the rules governing the logical accent. We discovered then that if a sentence consists of a subject and a predicate the accent is placed upon the predicate; in the example, "the grass *grows*" the accent is placed on the verb. If the phrase is supplemented by a direct object the accent is transferred to the latter "the grass grows *in the field*". If a modifier be added to the object the accent is shifted to this modifier, "the grass grows in the field *near the forest.*"

This is what syntax teaches us. In ordinary daily conversation the accent can be placed upon any word depending upon the psychological coloring to be imparted to the phrase or depending on the nature of the uttered thought. Let us take the phrase, "Today we shall be hearing some wonderful singing", as an example. If we are guided by the meaning of the phrase we should place the accent upon the direct object, that is, upon the word *singing*. Let us, however, imagine that the phrase is uttered by an effusive person whose room is plastered with portraits and autographs of the singer who is to appear; let us imagine him to be one who manages to fairly ooze over with rapture at every concert given by his idol. Now just imagine how such a person might utter that phrase and you will come to see that the expression that will accentuate the state of mind of that person will take the form of stressing the word *wonderful*. The phrase will then sound somewhat gushy and hence amusing, but it can not be uttered in any other manner by the above-described person.

Now let us suppose that an old conservatory professor is speaking of this concert. To him singing is a deep and subtle art demanding culture and the knowledge of many craft secrets. The professor speaks with contempt of many known singers but the person scheduled to appear today is to him a genuine artist, a rare phenomenon deserving special attention. It stands to reason that the professor will utter this phrase in an altogether different manner from that of the enthusiast above. We shall now hear an emphasis on the word *singing*.

And again, let us suppose that the same phrase is uttered by a person who has tried many times to attend concerts of this singer. Until the present he has failed but now he meets with success. Anticipating the expected pleasure he will accentuate the words *we shall hear*.

Or it may happen that in the course of a general conversation on art and music some one hits upon the idea of finishing off this pleasant conversation by a visit to the concert hall. In such a case the word *today* will stand out in the entire phrase.

We have shown how circumstances of life change the appearance of one and the same phrase, shifting the accent to any desired word and thus imparting a new psychological and sound coloring to the phrase. One can practise in just the reverse manner, i.e., deliberately place the accent upon any word and ask oneself the question as to the possible psychological justification thereof. A mechanically placed accent will force our fantasy to evoke into life the suggested circumstances, investing the given phrase with concrete meaning and thus creating a living, colorful, concrete thought. This process always takes place when trying to determine the underground sub-text of the lifeless text of the role. And at the same time such a process always constitutes a good exercise for the development of fantasy.

Such are, generally speaking, the conditions that contribute toward rendering speech colorful and precise, towards making it a living thing directed to the eye and not to the ear.

Stanislavski's

Method of Acting

By M. A. CHEKHOV

THE WORK OF THE SYSTEM may be divided into two parts: one's work upon one's self, a general training which must be carried on constantly; and work on specific roles. The former proposes to give the actor elasticity, full mastery of his emotions and control of his body. The following points are stressed in the general training:

OBSERVATION

The student must train himself to analyze his own motives and to detect the motives of other people. He must keep before himself the problem of determining other people's characters, professions and habits from their appearances.

INTELLECTUAL CONTROL

Everything in acting is not done mentally. Intellectual analysis determines what is demanded by a scene, and sets the problem for the actor as clearly as possible. But the way in which the problem is to be solved, the details and manner of the performance cannot be arbitrarily determined in advance. They have to be worked out as one plays. This is where the rich material of the subconscious, which holds much of the background and personality of the actor, makes its contribution. For example, an actor decides that the core of his activity in a scene is to subdue a mob. Then he concentrates upon doing this, but he must not try to settle for himself, prematurely, when or how he shall move, whether he shall shout at the mob or command it quietly.

When a rehearsal has been handled in this organic way, the director or the actor decides which details and developments are to be retained and developed still further for the final performance.

CONTROL OF EMOTIONS

This problem is more complex. The actor must have at his command all kinds of moods and feelings. One way of achieving a specific emotion is by using "affective recollections," that is, by awakening in the memory a definite feeling actually experienced in one's past, in order to recreate the feeling. Some people can do this simply by remembering a feeling. They think how angry they were at a certain time, and a real anger begins to stir in them at the recollection. It can also be done by concentrating upon the physical details and incidental circumstances which surrounded a moment of high feeling, until by association the feeling itself is recreated. Often a mood can be induced by simply stimulating through the memory sensory effects. A sense of lazy well-being, for instance, might be achieved in this way through a sense memory of sunshine sinking in through one's pores.

SCENIC FAITH

This term defines an actor's belief in the situation he is playing. If he lacks it, the audience will lack it. They may admire his performance and say, "Isn't he exactly *like* a hungry man?" but they will never believe he *is* a hungry man on a street corner. One step toward the development of such stage faith is illustrated by the following example:

"I have to play a scene in which a very dear friend is supposed to be lying ill in the next room, and guests come to call." This comment describes the very obvious but basic core of stage performance, "It is difficult to conceive why a dear friend should be lying ill here in this theatre, or why guests come here, or indeed why I myself am here. . . . This prevents my accepting the situation in full faith; it becomes necessary to resolve the bald incongruities.

"I have to invent circumstances to supplement those of the scene, so that I can come to believe in the unrealistic conditions. Such fictitious explanatory circumstances may be very silly, naive, and lacking in any life-like truth. I might justify the above scene like this: I find myself in the theatre with a sick friend. It happened because my landlord dispossessed me and I had to ask the director to let me stay in the theatre for a while. I am here on the stage because the manager was having all the other floors waxed. My friend came to see me on account of his leaving for Moscow today. He was taken ill and the doctor was summoned. . . . Such excuses are sufficient to smooth over all the unacceptable features of the scene. The student need not tell them to anyone since in the telling the naivete would be lost and the silliness of the fabrication would become apparent."

Having thus obtained a sense of the reality of the setting, the student will come to feel a certain intimacy with regard to it. This is one step toward the development of complete stage faith.

DISSECTING THE PART

The second half of an actor's problem is his work on specific parts. He learns to analyze the material, decide on its value for him and the meaning he wants to bring out. The process of building a performance is for the actor to merge with the character in his play.

The fresh approach and enthusiasm which accompany a first reading of a script are useful and should be prolonged. In this period of spontaneous reaction to the material, creative suggestions for the production are most likely to turn up. They can be stimulated by provocative questions about the characters, their backgrounds, the details of their lives. Which trait of the character is nearest to the actor? What animal does he suggest? What would he do in some situation outside the play? This sort of speculation will also clarify the actor's idea of the character.

Next the part can be broken into sections (also called *beats*). There is nothing formal about this: a part falls during a scene into a few divisions from each of which a different effect is desired. The effect desired may be one of amazement, then servility, then fear. But if the sections are labelled with nouns they must then be expanded into verbs, for one cannot perform "amazement" in general. Amazement can result because the character wants to understand something. Fear, he wants to avoid a danger. Servility, he does not want to be put out. In selecting the actions to produce the desired effects, account must be taken of the actor's personality as well as of the script, for the same action will not bring identical results in all actors.

Out of all the actions of the sections one may derive two or three, and finally from these a single one, which not only includes the separate ones, but which conditions and explains them. The three examples given above might be resolved into one. The character wants to ingratiate himself. And if the other main actions of the play were, the character wants to make money, and he wants to prove that he is on the side of the law, then the inclusive action of the play may prove to be, he wants to find security. This inclusive action is the basic drive of the character.

This is not always easy to find at the beginning of rehearsal. If it can't be determined at once, the actor can recall his own experiences which are analogous to those in the play, and use them as his starting point. In trying to give verbal definition to these "I wants"—the actor acquires a deeper understanding of the role. Each action sets him a problem similar to the ones in the work on affective feeling, and to be approached in the same way.

PLAYING FOR ONE'S PARTNER

There are three ways of playing a scene: to concentrate on explaining and demonstrating everything to the audience, to put on a performance for oneself, or to play for and with the other actors in the scene. The first is typical of stock company acting and is common even among the better Broadway performers. It consists of using gestures and mimicry in an effort to make clear to the audience exactly what the character is supposed to be doing and feeling, and what kind of person he is. The actor does not do or feel these things at all, nor is he aware of the other actors in the scene as real characters.

To play for oneself is to plunge into the contemplation of one's own feelings and actions. It is a particularly irritating kind of performance to an audience, since it leaves them mystified and out of it. It is the kind indulged in by certain arty, though very sincere actors, who are more interested in their own emotional contortions than in the scene itself.

The only satisfactory performance comes with the right relationship with one's fellow actors. If the actor, like a human being, makes himself clear and understood by his stage partner, the audience will understand him, the performance will become real. Suppose a character has to beg a favor from another. If the actress plays "for the audience" she will be trying to prove to them how much it means to her. If she is playing for herself she will churn up desperation inside herself and end by feeling sorry for herself—but the audience will not feel sorry for her. All she needs to do is actually to beg from the other actor, to concentrate upon convincing him of her need—then the audience can be convinced.

In achieving this relationship, the actor must make constant use of real things—the other actors, the setting, the properties. He must relate himself to them in a real way. If he really studies another person's face, there is at least one real thing happening on the stage which will make the other happenings seem more real to the actor as well as to the spectator.

All the above gives us the soul of the role, but not the body. And it is only through the body that all the thoughts and feelings of the character can be conveyed to the audience. Body and voice must be elastic and obedient to the will, so that they can reflect fully and easily every experience of the actor.

The external characterization must be selected for its expressiveness, interest, and appropriateness. It must not only fit the logical and psychological characterization which has been built up, but must take the latter for its starting point. Of course in creating what might be called the inner image, a means of externalizing it may suggest itself. If this happens, the job is to understand this association, and then to incorporate it in the performance.

But inner characterizations will not always suggest suitable outer ones. In most cases one has to invent for himself the most characteristic forms, but once these are selected they must be closely related to the inner characterization, and they must be justified. In performing the role of a shy and modest man, one can take as his characteristic feature a light and inaudible step. This must be related to the rest of the characterization. One must trace the origin of such a step, work out a series of exercises which will give full justification of this feature, and enable one to adopt this gait as one's own mannerism. Then this must be practiced until it becomes mechanical, but at the same time light and customary without demanding conscious attention for its execution. Such characteristic features must become an integral part of the actor. Then as soon as he begins to live the life of the character these characteristics assert themselves spontaneously; and vice versa, when acting these features, the actor begins to experience the feelings underlying them.

CLICHE

A cliche is a ready-made form for the expression of feeling. It is harmful because it forces the feeling into a set cast, and is likely to break up the continuity of the real experience. Some cliches are copies of other actors, some are repetitions of one's own devices. In showing a state of distress, for instance, one may invariably clasp one's hands regardless of whether this fits the part or the degree of intensity of emotion. Or a cliche may be a habit formed in real life. A certain actor always pulls his ear when he gets confused. This habit cannot suit every part—and besides it comes out of the actor's own confusion, not the character's, and should be kept off the stage.

In order to eradicate a cliche a real activity should be substituted. A cliche used to indicate deep thought is wrinkling one's forehead and looking at the ceiling. If the actor will stop and actually *think*—even if all he does is the multiplication tables—thought will be manifest in his face and body.

Of course the actor may find, in searching for external characterization, a cliche which will fit very closely into a situation or feeling. In that case it can be used, life must be put into it, and an inner relation to the content of the role must be found. Such cases are rare.

REPETITION OF PERFORMANCES

The actor comes to each performance of the same part in a different state of mind, and a different mood. This fact should be utilized in keeping his performance from becoming stale. Every time he sets out to play a part he should refresh himself by thinking over the principal intention of the character and relating it to his own immediate state. If, for instance, reaching out for family happiness is the dominant drive of the character, the actor should ask himself what aspect of this is nearest to him. If one evaluates his role from the aspect of his mood at each performance, each problem in it acquires a special coloring each time. In essence it remains the same.

THE CREATIVE STATE

The first thing in teaching the Stanislavski method is to make the student actor use it by going through the kind of exercises which were described in the first part of this article. It may be impossible, and it is not important, during this practical work, to have him understand the theory behind it. In the early part of the teaching the director has to modify his instructions and explanations to suit the individual actor. But, when emotional and physical control are achieved and the actor has understood the technique in relation to his own work, then he is ready for and needs a full and comprehensive understanding of the philosophy of the system. This, then, is the point at which to give the student reasons and explanations and a review of the system in its entirety. Since these were given in the first section of this article, with the instructions for exercises, we will not take time to review them here.

We will consider instead some of the concrete and controllable elements of what is usually referred to mystically as "the creative state." They are discussed broadly since they are part of the process of any creative work, writing, painting, composing, as well as acting.

CONCENTRATION

The first and absolutely essential element is concentration: strong and undeviating attention to the work at hand. When the artist's attention is distracted, he stops functioning as an artist. When the actor on the stage lets his attention become diffuse, he loses all hold upon the audience. Now at every minute of the day a man's consciousness is attacked by a multiplicity of stimuli. Whatever he sees, hears, touches, tastes and smells, competes for his notice. The attention, whether consciously or casually directed, focuses upon certain of these sense impressions, while the rest form a background that is almost disregarded.

Children's attention is of a reflex kind: they are attracted fitfully by sounds, colors, objects. Outer impressions control their attention. But a mature person can direct his attention as he determines.

For an artist the relevant is the connection between interest and attention. Of course when one is interested in a thing, a certain amount of attention to it is implied. But the reverse is also true: when one forces concentration on a thing, interest begins to appear. It is generally assumed that an object or idea has to have interest first, in order to receive attention from a person. But an object or idea *will become interesting* if one deliberately concentrates on it. For instance, concentrate on some object which ordinarily has no interest for you. Study a matchbox. It will begin to take on a new aspect, you will note details, a diversity of associations will come into consciousness. Finally *your attention will create an interest in it.*

This principle is very important, for one of the distinguishing features of an artist is ability to see the world freshly and differently. When he masters his concentration so that he can fix it at will on any idea or object, he will be able to work when he wants to on any subject he determines, without being distracted, without waiting for "inspiration," and he will find that from the starting point of concentration, interest and relevant imagination will grow.

In trying to concentrate on an object, it is fatal to try "not to see," "not to think about" distractive impressions. This directs the concentration to the things one is "trying to ignore." One has only to focus on the object itself, and the distracting elements disappear. Suppose you have a fit of laughing and you want to stop. If you put your mind on something quite irrelevant to your laughing it will stop of itself. But if you try "to stop laughing," the giggles will grow on you, because in concentrating on this act of will, you concentrated on laughter.

IMAGINATION

Every work of art is to a certain extent the product of imagination. To portray life without an element of fantasy is to make a photographic copy, not to recreate it. The more photographic a work of art, the less its value and its power to influence other people, and the less forcefully the creative idea is conveyed. Imagination being, therefore, one of the necessary and most important elements of creative work, the artist has to work to develop it just as he works for concentration.

M. A. CHEKHOV

Imagination, broadly, is the union and combination of diverse elements into a whole which does not correspond to reality. The materials of imagination are always taken from life. No one can think of an altogether new sensation, a new feeling, a new *thing*. Imagination consists in associating known objects, uniting, separating, modifying, recombining them. And the bolder the artistic imagination, the greater the power of the work. (The scientist, the architect, any craftsman, uses imagination; the scientist by combining phenomena to discover natural laws; the mechanic or architect combine data to find more stable forms of structure.)

The fantasy of the artist always has for its aim the expression of feelings and actions springing from them. And here he must be reminded of an old truth: if on the one hand, the quality of his imagination depends on his ability to combine his material so as to express theatrically and boldly the idea behind his work, on the other hand it also depends on the richness of the material which is under his control. This material is not in textbooks. He must learn to draw on life, study, seek out the most diverse aspects of it, create for himself conditions in which he will be exposed to manifold expressions of it—and not wait until life by chance thrusts some striking scene under his nose. And in whatever field he works, the artist must study all branches of art. The actor, for example, can utilize painting, sculpture, music.

NAIVETE

The quality of fantasy is conditioned by naivete. Now children and savages display more creative imagination than grown people in civilized surroundings. It is not a matter of natural endowment; it is the result of the fact that children and savages have very little exact knowledge. Their concepts are not systemized, and so they can combine the elements of their environment without worrying about whether such a combination has any counterpart in reality. They are guided by feelings only. A child, for instance, can invent or believe in a submarine kingdom, water spirits and fairies, since he does not know whether life is possible for human beings under water. And the fantasy of modern times is barren compared to the lore of the primitive. In other words, the savage and the child are naive and credulous, and that is why their fantasy is free and abundant.

This shows the place of naivete in the creative fantasy of the artist. The modern cultured artist, brought up on exact sciences, must cultivate those very qualities which a child or savage manifests freely. He must develop them by conscious effort and exercises.

That naivete and artistic achievement are inseparable is confirmed by the biographies as well as by the work of important artists.

Here are exercises for the three qualities under discussion. In practice, they cannot be separated although this has been done for purposes of analysis:

Exercises for Concentration:

1. Study the wallpaper pattern so that you can describe or reproduce it accurately.
2. Listen to a sound.
3. Do an arithmetic problem mentally.
4. Select and follow a single sound out of a confusion of noise.
5. Do several activities in succession: look at the pictures in a magazine, listen to music, dance, do arithmetic problems. Then turn rapidly from one activity to the next, making sure that the transference of attention each time is complete and genuine.
6. Note, in a few seconds, as many details as possible of someone's clothes.
7. Concentrate upon an idea or problem. Five or six people ask questions which must be answered without having the attention waver from this idea.
8. Master the contents of a book while others talk, laugh, and try to break up the concentration.
9. Concentrate on a tune in your head while other music is being played.

Exercises for Imagination:

1. Look for resemblances between objects and people; between people and animals.
2. Concretize music in fantastic images.
3. Given one word, or two, extemporize on them; do the same exercise within a predetermined mood.

4. One person makes a series of sounds of different kinds. Those who do the exercise sit with their backs to the first person and weave the sounds into a continuous story.

5. Break up into sections some route you follow frequently; imagine a story connected with each section; weave all those stories into a single plot.

6. Take a person whom you know little about; try to picture his life in full detail.

7. Let someone give you a word; try to fixate the impression, that is, your first reaction to it; then try to convey this impression in whatever way you can. Take any word: e.g., clock; try to break away from the crude concept of it, see what your imagination will bring forth at the first perception of it. The images will be striking and unexpected; a turret with a clock upon a magic turret, the image of some pitiless forces—the inevitable hour, or perhaps it is linked with an event in your life and will recall that. Learn to fixate such subtle, fugitive images of your fancy, and they will serve your creative expression.

8. Try to discover beauty everywhere: in every posture, position, thought, scene. This exercise is very important. A creative person must be able to see and extract beauty from things which a noncreative person overlooks entirely; and he must see beauty first, not deformity.

Translated by Mark Schmidt and arranged by Molly Day Thacher from Chekhov's notes. Chekhov wrote these notes in 1922 when he was working in the Second Moscow Art Theatre Studio under Stanislavski.

PREPARING
FOR THE ROLE

From the Diary of E. VAKHTANGOV

THE STANISLAVSKI METHOD AIMS to develop in the student those abilities and qualities which give him the opportunity to free his creative individuality—an individuality imprisoned by prejudices and stereotyped patterns. The liberation and disclosing of the individuality; this must become the principal aim of a theatrical school. A theatrical school must clear the way for the creative potentialities of the student—but he must move and proceed along this road by himself; he cannot be taught. The school must remove all the conventional rubbish which prevents the spontaneous manifestation of the student's deeply hidden potentialities.

Stanislavski showed the actor how to achieve for himself a creative state, to establish the conditions in which a genuine creation upon the stage becomes possible.

If all the conditions of the creative state are established, but the pupil still shows himself incapable of genuine creative work, if no movement takes place even after the way has been cleared for his creative potentialities—then it is not the fault of the school but of nature which has deprived the student of the one thing that might have given him the opportunity of expressing himself upon the stage—scenic talent.

If the school attempts a different task, if it does not bring out within the pupil the singular qualities which predetermine the possibility of creative work; but attempts to teach him creativeness itself, then it may ruin a scenic talent given by nature. Instead of freeing the pupil from prejudices and stereotypes, it will impose upon him a set of new prejudices, characteristic of a given school.

It is impossible to teach anybody how to create because the creative process is a subconscious one, while all teaching is a form of conscious activity which can only prepare the actor for creative work.

Consciousness never creates what the subconscious does; for the subconscious has an independent faculty for gathering material without the knowledge of the consciousness.

In this sense each rehearsal of a play is most effective when it serves to evoke the material for the following rehearsal. The creative work of refashioning the newly perceived material takes place in the intervals between rehearsals. Out of nothing, nothing can be created. That is why a role cannot be performed by inspiration only. Inspiration is the moment when the subconscious, without the participation of the consciousness, gives form to all the impressions, experience and work preceding it. The ardor accompanying this moment is a natural state. Whatever is invented consciously does not bear this characteristic. Whatever is created subconsciously is accompanied by a discharge of energy which has an infecting quality. This ability, the subconscious carrying away of the subconscious of the spectator, is a characteristic of talent. Whoever perceives subconsciously and subconsciously expresses it—that one is a genius.

THE SCHOOL OF INTIMATE EXPERIENCE

Critics of Stanislavski's doctrine often overlook the statement which takes first place in the system and methods of Stanislavski: that the actor should not be concerned about his feeling during a play, it will come of itself. They label as auto-suggestion and narcotic self-intoxication the help which Stanislavski gives to his students in recalling their intimate experiences. But Stanislavski maintained the opposite: don't try to experience, don't make feelings to order, forget about them altogether. In life our feelings come to us by themselves against our will. Our willing gives birth to action directed towards the gratification of desire. If we succeed in gratifying it, a positive feeling is born spontaneously. If an obstacle stands in the way of gratifying it, a negative feeling is born—"suffering." An action directed towards the gratification of will is continuously accompanied by a series of spontaneous feelings, the content of which is the anticipation of the coming gratification or the fear of failure.

Thus, every feeling is a gratified or a non-gratified will. At first, a desire arises that becomes the will, then begins to act consciously aiming towards its gratification. Only then, altogether spontaneously, and sometimes against our will, does the feeling come. Thus, feeling is a product of will and the conscious (and sometimes subconscious) actions directed towards its gratification.

Therefore the actor, Stanislavski taught, must think first of all about what he wants to obtain at a particular moment and what he is to do, but *not* about what he is going to feel. The emotion, as well as the means of its expression, is being generated subconsciously, spontaneously, in the process of executing actions directed towards the gratification of a desire. The actor must, therefore, come on the stage not in order to feel or experience emotions, but in order to act. "Don't wait for emotions—act immediately," Stanislavski said. An actor must not simply stay upon the stage, but act. Every action differs from feeling by the presence of the will element. To persuade, to comfort, to ask, to reproach, to forgive, to wait, to chase away— these are verbs expressing *will action*. These verbs denote the task which the actor places before himself when working upon a character, while the verbs to become irritated, to pity, to weep, to laugh, to be impatient, to hate, to love—express feeling and therefore cannot and must not figure as a task in the analysis of a role. Feelings denoted by these verbs must be born spontaneously and subconsciously as a result of the actions executed by the first series of verbs.

Desire is the motive for action. Therefore the fundamental thing which an actor must learn is to wish, to wish by order, to wish whatever is given to the character. An actor who is a mere journeyman does the opposite of what nature demands from him and what the school of Stanislavski teaches. He grasps with bare hands at feelings and tries to give a definite form to their expression. He always begins from the end; that is, from the final ends of his part, Stanislavski used to say.

In life a man who weeps is concerned about restraining his tears—but the actor journeyman does just the opposite. Having read the remark of the author (He weeps), he tries with all his might to squeeze out tears and since nothing comes of it, he is forced to grasp at the straw of the stereotyped theatrical cry. The same is true of laughter. Who does not know the unpleasant, counterfeit laughter of an actor? The same takes place with the expression of other feelings.

Thus we may say that Stanislavski did not invent anything. He teaches us to follow the road pointed out by nature itself.

"AGITATION FROM THE ESSENCE"

An actor who is a mere journeyman becomes agitated (emotionally aroused) from the very fact of coming out on the stage and he accepts this "professional agitation" as the "feeling" of the character. His temperament is directed not towards the essence of the circumstances in which the acting person of the drama finds himself. This "professional agitation" or "muscular experience" as Stanislavski called it, does not react upon the audience very deeply; it touches only the periphery of its nervous system.

The feeling of the actor must not be ready-made beforehand somewhere on the shelf of his soul. It must arise spontaneously on the stage, depending upon the situations in which the actor finds himself as the acting person of the drama. This is what is meant by the *agitation from the essence.*

We have to obtain the awakening of the temperament without any external stimuli towards such an agitation. The actor must work during rehearsals upon whatever surrounds him in the drama, he must make this become his atmosphere, so that the problems of his part become his own problems, i.e., the acting out of the character must become the actor's natural need—then his temperament will speak from the essence. This temperament from the essence is most valuable because it alone is convincing.

If the actor does not make the essence of the drama his own essence, if he really does not believe that the secret of true creativeness lies in his confidence in the subconscious (which itself reacts from the essence), he will play according to past patterns, patterns evolved by bad rehearsals. The audience will know beforehand how the actor is going to play. Everything will be tedious and familiar.

The actor must come to realize the necessity of actions pointed out by the author—they must become organic. The actor must agree with the author in everything. He must understand the inevitability of such actions and not of any other.

The actor will realize the necessity of the actions pointed out by the author if he will come to know the conditions of life of a given character. The conditions of the life of a character must be known as well as you know your own mother. When you speak about your mother you feel that you know her with your whole being.

Whatever I as an actor speak or do on the stage must be necessary to me in an organic way—to me, and not to somebody else (not to the imagined character)—it must be necessary to my nerves, my blood, my thoughts.

In order that such an *agitation from the essence* arise, it is necessary to live your own temperament on the stage and not the supposed temperament of the character. You must proceed from yourself and not from a conceived image; you must place yourself in the position of the situation of the character. You must be serious and not feign seriousness. You must come to believe that whatever arises within you under the circumstances which are given by the author to the character are yours and not those of the character, that they will make you remake yourself, that is, they will make you the character.

To create and not to be oneself is impossible. It is essential not to distort oneself on the stage, inasmuch as the actor retains his own personality on the stage. You must remove whatever is superfluous as far as the character goes and not add what you do not possess. You cannot seek the character somewhere outside yourself and then fit it on—you must make it up out of the material which you yourself possess.

SCENIC FAITH

The ability of the actor to show toward the circumstances suggested in a play an attitude as serious as though they really existed, is called by Stanislavski *scenic faith*. *Scenic faith* predicates the truthfulness of passions realized not only by the playwright through the verisimilitude of the situations and the truth of the dialogue, but is also established by the actor through the credibility of his behavior on the stage.

If there is no will to believe, then the actor becomes a mere journeyman. The actor must take for truth whatever he creates out of his own fantasy. The faith of the actor is that quality which transports the audience. Thus at the very foundation of the theatre there lies the *scenic faith* of the actor and his ability to transform a theatrical fiction into a truth new to himself and to the audience. The more there is of this fiction on the stage, the richer and broader the creative potentialities of the actor. And the reverse; the less of this fiction, the more there is of the naturalistic truth—the narrower the confines of the actor's creative potentialities.

RHYTHM

Everything related to the domain of the means of theatrical expression—sound, words, phrases, gesture, body, rhythm—must be understood in a special theatrical sense, must have an *inner justification* proceeding from nature itself.

The elements of scenic craftsmanship are thus subordinate to organic and not mechanical laws. Usually in speaking about the external means of expression we forget about the *inner justification* proceeding from nature. We study the mechanics of the law to which the means of expression are subject; but the external means of expression are to be understood only by grasping their connection with the organic life of human beings as a whole.

The feeling of rhythm is not only the primitive ability to subordinate one's physical movements to a rhythmic count. The actor must subordinate his whole being, his whole organism to a given rhythm—the movement of his body, of his mind and of his feelings. Rhythm must be perceived from within. Then the physical movements of the body will become subordinated to this rhythm spontaneously. The task of the school consists in training the pupil in this sensitivity to rhythm, and not in teaching him to move rhythmically.

(The rhythmic exercises which Vakhtangov suggested to his pupils did not consist in beautiful movements specially invented for that purpose, but were subject to the principal of practical expediency. Students would move furniture in a certain rhythm accompanied by music, would clean the room, serve the table and so on. Vakhtangov would try to see that it was done with the freedom, lightness, and spontaneity with which such movements are executed in life. The pupil had to understand that a rhythmic movement is not only something which is studied during the lessons of rhythmic gymnastics. Rhythmicality is the property of each and every movement in nature. It is necessary to learn to live in a given rhythm and not only to move in it. To eat, to drink, to work, to gaze, to hear, to think—in other words—to live rhythmically.)

Every nation, every man, every phenomenon in nature, every event of human life—everything has its own characteristic rhythm. Therefore, every drama, every role, every part of a role, every feeling—has its own rhythm. Given the rhythm of a certain scene it will be played correctly. To perceive the rhythm of a character means to understand the role. To find the rhythm of a drama is to find the key to its presentation.

What has been said about rhythm applies equally well to *plastic*. *Plastic* is generally thought of as a specifically elegant movement; but nature has nothing in it which is not plastic. An actor who violates the law of nature on the stage will become non-plastic. An actor must occupy himself with *plastic* not in order to be able to dance or to have beautiful gestures or an elegant position of body, but to communicate with his body a feeling of plasticity. Plasticity is not movement only. It is to be found in a piece of cloth thrown upward, in the surface of a quiet lake, in a cat slumbering peacefully, in a wreath of flowers and a marble statue. The surge of the wave in the sea, the swaying of the branches, the trotting of a horse, the alternation of day and night, a sudden storm, the flight of a bird, the repose of a mountain space, the mad swirling of a cataract, the heavy tread of an elephant—all of this is plastic. An actor must be ingrained with the conscious habit of being plastic in order to bring it out subconsciously—in the way he wears his suit, in the power of his voice, in the physical transformation of himself to the character portrayed, in his ability to distribute expeditiously his energy to the muscles, in his gestures, in the logic of his feelings.

How often does it happen that actors who study rhythmic gymnastics diligently and successfully become non-rhythmical on the stage? An actor who performs the most difficult dancing steps moves on the stage in a non-plastic manner. The cause lies in the fact that he tries to perform a given exercise correctly in a mechanical sense while each and every exercise must be considered as an example in which the general law of rhythm and *plastic* manifests itself.

Immobility must be justified from within. It will not seem artificial or invented to the audience if each actor who participates in a given scene will justify for himself the halting of a movement. If the actor discovers for himself what brings about the sudden stoppage naturally, it will become organically inevitable.

At the same time there must be an inner dynamic in the externally static. A figure halting his movement must be expressive, must be dynamic in his immobility. In mass scenes the composition of bodies makes a sculptural group expressive in its immobility and serves as the background against which one person moves and talks.

Everyone has seen how a man putting a spoonful of soup to his mouth will halt the movement already begun and while interested in the story of his neighbor, hold the spoon carefully showing a subconscious concern about the contents of the spoon. One can also observe frequently how a man rushing somewhere will stop suddenly, turn around and without changing the direction of his body, will gaze for a long time on the object which made him stop. The external halting of physical movements on the stage must not break up the continuity of the inner movement, must not break up the line of the inner life. The inner movement may change its rhythm and character, but the movement of the inner life must not stop from the moment an actor appears on the stage until he leaves it. To be immobile does not mean to die altogether. Just the reverse, the more immobile, the more studied the play of the actor, the more intense must the inner life become.

"ARTISTICALITY"

True creativeness can be realized only when an inner impulse to work is present. Everything created in art is of value insofar as it is brought out by an inner need; by the sincere will to create. This constant readiness towards creative work, this will to work, Stanislavski calls "artisticality." In order to develop within oneself this ability, the actor must learn to seek something new at each and every rehearsal and not to reiterate what was discovered at previous rehearsals. The backlog of material acquired at the previous rehearsals will come to life by itself.

(At the eighth rehearsal of one of his plays, Vakhtangov said to the actors: "You have exhausted yourselves during these seven rehearsals; your own personal colors have been utilized and I don't want to impose upon you any longer. You must understand that each and every rehearsal is a new one. But you are too weary to search for the new. You are tired of the old and as a result there is no desire to play. An actor will have the desire to play only when he learns to come on the stage with the inner readiness to react to everything taking place on the stage as though it were a surprise to him. One partner must never tell the other what he is going to do on the stage. Everything on the stage must be unexpected. You must react to it spontaneously. There must be more confidence in your own subconscious.")

Only when such a readiness to react to everything as a surprise exists is the birth of new colors in a spontaneous and unexpected manner possible. Only under such conditions will the actor avoid going through the same "adjustments" which have already become stereotyped. Only given such conditions is the joy of creation possible.

The role is ready when the actor has made the dialogue his own dialogue. The words of a part will become his own words only when the actor truly understands what is contained within those words. Words contain thought by which a given character lives.

A thought underlying the text may not coincide with the direct meaning of a word. The aim for which a man utters words manifests itself usually not in the meaning of the words spoken but how he says them. Therefore it is necessary to know the reason for which the words are being spoken in order to read the words of the part correctly. For example, the phrase "What time is it?" is seldom asked to find out what time it is. This question may be asked for various purposes—to rebuke someone for coming late; to hint to someone that it is time to leave; to complain about boredom, to ask for sympathy, etc.

The actor must speak not words but thoughts. The work of finding those thoughts which underlie the word text we call *disclosing the text*.

Thus in order that the words of a role become your own words it is necessary to make the thought which a given character lives your own thoughts.

These notes from the diary of Vakhtangov originally arranged by B. E. Zakhava are published here for the first time. They have been adapted from a translation made for the use of the Group Theatre.

CASE-HISTORY

OF A ROLE

By A. S. GIATSINTOVA

THE WORK IS HARD but delightful. It consists not only of creating a part (and of training one's self) but also of creating a theatre.

The most remarkable feature of our work is its uninterruptedness. If I am preparing a part, I cannot discard it on my day off; it continues to live within me whatever I may do, whether I am at home, or out skiing, or taking a walk. It is a hard task to steal up on this enemy and to win him over. To conquer the fear of a new part is difficult and requires much skill.

Here before me is a part. I don't as yet know anything of what is hidden behind those black lines. Nothing seems to grow out of the words; only cold, logical phrases register in my mind. I am quite familiar with the play; but just the same, I am still completely in the dark. My heart beats heavily in face of the unknown as I gaze upon the strange words. A part has the capacity of blotting out everything that is calm and lazy in an actor's life;. and everything that has no connection with the part will disappear for the time being. I shall now live with only a small fraction of my being.

That fraction of me that is actress continues working under all circumstances, secretly gathering together all that may be useful. This phase, however, does not come at once. At the beginning there is some sort of protest and fear. You want to find out this or that; you throw side-long glances at the part but you are still afraid to really tackle it. While walking along the street, perhaps, you begin to wonder about the character, "What type is she? What are the surroundings like? What did people think of in those days? How did they live? What kind of hairdress was in style?" I ask all these questions without any logical sequence. But before I think, I must see. First of all, I must dig a passage to my imagination.

But the words of the part are, as yet, so strange, and I don't know which of them is the most important. They all seem indifferently logical. But I must love devoutly, hate fiercely; I have to accept and repudiate; I have to act! *Will, Will, Will!* The iron will of the actor. I must forge the keys to my imagination, to my thoughts, to my will.

It is helpful if a part is given to you in the spring and rehearsing is to begin in the fall. Not that that makes it easier to prepare a part, but because it gives one more time to think about it. For after all, a part acquires form from the play as a whole, and from daily rehearsals with the whole group with the director at the head.

Supposing that I could get no help at all from the words; but my partner has already understood something, and shows it in his part: that gives me a lead, and I begin to feel my way about. Usually at our discussions of a play, so much is said that is of value, and said with so much heat and effort to solve the problem at hand, that I cannot imagine how it is possible to prepare a part when removed from that atmosphere. It is true, nevertheless, that a part has a capacity to acquire life within the heart of the actor as soon as he has encountered it or has merely heard his name read as the parts were cast. During the summer a part can hibernate within the actor, so to speak, and only every now and then remind him of its existence.

You begin to think, or rather, to wonder. These wonderings have an unusual capacity to make you comprehend the form of the character. It becomes more familiar, more intimate. To conquer the fear of a new character is a difficult step. It is not the fear of egoism. (Will I make it or not?) It is, rather, complete blindness. But I must gain vision. To that end I ask myself questions, read my part, read the whole play.

If the play is historical or foreign, if it requires some special knowledge I calmly, as if without any purpose, read the necessary books. This is extremely interesting. The necessary atmosphere is absorbed, and the circle shrinks painlessly. At first appears the general idea of the part which I begin breaking up until I remain with a fraction of it; but in the work I keep adding to it until it is whole again.

The work of the actor consists of making the outwardly probable character inwardly complete. I must become a certain specified person—I must not merely imitate her, neither must I imitate myself. I cannot portray a character by giving him my personal habits or feeling—by doing so I should fake the character and minimize my task as an artist. It is true that such acting intrigues and pleases the interest of a great many—but such acting is predominantly physiological: tears flow copiously, the spectator pities the actress, she quakes his nerves, but awakens neither his thinking power, nor his imagination.

> *The words were flowing as if being born*
> *not by timid memory but by the heart.* (Pushkin).

It is exactly so that I would like to act.

In our theatrical childhood we used to try to work up an emotion and then timidly force the words, fearing to fake or scare our own emotion. The emotion must be genuine, and I myself must be genuine: and in those days I used to try my best to become upset by thinking of the death of someone near to me; but I haven't yet met death face to face and so have remained cool and indifferent to all corpses. And so, at the death of the Duke Andrei, in *War and Peace*, I cried and only later finally understood to what purpose I was there.

Like a traveler in a strange city, curiously absorbing the sights I try to gather my impressions and store them in my heart. When necessary I shall summon them and re-examine them—then within them I shall act. The strange unfamiliar impressions flow freely into the heart: but I, myself, (so to speak) remain aloof. Of course I do not mean to say that during this period I accept the world without a point of view of my own, without an estimate of what I see: but my mannerisms and habits, my worries about myself are almost of no concern. They also must not hinder me when I am forming a character.

And to form a character one must have a comprehension of the world, one's own point of view, taste; one must do everything simply, and above all know and feel the essence of the business on hand. Of that Gogol speaks very simply, "It is not difficult to color a part: that can be done afterwards. The difficulty lies in understanding the essence of the business at hand—the purpose of the presence of this or that character." And as for taste and simplicity— how these two priceless qualities of the actor were formerly looked down upon! It is only recently that the critics have begun to appreciate simplicity (the spectators have always been inclined towards it), but even now taste often remains unrewarded.

But let us now go back to the part itself. While working on it you create various details. Supposing that in some scene I stop talking in the middle of a sentence and begin thinking. That helps me very much. And so, a great temptation arises to pause in that manner as often as possible. It may be pleasing to me, but how about the audience? How can one guard against tastelessness? Only through consciousness of the whole. One must not lose sight of the horizon and at the same time he must look under his feet. It is only when you do not think that you are alone, all-important, and independent that a sense of artistic taste will be born.

Simplicity is the same as depth. The deeper and the more sincerely you look at something the more interesting that object will appear; the more complex and yet the more simple. But complexity does not consist of mannerism. Great power is required to express it; and power can only be simple. Clarity of form also comes from depth —in order to be simple and deep one must see, feel, and understand.

Everything that the artist sees, he must inscribe in his heart. He must not dare to be blind and self-satisfied. Conceit makes an artist so dull that he is ridiculous, even outwardly. Some time ago, in the heat of a discussion, I advised a certain playwright to compare himself to Shakespeare because he keeps himself in a happy mood by comparing himself (favorably, of course) with everything that is second-rate, or even preferably, mediocre. He feels so content! If he would compare himself to Shakespeare his spirits would not be so high, but he would begin to write much better! And it is not simply a matter of good character. Our character is no better or worse than that of other comrades. The matter is in the seriousness of our attitude toward our work. If one has seriously made for himself a great goal then whence is that satisfaction to appear? Our country has given itself tremendous problems and the actor (the conceited one) has given himself a very tiny one (let us assume that he has even solved it), and is terribly satisfied. But the point is that he dares not merely solve his own problems—he must also solve the problems of the theatre as a whole. The work of the actor consists not merely in creating a part, but in creating the whole theatre—the theatrical organism. The cure for conceit, light-mindedness, lazyness, and the "elegant" cynism of the actor, lies precisely in this work.

We must work toward bringing to a higher level the life of the theatre. The creativeness of everyone is required for that purpose. But whence shall this demand for creativeness arise? Only from a clear perception of the world; from the understanding of one's duty; from the ear of the artist who, hearing the march of time, enters the ranks of fighters and falls in step. But time is short; time flows by and I must build a strong foundation for my theatre. I must express the best that is in me. Also I must help bring up the youth. And I must not be concerned with only a fraction of the work by merely preparing them for the stage. It is necessary also to teach the youth a feeling of responsibility and devotedness to our work. The training begins from the first step into the theatre lobby. A creative atmosphere, cleanliness, quiet, respect to the collective, and chiefly respect to each comrade must predominate in the theatre. The atmosphere of the theatre depends a lot on the preparatory work of the actor at home. He comes from home with a new idea and h must express himself. He must be listened to, and listened to creatively.

It is necessary to learn to create collectively. That is very difficult; but I must understand that the person with all the shortcomings that irritate me, is along side of me building the theatre and I must work along with him. I must understand that in his creative moments he contributes the best of what he possesses. Therefore I must respect him. This may be difficult but, I must repeat, it is necessary. I must exploit all my personal ambition for the common good. I must also understand, and this too is difficult, that there is no stronger comradeship than that of common work. Associating as actors, working toward a common objective creates a warmth in relationships and a concern of one for the other. One never knows the "creative ceiling" of an artist that he may be associating with. A new accomplishment in his art makes a new person of him.

The work of the actor is a new expression of our marvelous age, in which individuality blossoms while individualism is dying out; in which individuality unites people instead of forcing them apart.

FROM THE PRODUCTION PLAN OF *OTHELLO*

By CONSTANTIN STANISLAVSKI

ON OCTOBER 29TH, 1928, the 30th birthday of the Moscow Art Theatre, Stanislavski played the role of Vershinin in Chekhov's *Three Sisters*. This was his last stage appearance for he was taken ill during that very performance. In May, 1929, when the acute stage of the illness had passed, he went to Nice on doctor's orders. There on the Mediterranean shore, far from his friends, from the theatre, he pondered over an unfinished work, an old dream of his, to stage *Othello*. Taking up his pen he there and then compiled a detailed director's plan of this tragedy.

That is how the book, *Production Plan of Othello*, finished in 1930, came into existence. On the left-hand page is Shakespeare's text, on the right Stanislavski's commentaries, opposite the part of each character. Sometimes they develop into several pages without a break. Stanislavski resorted to an unusual form of inserted short stories in order to describe the past of Othello, Iago, Cassio and Roderigo, and what occurs between the acts: he expresses his thoughts on the tragedy and closely follows the conflict of passions in the human soul.

Stanislavski's ideas about Shakespeare have taken the precise form of literary commentary.

Stanislavski wanted the settings for Othello to be mounted on a revolving stage and for the scenes to follow each other without intervals. At the same time the producer warned against exaggerating the effect by too much mechanical smoothness.

Stanislavski held that modern stage technique should be so employed as to show the sweeping scope of Shakespeare's tragedies without being cramped by unity of time and place. The first act has been given an extensive commentary. Following his usual method, Stanislavski wanted the actor to feel his part, identify himself with his hero, gain a clear idea of his fate, his past life and character and only then, with this as a basis, determine his stage behavior. Who are Roderigo, Iago and Brabantio?—he asks, and then goes on to dwell in detail on the characters of the first scene. Concluding his introduction to the tragedy, Stanislavski notes that "the first scene is not a simple, tranquil exposition of the play as it is usually interpreted. The scene is vitally essential. It immediately and clearly delineates the villainous part of Iago, who, throughout the play, carries on his intrigue and campaign of vengeance against Othello and all he holds dear."

T. C.

Act I
Scene I
Brabantio's House
Iago and Roderigo in a gondola

What is the *past* which justifies the *present* of this scene: Who is Roderigo? I imagine that he is the son of very wealthy parents, landowners who took the produce of their village to Venice and exchanged it for velvet and other luxuries. These goods were in turn shipped to other countries, including Russia, and sold at great profit. But now Roderigo's parents are dead. How can he manage such a tremendous business? All he is capable of is squandering his father's wealth. It is this wealth which made his father, and consequently himself, acceptable in aristocratic circles. Roderigo, a simple soul and a lover of gay times, constantly supplies the young blades of Venice with money which, obviously, is never returned. Where does this money come from? Well, thus far the well-established business, managed by old and faithful workers, is still running through force of inertia; but certainly it cannot continue like this much longer.

One morning, after the usual drinking bout, Roderigo is moving down a canal when he sees, as though in a dream, the young and beautiful Desdemona stepping into a gondola at her father's house. She and her nurse are on their way to church. Roderigo is spellbound. He stops his gondola and stares at the beautiful vision. The nurse, noticing both his attention and the traces of the previous night's revelries on his face, covers Desdemona's face with a veil. Roderigo pursues the gondola of the beautiful young lady. He follows her into the church. His excitement sobers him completely, except that there still remains a trace of uncertainty in his walk. He does not pray; he is absorbed in Desdemona. Her nurse tries in devious ways to shield her from his eyes, but Desdemona herself enjoys this little adventure. It is not because she finds Roderigo attractive, but simply because it is boring at home and in church and because she yearns for excitement. During the service Brabantio joins his daughter. The nurse whispers something to him, pointing to Roderigo. Brabantio glances sternly in his direction; but this in no way embarrasses brazen Roderigo.

When Desdemona returns to her gondola she finds it covered with flowers. The gondolier is reprimanded for gossiping with the other gondoliers rather than watching his boat. Brabantio has the flowers thrown over the side and orders his daughter home. But no sooner does the gondola turn the first corner then they discover Roderigo. His gondola precedes them. All along the way he casts flowers into the water, paving, so to speak, the path of the beautiful lady with blossoms which he has bought from the flower girls near the church. Such originality and generosity pleases the young lady. Why? Simply because it is fun, it is flattering, and besides it makes one's nurse angry.

Roderigo loses his head completely. He thinks of nothing but Desdemona. He serenades her beneath her windows. He sits in his gondola all through the night in the hope that she will look out. And it actually happens once or twice. She even teasingly smiles at him. But he, being a simple soul, interprets it as a sign of success. He is at a loss as to how to show his gratitude. He begins to write poetry. He bribes the servants to deliver his rhymed declarations of love. The bribes are high, yet no one can be certain that his messages ever reach their destination. Finally Signor Brabantio's brother warns Desdemona's persistent admirer that if he does not cease his wooing measures will be taken. But Roderigo continues his pursuit—and measures are taken. Servants are sent to drive away the unwanted suitor. They perform their duty in a most unceremonious manner: they pelt him with orange peels, kitchen slops and other garbage. Roderigo patiently puts up with all this. Once Roderigo intercepts Desdemona on a dark canal. He catches up with her gondola and tosses her a large bouquet with his madrigal attached to it. But oh, bitter fate! Desdemona, without so much at glancing at him, throws the bouquet with its madrigal into the water. Then, turning her angry face away, lowers her veil. Roderigo feels mortally wounded. He is in despair. The best way he can find to revenge himself on that cruel beauty, is to plunge into a week-long orgy of drinking. After that, again with the purpose of avenging himself, he decorates his gondola with expensive trappings, flowers and lanterns, fills it with an assortment of beauties of doubtful reputation and with much laughter and gay song floats back and forth in front of Brabantio's house, or cruises on the Grand Canal where Desdemona usually takes her daily outing. But as soon as his intoxication wears off he is once again seized by unhappiness. He broods in his gondola in front of Desdemona's house until the servants are sent to drive him away.

Things go on this way until the appearance of Othello. Desdemona first meets him in a crowded street. Since Othello's return to Venice as a conqueror, military men have become the rage. Having conquered the Turks, they are now the conquerors of women's hearts. Roderigo, himself, wants to become a soldier. The warriors are the favorites of the courtesans at the nightly orgies. During such revelries Roderigo pays all the expenses. This brings him into the company of all the officers, including Iago. At one of the orgies, some of the intoxicated officers would have trounced him thoroughly had it not been for Iago's ardent defense. Roderigo, filled with gratitude, offers Iago a generous reward, but Iago declines, assuring him that he acted out of sympathy and a feeling of comradeship. This is the beginning of their friendship.

By this time the romance between Othello and Desdemona has flowered. Cassio, who is the go-between for the lovers, knows about Roderigo's love for Desdemona. He, too, meets Roderigo at one of the nightly revelries. Well aware of Roderigo's simple-mindedness and knowing the relationship between Othello and Desdemona, he finds Roderigo's dreams of a reciprocated love ridiculous. Cassio therefore constantly makes sport of Roderigo and plays tricks on him. He misinforms Roderigo as to where Desdemona is planning to take her walk that day, or he tells him that she will be expecting him at a certain rendezvous. And poor Roderigo spends hours vainly waiting for his love. Hurt and humiliated, he runs to Iago who vows to defend and avenge him and to arrange his marriage, for he does not believe in a love affair with a black devil. This compels Roderigo to cling to Iago even more, and to shower money on him.

What of Iago's past? He is a plain soldier by origin. He appears crude, good-natured, faithful and honest. He is a truly brave warrior. In every battle he is at Othello's side; on several occasions he saves his life. He is clever. He quickly grasps Othello's tactics, conceived through sheer military genius and intuition. Othello consults him before and during every battle, and often Iago gives him masterful and useful advice. There are two beings in Iago: one which he shows the world, and the other his true self. One—kind, simple, good-natured; the other—cruel, and repulsive. The assumed nature deceives everyone (even his wife, to some extent) so completely that he is regarded as most trustworthy and kind-hearted.

Othello, who has seen Iago in battle and knows his courage and cruelty, is also deceived by Iago's act. He is aware that in battle men turn into beasts, for he, himself, is that way. This, however, does not prevent him from being soft, tender and almost shy in normal life, and he attributes the same qualities to Iago. Moreover, Othello highly values Iago's keenness and cunning which more than once proved extremely helpful in battle. In the field Iago is not only an advisor but a friend. Othello shares his misfortunes, his doubts and his hopes with him. Iago is his lackey, his chambermaid, and when necessary, his physician. He knows better than anyone else how to dress a wound, and when it is time to hearten, to entertain, to sing an obscene song and tell a salty anecdote. Many, many times Iago's songs and off-color stories proved of great service. For instance: the troops are tired, the soldiers are complaining. Iago appears, sings a song which by its obscenity shocks even the soldiers, and the whole mood changes. On another occasion, just at the proper moment, when it is necessary to give some satisfaction to the enraged soldiers, Iago is capable of devising such beastly and cold-blooded torture and execution of captured barbarians that it satisfies and pacifies the rebellious spirit of the troops. Needless to say, it is done without Othello's knowledge, because the noble Moor does not tolerate brutality. If necessary he will chop a head off, but with one clean stroke, without torture.

Iago is honest. He will never take money or property belonging to the crown. He is too clever to risk it. But if it is possible to take advantage of a fool, and there are many besides Roderigo, he does not pass up the opportunity. He takes anything from them: money, gifts, women, horses, dogs—anything. This supplementary income is sufficient for a gay life. Emilia does not know about it, although she may suspect. Iago's closeness to Othello, his promotion from ordinary soldier to lieutenant, the fact that he sleeps in Othello's tent and is his right-hand man, doubtless wins him the jealousy of the other officers and the admiration of the men. But everyone fears and respects Iago. He is truly an ideal soldier and warrior.

But in Venice, among the glitter, the haughtiness and the stiffness of official life, among the high and mighty with whom Othello has to deal, Iago is completely out of place. In addition Othello lacks a knowledge of the sciences, he cannot write and his education is meager. He needs someone to fill in these gaps, an adjutant whom he can send, without any misgivings, with a message to the senators or to the Doge himself. Could he possibly appoint the rough soldier Iago to this position? Certainly the learned Cassio is far more suitable. He is a Florentine, and in those days Florentines, like the Parisians of today, are the epitome of social grace and sophistication. Could be possibly employ Iago in dealings with Brabantio or for the preparations of secret rendezvous with Desdemona? Cassio is admirably suited to these tasks. There is nothing surprising, then, that Othello makes him a lieutenant and appoints him his adjutant. Moreover, it never occurs to the Moor that Iago is a candidate to such a post. Why should Iago aspire to this role: He is already close to Othello, a confidant, a friend. Let him remain so. Why put him in the compromising position of an uneducated, uncouth and coarse adjutant who would be the laughing stock of everyone? This, most likely, is Othello's reasoning.

But Iago is of a different opinion. He reasons that for his service, his courage, the numerous times he has saved his General's life, for his friendship, devotion—he, and no one else, is entitled to be the General's adjutant. It would not have been so bad had he been substituted by some outstanding man or officer from among his military friends. But Othello choses the first pretty little officer who does not even know what war is like. Othello favors a mere boy only because he can read books, chatter with ladies, and bow smartly before the mighty ones. Such logic Iago cannot fathom. That is why Cassio's appointment proves such a blow, an insult, a humiliation, an injury, an ingratitude that Iago cannot forgive. And what really hurts Iago is the fact that his General hides from him his love for Desdemona, the kidnapping, and entrusts all this to the boy Cassio. It is therefore not surprising that after Cassio is appointed adjutant, Iago, out of bitterness, begins to drink and indulge in orgies. At these orgies he meets and becomes friendly with Roderigo. The favorite topics of the heart-to-heart talks of these new friends is, on the one hand, Roderigo's dreams of abducting Desdemona, which Iago is to arrange, and on the other hand, Iago's complaints concerning the injustices he suffers at the hands of Othello. In order to lighten and at the same time perpetuate his mood, Iago dwells on his past services and Othello's ingratitude. He even recalls the barrack rumors concerning Emilia.

When Iago was close to Othello there were many who envied him. And so, in order to sooth their jealousy, they sought a reason that would explain Othello's favor. The rumor that something was going on between Othello and Emilia was started and, of course, they did everything to let it reach Iago's ears. But at that time he paid little attention to it. Iago never really loved Emilia. He was attracted by her robustness, she was a good housewife, she could sing and play the lute, she was gay and had some property, she came from a good merchant family. At that time, even if there had been something between Othello and Emilia (and he knew there wasn't) he wouldn't have been upset.

But now, having suffered insult, he recalls the rumors. He wants, indeed it is necessary for him to create that relationship between the General and his wife. It gives him the right to hate more, to seek revenge. Now Iago craves to believe this rumor because in reality he knows it to be a lie. Emilia has always thought well of Othello. He is kind, lonely, uncared for. In the field his bachelor quarters lacked the feminine touch. That is why the wifely Emilia often came and set them in order. Iago knows this. He frequently saw her at Othello's but never attached any special significance to it. And now he has to pay for it. In a word, Iago has hypnotized himself into believing what never existed. This gives the knave in Iago a pretext for malice, for finding fault, for accusing the innocent Othello, and for inflaming within himself hatred and bitterness. This is the condition in which Iago learns of the unbelievable and unexpected news of the abduction of Desdemona. He cannot believe his eyes when, arriving at Othello's apartment, he sees the heavenly beauty embracing the black monster and devil, as the Moor now appears to him. The blow is so great that for some time his mind is blank. When it is finally explained to him how craftily the lovers, under the direction of Cassio, tricked and deceived even him, and when he hears their gay voices laughing at him, he has to flee in order to hide the fury which consumes him.

The abduction of Desdemona not only humiliates Iago but puts him in an extremely embarrassing position *vis a vis* Roderigo, for while milking him of his money the scoundrel was promising to arrange a match with the beautiful Desdemona or, failing to obtain her father's consent, to steal her away from her home. And suddenly he finds himself in this situation. Even the simple-minded Roderigo understands that Iago is leading him by the nose. Roderigo is stupidly, stubbornly, childishly, foolishly infuriated. He even forgets that Iago had saved him from a beating at the hands of some drunken rogues.

Long before the prearranged date for the abduction of Desdemona, Cassio had begun an intrigue with one of the chambermaids of the Brabantio household. Frequently he met her at the back porch and took her out in his gondola for a rendezvous. On the appointed night, at the hour of the usual rendezvous, it was Desdemona, and not the chambermaid, who stepped into his gondola. Before this, the maneuver was employed to arrange meetings between Desdemona and Othello.

It should not be forgotten that Desdemona is not at all the woman she is usually portrayed on the stage. She is always portrayed as a kind of shy, frightened Ophelia. But Desdemona is entirely different. She is determined and brave. She does not want the usual marriage of convenience. She wants a fairy prince.

However, we will discuss her at the proper time. In the meantime this will suffice to explain why she chooses the path of a risky and daring abduction.

When Iago learns of these events he is determined not to give in. He believes that not all is lost and that if he can create a scandal that would arouse the entire city, Othello would fail. The marriage might yet be annulled by orders from above. Who knows, maybe Iago is right? As long as the question of war is not yet resolved, Iago is correct in reckoning on an annullment.

It is important not to lose time. When it is necessary to act, Iago possesses Satanic energy. He works from all directions. Having regained his calm, he returns to the newlyweds, offers them congratulations, laughs with them and calls himself a fool. Then he rushes to Roderigo. When Roderigo learns the news the poor fool first cries like a child, then curses his friend with every obscene word and decides to break with him. It takes titanic efforts for Iago to convince him to cooperate in creating the scandal that will arouse the city and result in the annullment of the marriage.

We meet our friends at the moment that Iago, almost forcibly, puts Roderigo into the young man's gondola (very luxurious, decorated with fine fabrics, as befitting a wealthy loafer) and takes him to the Brabantio house. They arrive. The gondolier comes out, ties the gondola and waits. It is time to begin, but Roderigo still resists, he doesn't want to give in and hardly speaks to Iago.

From everything said above it is clear that this first scene is not a simple, tranquil exposition of the play as it is usually interpreted. Neither is it a scene in which the performer of Iago's role must display his malice and temper. The scene is vitally essential. In its essence it is a scene of action. It immediately and clearly delineates the villainous part of Iago, who, throughout the play carries on an intrigue and a campaign of revenge against Othello and all he holds dear. The action of this scene lies in its simple, elementary, semi-physical task, that of making Roderigo, at any cost, speak, beguiling him to make him create a city-wide scandal, to make him yell and shout. Only he can do this. Iago, being in the service of Othello, cannot conveniently do it. The actor who plays Roderigo must resist in all earnestness and really break his ties with his former friend Iago. This will make the performer of Iago's role come forth with such unusual ingenuity, methods and approaches, the credibility of which would be completely believable to the performer of Iago and the performer of Roderigo. In the solution of this task, namely, how and by what means to compel the stubborn fool to do what Iago wants, lies the work of both performers in this scene.

From everything said above it is clear with what nervous and rapid tempo the play starts from the very outset.

Roderigo is very, very angry with Iago.

Iago is quite taken aback and tries to improve the situation. First, because Roderigo is his money-bag, and then, because he needs Roderigo today to arouse the entire city. There is no time to lose, otherwise the wedding night will pass and it will be too late, all will be lost.

Roderigo sits in the best seat in the gondola. He is angry. He turns his back on Iago. The latter tries every trick to make him talk. His fervent arguments are suddenly met with loud, almost rude replies. Iago tries to stop him for he is afraid that they will be overheard or that he will be seen with Roderigo.

Stanislavski and the

Moscow Art Theatre

12 PHOTOGRAPHS

I. 1899—The Original Company of the
Moscow Art Theatre

Seated in the center are the two founders of the Theatre, C. Stanislavski
and V. Nemirovich-Danchenko. Standing in the second row, third from
the left is Olga Knipper-Chekhova, widow of Chekhov and last surviving
member of the original company.

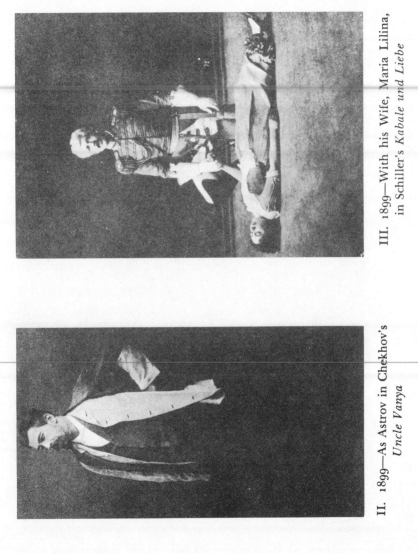

III. 1899—With his Wife, Maria Lilina, in Schiller's *Kabule und Liebe*

II. 1899—As Astrov in Chekhov's *Uncle Vanya*

IV. 1901—As Vershinin in Chekhov's *Three Sisters*

V. 1902—As Satin in Gorky's *The Lower Depths*   143

VI.   1910—With V. Kachalov in Ostrovsky's
Enough Stupidity in Every Sage

VII. 1911—As·Prince Abrezkov in Tolstoy's
The Living Corpse

VIII. 1912—With his wife, Maria Lilina, in Turgenev's *Provincialka*

IX. 1913—As Argon in Moliere's
Le Malade Imaginaire

X. 1924—As Famusov in Griboyedov's
Wit Works Woe

XI. 1938—Sketches by Stanislavski from his
Production Plan for Othello

XII. 1938—One of the last photographs of Stanislavski (Stanislavski shortly before his death)

STANISLAVSKI DIRECTS

GOGOL'S *DEAD SOULS*

By V. O. TOPORKOV

All through his life in art Constantin Stanislavski, that consummate master of the stage, founder of the Moscow Art Theatre, nursed the idea of producing Gogol's plays in a manner worthy of them. Twice he tried his hand at staging *The Inspector General*. In each case he felt he had achieved only partial success. Neither production quite satisfied this exacting artist, and he persevered in his efforts to perfect the technique of acting so as to be able to solve the difficult problem of presenting Gogol on the stage.

In 1932 the Moscow Art Theatre decided to put on *Dead Souls*. The dramatization of the poem was entrusted to the talented Soviet writer M. A. Bulgakov. I was cast for the leading part of Chichikov.

I permit myself a brief summary of *Dead Souls*, the plot for which was suggested to Gogol by the great poet Alexander Pushkin. Pavel Ivanovich Chichikov, a petty official of the rank of collegiate councillor, conceives a shady scheme for getting rich quickly. The events described in the novel take place under serfdom, when the property rights of the landed gentry extended to the serfs as well as to land. The landlords exploited their peasants, whom they bought and sold like chattel. The government kept a register of the serfs. From time to time these registers were revised, for which occasion lists of the deceased would be drawn up and the "dead souls" struck off the register, the landlord then being released from paying taxes on them. Not until the next revision came around would a deceased peasant be struck off the register. This meant that in the intervals between revisions, each landlord would gradually find himself "burdened" with quite a large number of "dead souls," who, officially, continued to be counted as alive.

Chichikov conceived the idea of taking advantage of this circumstance. He bought up dead peasants who still figured as alive with the object of pawning them, so to say, of obtaining a loan from the government council of guardians on their account. This was, of course, a criminal action, but one that was extremely hard to detect, as from the formal point of view the documents were all in order and the whole procedure had the appearance of legality.

Nevertheless Chichikov's scheme fell through. He was caught in the act and thrown into jail; only by paying a huge bribe to the municipal authorities was he able to escape trial and fly from the town.

To buy up his "dead souls" Chichikov travels from landlord to landlord all over the vast expanses of Russia, and this gives the author of the novel the opportunity to lay bare all the ugly sores of feudal Russia and to draw a whole gallery of portraits of the representatives of the landed gentry, to describe their life and customs.

The most interesting and vivid of Gogol's portraits is that of the landlord Plushkin—the quintessential image of a miser. In the world literature you can hardly find so brilliant, so artistically true an expression of avarice, or passion for gain.

The preliminary work on the production was conducted by stage-director V. G. Sakhnovsky, and as things worked out, Sakhnovsky carried the work nearly to completion, right up to the dress rehearsal, thus creating the first version of the production. The dress rehearsal left Stanislavski dissatisfied with our performance, whereupon he zealously set about revising the production, creating a completely new version.

"Constantin Sergeyevich's direction of all the performers in the scenes from *Dead Souls*," Sakhnovsky subsequently wrote in *Sovietskoye Iskusstvo*, October 15, 1932, "will constitute one of the remarkable chapters in the history of the Art Theatre. Some of the rehearsals were recorded in full, others only in part. All the performers will remember those rehearsals not only as instances of wonderful direction of actors in a Gogol play by a brilliant master, but also as examples of instruction in new methods of working on a role, in general. At some of the rehearsals the performers wildly applauded Stanislavski when he brought to light totally new facets of old familiar things."

V. O. TOPORKOV

In those days, not so long distant, many of our theatres were still held in thrall by formalistic tendencies. To achieve greater "expressiveness" they indulged in an "acute" form of external exaggeration which they defined as "grotesque," a word then fashionable. The harmonious, monumental works of our great classical playwrights would be chopped up into small pieces or episodes, which would then be refashioned into a "work" bearing every resemblance to a patchwork quilt. At the whim of the stage director the characters of the dramatis personae would be distorted beyond recognition, contrary to the sound sense of the author's character portraits.

Indeed, the aesthete-minded dramatic critics upheld that "new trend," and attacked the Moscow Art Theatre, which, in addition to preserving its realistic traditions, was also striving to develop them in the direction of socialist realism, as its production of Vsevolod Ivanov's *Armoured Train 14-69* so clearly proves.

Nevertheless, when he started to work on Gogol, Sakhnovsky made allowances for a certain degree of the "grotesque" element. He talked to us for hours on end, making very witty conjectures as to Gogol's personality, his philosophy, his relations with contemporaries and so on, and so forth. We haunted the museums to study the various portraits of Gogol, dug into his works, letters and biography. This was all very interesting, but not very concrete, and gave us but little help with our practical work. For all that we worked with great enthusiasm, now seeming to find some thread, now losing it again, to the very day of the dress rehearsal attended by Stanislavski we groped about in the dark for lack of guidance.

I shall not describe that rehearsal in detail, except to say that it reduced Stanislavski to a state of consternation. He told the stage directors he had not been able to understand a thing; either all the work on it would have to be started all over again or else the play would have to be dropped altogether.

As I now recollect the smallest details of Stanislavski's work on *Dead Souls,* and all the instructions he gave us in the course of our rehearsals, I venture to believe that I can accurately outline the method he employed to save the play.

Without doubt his first task was to find the dramatic keystone for this raw piece of work. What was the story to hinge on? What lines of development was the spectator to follow? None of the dramatized versions of Gogol's immortal novel (and there were more than 100 of them) had ever been successful for the reason that they were too loosely constructed. Individual scenes from *Dead Souls* had been enacted beautifully at various times, but no sooner were they strung together to form a complete play than this series of scenes, representing so many repetitions of the one act of purchasing dead souls but lacking a definite, unifying line of development, failed to hold the spectator's interest. By the middle of the performance the audience would begin to feel bored despite the participation of such fine actors as Varlamov, Davydov, Dalmatov and others.

The most thankless role in all the versions was that of Chichikov, for all that Gogol himself had drawn a brilliant portrait of him. He appears in all the scenes, but because in each of them he does the same thing, the audience soon gets tired of him and transfers its attention elsewhere.

It was on Chichikov, however, that Stanislavski resolved to pivot the play. "Chichikov's career," he decided, was to form the subject of the play, the line of development that the spectator was to follow. Stanislavski was well versed in the laws of the theatre and knew that the better a play is constructed dramatically, the better it puts its ideas across. If the play happens to be imperfectly constructed, it is the duty of the director to improve on it, not, however, by adding accessory decorations that detract the spectator's attention from its essence, but by strengthening its line of action.

"What are we to do with Chichikov?" Stanislavski exclaimed at one of the rehearsals, "How are we to avoid monotony of his perpetual arrivals and discussions of one and the same topic? Only by means of through-action. We have to show how a chance word suggests to Chichikov the idea of buying dead registered souls, how his plan grows and expands, how it reaches its culminating point and then swiftly falls through. All honor and glory to you if you master the through-action in this role, but it's going to be very hard to do."

The task had both its general and specific difficulties. Having selected Chichikov as the leading figure, Stanislavski still lacked a suitable performer for the part. My qualities fitted me for the "grotesque" interpretation of Chichikov we had aimed for before Stanislavski stepped in, but were absolutely unsuited to the real Chichikov portrayed in Gogol's novel. Besides, our attempts to "point up" this sharply pointed image had, naturally, distorted my own sense of truth and verisimilitude and paralyzed my true artistic intuition and creative will.

By allowing ourselves to be influenced by the theatrical "fashion" of the day, we got into a blind alley and only a man of great practical knowledge of the theatre could rescue us from it.

"All your joints are dislocated," Stanislavski told me at our first discussion after the dress rehearsal. "You haven't got a single sound organ. First you have to be cured and have all your joints set right; you have to be taught anew how to walk, not to act, but just to walk."

Of the big problems he himself had to tackle in this play he told us nothing at the time. It was ever his system to say nothing beforehand.

"Are you good at bargaining?" he asked me.

"Bargaining?"

"Yes: buying cheap and selling dear; can you humbug the other man, play up your own goods and belittle his, guess his lowest price, play poor, call God to witness, cajole and so forth, and so forth."

"No, I'm absolutely no good at that."

"Then you'll have to learn. That's the most important part of your role."

At the first few rehearsals Stanislavski worked with me alone in order to "set my dislocated joints." He instructed me very attentively and carefully, treating me as a doctor treats a patient, and as I realize now, the main purpose of our studies was to organize and mold the organic lines of Chichikov's physical conduct, in other words, the practical application of his method of mastering the scenic image in its entirety, or what subsequently came to be called the "method of physical actions."

It was as though Stanislavski had made us come down from the clouds. The questions he put were astonishingly simple, lucid and concrete. I was even a little disappointed and nonplussed—it was all so extremely simple and ordinary and so far removed from the goals our fancies pictured. In addition, my previous efforts had so confounded my mind that I was sometimes hard put to it to answer the simplest questions.

"Why, please tell me, should Chichikov go about buying dead souls?" was one of the questions Stanislavski popped at me one day.

What could I answer? This was something everyone knew, and yet . . . .

"What do you mean 'why'? It tells us in the novel: he meant to offer them as surely as though they were alive and receive money for them."

"But what for?"

"What for? It was profitable . . . he would get money for them."

"Why?"

"How 'why'?"

"Why was it profitable for him, what did he need money for, what did he mean to do with the money? Have you ever thought of that?"

"No, I've never considered it so closely."

"Well, think it over."

(A long pause.)

"Well, the souls are 'pawned' and the money received—what next?"

(Another pause.)

"You have to know exactly and correctly, in every possible detail, the final goal of all your doings. Consider the matter well, trace Chichikov's biography to glean material for your practical work on the role."

Very subtly, very ably, Stanislavski directed my thoughts to the required channel, but he never pressed any ready-made formulas upon me. He simply prodded my imagination with a skilful hand.

"Put yourself in Chichikov's place. What would you do in his circumstance?"

"Yes, but I'm not Chichikov, I'm not interested in getting rich."

"But if it were something that did interest you in the highest degree, what would you do then?"

The simplest things concerning the most vital factors in Chichikov's life were settled in the course of these talks. There was none of that vagueness, none of the abstruse interpretations the formalist of the time had so great a weakness for.

At first Stanislavski was interested in the hero's simplest concerns and affairs. How much money did Chichikov have when he bribed the council of guardians and how big was the bribe, etc. In brief, he wanted me to know every smallest detail of my hero's life. I had to settle all these problems myself, and so I did, waiting, meanwhile, to begin work on my role, never suspecting that this work had already begun, but that the method was a most unusual one.

Once, at one of the rehearsals in Stanislavski's study, we got to discussing the new trends in the threatre. By that time, Stanislavski was no longer going to the theatres himself and he listened to our accounts of the plays then running in Moscow with keen interest. We told him about the formalistic devices resorted to by the directors of several theatrical groups which were all the rage at the time and which considered that it was their mission to replace the outmoded academic style of the Art Theatre.

"We have to take all this calmly and bravely," said Stanislavski. "We have to go on perfecting our art and our technique. Sometimes false

V. O. TOPORKOV

quests and trends in art seem for a time to be an important find and threaten the foundations of high realistic art, but they are powerless to destroy it altogether. Formalism is a temporary fad; we have to wait for it to pass over, but at the same time we have to work and not just sit with folded hands. Somebody has to take care to preserve the shoots of the genuine, great real art which are now being choked by weeds. But you can rest assured that the time for their growth and luxurious blossoming will come. The weeds will be destroyed, but you have to preserve the shoots. This difficult task lies on our shoulders. It is our sacred duty, the duty we owe to art and to our country."

*   *   *

Stanislavski's work on the scene *Chichikov and Plushkin* is the most striking example of his realistic skill as a director, of his ability to penetrate to the heart of human passions and find exact forms for their scenic representation.

The chapter on Plushkin, so remarkable in Gogol's novel, loses much in the dramatized version. Plushkin sits in his room. Chichikov enters and takes Plushkin for the housekeeper. After a while the misunderstanding is cleared up and Chichikov, presenting his scheme in the guise of an act of charity towards this unhappy old man, wins the latter's consent to sell his dead souls. Plushkin was played by L. M. Leonidov, a wonderful actor eminently suited to represent this type. His age, his penetrating, suspicious glance, his strong voice with the occasional tenor notes that made it sound womanish at times, his bent for tragedy all indicated that the part of Plushkin was in the right hands and the theatre would succeed in presenting the deeply tragic image of this Russian landlord, once a man of some moment, a fine farmer and a respectable family man, but now consumed by his fatal passion. But how were all the complex features of this character, so minutely, lovingly and richly described in the novel, to be brought out on the stage? Gogol's beautiful descriptions and poetic digressions could not be incorporated into the stage version. In the play this is only a brief episode, merely a business-like interview concerning the sale of dead souls, and nothing more.

This circumstance kept Leonidov in a state of nervous tension. He felt that it would not lend wings to his temperament and to his potentialities as an actor.

Leonidov held Stanislavski in great esteem. Every rehearsal with Stanislavski was a stirring event to hm. Anxious to make a decent showing at the first presentation of this scene before Stanislavski, he worked very hard and was very exacting of himself and of me as his partner. My role was coming along poorly and he did his best to help me, being well aware that the absence of a good Chichikov could ruin him completely.

It was obvious that we were not getting anywhere with the scene. At times Leonidov's intonations were exceptionally vivid; now and then his portrait of the miser was very convincing, and yet the scene was interesting only in parts. As a whole it was quite boring and failed to hold the spectator engrossed (I refer to the few spectators who were always present at rehearsals).

The day came when we enacted the Plushkin scene for Stanislavski for the first time. I doubt I had ever before seen Stanislavski show such concentrated attention at a rehearsal. This time all his attention was fixed on Leonidov. I played poorly and was aware of my feebleness, but he ignored me completely, I just did not exist for him. He followed Leonidov's acting intently, afraid to miss a single gesture, sigh or intonation. He sat as still as a statue, but his thoughts were plainly to be read on his face, at which, I must confess, I glanced from time to time. In most cases what I read there was not in our favor.

When we finished there ensued a long and painful pause. Stanislavski took off his glasses and stared ahead of him as though he were weighing the words in which to couch his sad diagnosis. Leonidov stood waiting with blanched face and downcast eyes. For my part, I was so utterly devoid of hope that I could feign cool indifference. The directors and their assistants made ready to take down Stanislavski's remarks.

"Hm . . . hm . . . very good . . . You have hit upon many good touches, Leonid Mironovich . . . [A long pause] But the whole thing is rather amorphous, it is all 'in general.' There is no pattern and your good colors lack lustre. The scene has no beginning, no development, no culminating point, no end. Plushkin is a miser; take the trouble to seek his kind side . . . no, not kind but even generous, prodigal, a very wastrel, and make that the high point of your role. That will give sparkling color to your miserliness and particularly fine emphasis to the phrase: 'No, I shall leave it (the watch) to him in my will that he may remember me when I am dead.' How can you give expression to your miserliness? Only by means of the things that happen to you. But you pay too little attention to them; you are wholly engrossed in yourself, in your inner world; all through the scene you are afraid of spilling your feeling of miserliness, and that is wrong. You should proceed from the

158

happenings of today. Play each episode to the end, in all its details. That is the only way you can show the character.

"What has happened? Plushkin has come home after his usual round of junk-collecting and has brought home a basketful of trash to add to the heap already lying on the floor of his room. But for him this is not junk or trash; it is a rich collection of the rarest antiques.

"He has been away a long time, leaving his house unprotected when the entire neighborhood, he believes, is a nest of bandits. What a hard time he had getting home with his basket of 'treasures' without being robbed! When he enters the room he casts an anxious glance around it to make sure that nobody has been there in his absence. Somewhat reassured, he settles himself near his junk pile and begins to sort and count the specimens of his collection. On this the curtain rises and your scene begins.

"This is the beginning of the action. The audience sees Plushkin and his room for the first time and will be interested. You have no need to hurry. You can play a big scene here: *Plushkin examining his treasures.* Can you play that, and only that? Do you see what excellent material this is for skillful acting? By playing this scene in all its details, all its organic qualities, you can hold the audience spellbound without saying a word. But you let the opportunity slip by, ignore it in your haste to reach the dialogue with Chichikov.

"You think your salvation lies there, but you are mistaken. Long before Chichikov says a word Plushkin has so many things, so many emotions to live through, and all of the highest interest to the audience. We see an old man who looks like a woman rummaging in a pile of junk, closely and lovingly examining each object, whether a horseshoe or the torn sole of an old shoe. He is engrossed in what he is doing and does not notice how Chichikov cautiously pushes the door open and comes in and scrutinizes Plushkin, unable to make out whether he is a man or a woman. Feeling the stranger's glance Plushkin turns around and their eyes meet.

"What does this mean to Plushkin? Why, it is just what he has feared most, what has haunted him like a nightmare: a bandit has stolen up to his treasures. And what a bandit—not one of those who lives here, near his estate—he knows all those well—no, this is a newcomer, a stranger to these parts, and evidently a well-known robber and murderer.

"What should he do? After his first moments of consternation Plushkin takes a whole series of precautions to save his life, carefully concealing his fears from the bandit, however, in order to outwit him and escape from the room to summon assistance.

"Under these circumstances it is very difficult for Chichikov to address him, and this mutual misunderstanding, their conflicting impulses (the one to start the ball of conversation rolling, the other to escape from the room) also offers a very interesting scenic picture.

"At last the first words are spoken, the situation is more or less cleared up and the dialogue begins.

"But what you do is to plunge straight into the dialogue, skipping the most interesting part, the moment of orientation, of mutual adaptation.

"In real life you would never skip this moment, but for some strange reason on the stage it is always being done. I assure you that it is very important, it is most convincing to the audience and sets the actor on the right road, making him believe in his actions, and that is the most important thing.

"Moments of orientation may be brief, barely perceptible, or sometimes, depending upon the circumstances, just the contrary. The moment of orientation, of feeling each other out, does not necessarily cease when your partner starts talking. In the first few phrases the tone is generally still a little uncertain because neither of the partners has yet made his preliminary estimate of the other. They continue to feel each other out so as to decide upon the most suitable mode of approach. This would be particularly true of so suspicious a person as Plushkin.

"Remember that before he realized who Chichikov was and came to believe that he was veritably a messenger from heaven who has come to reward him for his great goodness and humility, he took him first for a bandit, then for a landlord who wanted to be treated to a good dinner, and then for a ruined hussar who has come to borrow money, and so forth. All these are moments of orientation, adaption and then reorientation and re-adaptation to new circumstances.

"All this may be taken as the introduction, the first part of the scene: *Plushkin gets to know Chichikov.* For the time being that is all you have to do. Forget everything else, give all your attention for the while to doing this and note your impressions.

"Part two: Plushkin has at last realized that he has to do with a benefactor. How can he thank him, how win his favor so that he may go on showing his mercies? This is where Plushkin organizes a 'feast': he orders the samovar to be ready and the dried crust of a cake presented to him by a relative three years ago brought in. Now he is a rich, hospitable landlord giving an incomparable feast. Here you must play a generous, spendthrift Plushkin; forget about his being a miser and set yourself the one problem of regaling your benefactor, of impressing him with your great generosity and, simultaneously, accelerating the conclusion of the deal for the sale of your dead souls.

"There are two critical moments in the course of this second part of the scene when the whole deal is in danger of falling through: once because Plushkin cannot go to town, and the other time because of the loss of the clean sheet of paper. These are very serious moments; do not let them escape you; play each one out to the end.

"The loss of his clean sheet of paper is a matter of importance to Plushkin. Your main problem here is to know how to look for it properly. It is only by your manner of searching that you can convey the depth of your emotions. It requires a high degree of collectedness, true attention. In short, you must be acting, not showing your emotions.

"At last all the obstacles are removed and the deal concluded: this amazing benefactor, Pavel Ivanovich Chichikov, has bought the runaway as well as the dead souls.

"Now the third part of the scene: Plushkin is eager to see off with all honors this extraordinary man who has topped his kind deed by refusing all refreshments. This is a whole scene: *Seeing Chichikov off.*

"Think only of how to express your love, your respect, your gratitude to your guest. Forget completely the Plushkin who is a misanthropic Plushkin. No, now he is exceedingly affable, brimming over with love for man. Act Afanasi Ivanovich from *Old-World Gentlefolks.*

"And now the final part of the scene: Plushkin is alone again. At first, by inertia, he is still preoccupied by his anxiety to propitiate his dear guest. Suddenly he fears that he has not shown his gratitude sufficiently. He keeps running from the window, where he can see Chichikov climbing into his carriage, to his junk pile and his desk, struggling with the desire to do something.

"Finally, his kind, elevated feelings gain the upper hand, he reaches a decision and while he feverishly rummages the dusty drawers of his desk, he exclaims: 'I'll give him a pocket watch.' At last he finds the watch. 'He is still a young man, he needs a pocket watch to please his bride . . .' etc. He blows the dust from the watch, examines it carefully, and starts for the door in all haste to intercept his departing guest, but suddenly he stops short.

"Here you may have what is called a 'histrionic pause.' A man who was just burning with eagerness to present a gift is struck with horror at the realization that he was on the verge of the most inexcusable extravagance; an extravagance that might well have ruined him. It is not an instantaneous realization. Its birth and development must be expressed in the pause. When he does finally grasp the full significance of his act, there arises the problem of finding the safest possible hiding place for the treasure that has nearly slipped out of his hands. He shifts the watch from one place of safekeeping to another until he is finally sure that it is well hidden, and only then does he regain his composure.

"At last the watch is safely put away. . . . But what about the benefactor? Never mind: 'I'll leave it to him in my will that he may remember me when I am dead.'

"And so Plushkin again becomes Plushkin. Anxiously he turns to his property: hasn't the unexpected visitor carried anything off?

"On this scene the curtain comes down.

"Each one of these pieces must be played so that it appears true to life, with its events and emotions following each other in logical sequence; each scene must be the development of the one before and all of them should be linked in an unbroken line of cumulative action.

"Do not think about the image, about your emotions. You have a number of episodes of widely varied emotional tone to play. They should not all be colored by the one tone of miserliness, gloom, etc. Kindness, generosity and joy also appear here. Plushkin's actions differ correspondingly. The unexpected alternation of often totally opposite kinds of actions will bring out the miser's energetic pursuit of gain. Round out each episode in full, make everything an event. First of all plot your physical conduct in each episode and then link them together in a single line of action. This is the surest means of giving embodiment to the idea behind Gogol's portrait of Plushkin."

"And what is my line to be, Constantin Sergeyevich?" I asked.

"You must in every case be able to adapt yourself to the character of your companion.

"Plushkin is a hard nut to crack, but you have to be able to see through him, too, and to find the means of making yourself pleasing to him as well. How? Put yourself in his place and think: what does he want? Everyone counts him a miser, but you marvel at his kindness, his thrift, and do it so that he believes you. Remember what he says about his neighbor, the captain? 'He calls me his relative, it's all "uncle, uncle," and he kisses my hands; but I'm no more his uncle than he's my grandfather.' You see—for all his hand-kissing he doesn't believe the man. Consequently, you have to be more subtle.

"You must sincerely make all Plushkin's cares your own, understand them, sympathize with him, turn your own self into Plushkin for this while.

"Perhaps, in general, it would be good for you to spend some time rehearsing not Chichikov, but all the landlords he has dealings with. Yes, that would certainly be of benefit."

* * *

B. Y. Petker, who, like myself, had come to the Art Theatre from the Moscow Theatre of Comedy (formerly the Korsh Theatre) was being trained as Leonidov's understudy in the role of Plushkin. Although he was still young at that time, he was very good in character parts and when the question of an understudy for the part of Plushkin arose he was chosen for it. In addition to all else, this gave Stanislavski the opportunity to see our new actor at work.

After the stage directors E. S. Telesheva and V. G. Sakhnovsky had drilled him for some time, a rehearsal with Stanislavski was arranged. Petker was asked to come an hour or two earlier and he told me the story of what happened in my absence.

On the dot of the appointed hour Petker turned into a small yard where he found Stanislavski sitting at a table in the shade of a large canvas umbrella. Stanislavski welcomed Petker very kindly and asked the directors to tell him about the progress of the rehearsals, about what was coming along well and where they were meeting with snags.

Receiving satisfactory replies to a long series of questions, he then asked:

"But what about the difference in age? Don't forget that Plushkin is at least seventy years old. That's a very difficult thing to do."

But on this point, too, the directors tried to reassure him.

"Hm . . . Hm . . . I'm very much afraid it may turn out to be one of those cases of 'acting an old man,' with everyone marvelling to see so young a man do old age so well. That would be very little and altogether uninteresting in comparison with Gogol's image—that personification of all the miserliness in the world. . . . Well, let us try. I'll speak Chichikov's words. And so, let us begin."

Petker did his best, employing all the tried and tested means, to represent a decrepit, old miser. Stanislavski gave all the cues and watched Petker closely. Suddenly he stopped short and asked:

"Whom are you talking to? Who sits facing you now?"

"Constantin Sergeyevich Stanislavski . . ."

"Nothing of the kind; a rogue . . ."

"What!"

"See! Already you are looking at me more closely than when you were acting the scene. There's a hint of life here now. If you know me to be a rogue, how will you watch me during our conversation? Why, your attitude to me will simply be that of one to a rogue. You will try to anticipate my moves and intentions. Suppose I have a knife hidden about me? You will review the location in the yard of the things you most fear for. Don't act anything, just think to yourself. You are intent on acting something. You can't act anything yet, just accumulate thoughts."

As he said this Stanislavski reached for a pen on the table to jot down a note, but Petker's hand shot out and moved the pen out of reach.

"Quite right. Now try to anticipate my next move. Watch me. No, don't act, just watch me really and truly. Again he's acting. . . . Come, let us stroll about the yard. I am your neighbor and this is your estate. Tell me about your affairs in detail. What barn is this?" he asked in a serious tone of voice, pointing to a shed.

Petker invented some vague reply, but Stanislavski was not satisfied and enquired about each thing in greater and greater detail. In the midst of this a carter drove into the yard with a loaded cart. Stanislavski immediately headed for it, asking Petker what it was and what he needed it for.

Petker gave him some explanation. Stanislavski listened intently, but questioned him more and more closely until he finally received a suitable reply. And so they walked about the yard playing this game very seriously. Then they sat down at the table and continued to discuss such problems as hay making, the crop, the peasants, etc.

I arrived at the rehearsal in the midst of this conversation. Finding Stanislavski engaged in a serious conversation with Petker and never imagining that they were rehearsing, I stopped a short distance away, waiting for a convenient moment to present myself.

Glancing at me out of the corner of his eye, Stanislavski softly whispered to Petker:

"Look who's come! Be careful of him, keep him at a distance—he's a rogue."

I realized what they were doing and joined the game at once. Leaving the field of action to us, Stanislavski quickly reconverted himself from landlord to director and observed us attentively.

I approached Petker, but he jumped up and ran away.

"Hm . . . hm . . . You 'acted' that, Boris Yakovlevich. You need only back away a little, that's all. . . . Then Chichikov will see at once that you are afraid of him and you will have done only what is necessary to place yourself in safety."

Gradually Petker and I got to talking, first improvising, and then slipping into the text of the play. Every time our conversation assumed theatrical forms and lost its organic flow, Stanislavski interrupted us. Again and again he brought us back to the truth:

"Nothing should be acted. You just listen and try to grasp what Chichikov is driving at. All I want now is your attention. . . . Try to guess the object of this unexpected visit. Now invite him to be seated. . . . No, not that way: he might stick a knife into you. . . . And that's wrong, too . . . find a more convenient . . . and safer way."

Step by step Stanislavski unearthed all the actor's vital qualities and dislodged all his theatrical, professional habits. Already Petker had lost his special senile "tone," had overcome his usual manner of acting. His face was already coming alive and his eyes peered forth attentively and distrustfully. I was evidently responding in the same manner and we both felt bound by a thread of mutual interest in each other.

Cautiously, I began to explain my offer to him. He listened to me and tried to grasp its point.

We felt good. The few spectators present listened to us and followed the development of our conversation.

Then there came the moment when the realization of the great boon that is being offered to him penetrates Petker-Plushkin's mind, and as Chichikov said: "Because of my esteem for you I will pay for the purchase-deed myself" his face seemed to light up. For some moments he stared at me in amazement. Our audience awaited further developments with interest. Petker's face twitched convulsively. Stanislavski, who had sat silent all this time, unwilling to interrupt the scene now that it had at last taken the right course, softly prompted:

"Now you can work your face as much as you like. You've earned the right to it, now. Wrinkle it as much as you can—more . . . more . . . don't be afraid now. . . . There, that's right!"

He shook with laughter as he spoke and all the others were laughing, too. With this Stanislavski brought the rehearsal to a close.

"Well, it's very good. . . . Do you see how carefully you have to feel out the role, to weave the fragile gossamer thread of the living, organic fabric of the character's behavior, how very carefully you have to weave it lest it should tear? Don't go poking the coarse rope of professional acting into it. Patiently weave these gossamer threads into the fabric of high organic art; with time it will gain strength and then you will no longer need to fear for it. Keep on working, don't force the pace, carefully start out from the simplest, lifelike, organic actions. Don't think about the image for the time being. As a result of your correct actions the image will develop of itself. You have just seen an example of how you can carefully pave your way by proceeding from one small truth to the other, how you can check yourself, give rein to your imaginative powers and achieve vivid, expressive scenic action. Keep on working along these lines.

"Do you understand what you have to do?" he added, turning to the directors. "After a while come and show me the scene again."

* * *

Addressing the performers before the presentation of *Dead Souls* on the stage, Stanislavski said:

"I am putting the play on although it is not quite ready. . . . It is not yet *Dead Souls,* not yet Gogol, but in what you are doing I can perceive the living shoots of a future Gogol production. Follow this path and you will find Gogol. Only it will take a long time yet."

And to me he said in private:

"You have only just recovered from your illness; you have learned to walk and to act a little. Strengthen this living, but still weak line of action. Some five or ten years hence you will present a true picture of Chichikov, and some twenty years hence you will appreciate Gogol properly."

As Stanislavski foretold, the production of *Dead Souls,* whose living shoots of genuine, profound art were tenderly nurtured by this great master, would go on developing. For nearly twenty years it has held our stage with invariable success.

FILM ACTING:

TWO PHASES

By V. I. PUDOVKIN

WHAT ARE THE BASIC METHODS the actor finds? We have already seen that the theatre supports him in his fight for organic unity of the acting image by means of a detailed methodology of rehearsals.

In these rehearsals, obedient to the will of the actors and producer, the stern temporal conditions limiting the players are for a space removed and substituted by more unified and uninterrupted work aiding the actor to link, in whatsoever direction may be necessary, his live personality with the image he plays.

At rehearsals the actor, free from breaks in time or position, can link the separate pieces of his role into one whole, can concretely live into his image, checking it by a series of pieces of his role outside the play, but undoubtedly organically belonging to the image. In short, at rehearsals he can do all that work which will enable him later on to feel every separate piece of his role, however interrupted it may be mechanically in the course of the performance, as his own, belonging to him, and if not uninterrupted in the sense of his physical presence on the stage, at least inwardly uninterrupted in the unity of his feeling and understanding of the role.

What do we do in the cinema in the way of providing technical help to the actor in his difficult creative work? It must be admitted that this assistance, where it is even given at all, is in most producing collectives of an exceedingly perfunctory character. Sometimes there are attempts at just a preliminary working-through the script with the actor by the director. The role is discussed, the role is, in fact, talked all round and about, so-called actor and director "role-conferences" take place. Something on the lines of so-called "round-table conferences" in the theatre (work in the theatre preliminary to rehearsals) takes place in the cinema to a greater or lesser degree. But no practical preliminary work with the actor on the lines of linking the image found at the "round-table conference" with its outer expression, actually the basic starting-point of the work needed to transform an actor thinking about a role into an actor acting it, has ever been used as a normal course.

In his preliminary work on the image the actor has, quite ridiculously and unnecessarily, been mechanically separated from practice, from the concrete work on himself as a live, connectedly and unitedly moving and speaking human being. The actor has approached the work of being shot, a process already requiring technically fixed and defined methods of execution, quite unaided, and able only academically to image to himself the general meaning of his role, in no way having linked it to his concrete live individuality. Such has been the position in the best cases; in the worst, the actor purely and simply has not known anything about his role apart from the sum total of directorial instructions restricted to each piece being shot. Naturally, each shot is proceeded by a sort of travesty of a rehearsal, but this cannot be considered seriously, for no antecedent work has ever been done upon it to give it an inner link to the actor's image.

It is this incorrect attitude to the tasks of acting work that has given rise to the pseudo-theory of the *montage* (edited) image (a theory for which no single individual is responsible). This theory deduces, from the fact that an impression of acting can be composed mechanically by sticking pieces together, the illegitimate assumption that separate pieces, not connected inwardly within the actor, will necessarily give an optimum result.

The true significance of the edited image is quite different; it has considerable importance for the cinema actor, and we shall speak of it later.

Just as in the theatre, so in the cinema, the methodology of rehearsals is all-important for the actor.

In fact, as we have already observed, this methodology is even more important in the cinema than in the theatre, since the hyper-discontinuity of acting work in shooting desiderates a correspondingly especially clear, definite, and detailed absorption by the actor of the wholeness of his role.

Systematic rehearsal work in the cinema prior to shooting has so far been conducted only by way of experiment. I cannot speak of the work of the Experimental Film Collectives, as they have made no verbal or written record of their experiences. I shall discuss the experiment of Kuleshov in his film: *The Great Consoler.**

Kuleshov wrote a shooting script, that is, a script worked out in technical detail as it is to be shot on the floor and edited afterwards. All the shots in this script, numbered and with their numerical order preserved, were transferred to a miniature studio floor. In fact, prior to the shooting of the film, he staged a performance consisting of very short scenes each in length identical with the piece later to be edited. As far as possible Kuleshov played each scene through on the studio floor in such a way that subsequently, after a most careful rehearsal, it could be transferred back to and shot without alteration on the actual floor used in shooting.

His rehearsal system attained three results. First, it achieved the preliminary work with the actor to the deepest possible degree. Second, it gave the executives the opportunity to "see" the film, as it were, before it was shot, and make in time any correction or alteration that might be required. And third, it reduced to a minimum the waste of time during the preliminaries to each shot, which, as is well known, in general run away with a great deal of money.

The combination of these results gave Kuleshov's work a somewhat peculiar style. First and foremost, in striving at all costs to make the rehearsal performance an exact pattern of the future screen performance, Kuleshov undoubtedly not only rehearsed his actors, but also to some extent adapted his film to a form more convenient and simple for the carrying out of the rehearsal.

It is not a coincidence that Kuleshov's film contains few dramatis personæ. It is not a coincidence that Kuleshov has no crowd scenes. It is not a coincidence that the extremely sparse and limited exteriors take the shape either of empty country roads or of city streets on which one never meets a living soul except those few dramatis personæ.

*A film blended of O. Henry's life and *Alias Jimmy Valentine.*

Kuleshov, of course, wrote his script in this way, set the action in these scenes, chose this subject and this number of characters precisely to give himself the chance to fit the film rapidly and easily into the framework of a stage performance, one, moreover, of necessity played on a stage rather especially primitively fitted out.

I do not think this work of Kuleshov should be treated as wrong in principle. The effort was undoubtedly a most interesting experiment. The experiment was not wrong, but any mechanical deduction that might be made from it along the line of converting the method into a dogmatic recipe to be used in the shooting of any and every film would most undoubtedly be wrong.

Our task remains, of course, the finding of such ways, such forms, and such methods of adjusting a rehearsal period as will in no wise handicap the film in the field of its exploration of every possible wide and rich development.

We are still faced with the problem how to organize preparatory rehearsal work on a film which definitely and markedly strives to develop along cinematic lines, that is, including a series of scenes embracing a large spacial canvas, locations, and circumstances such as cannot be reproduced on a rehearsal floor.

We must not and cannot pander to a desire to play the future film through on a rehearsal floor to the extent of eliminating from it elements which, though they have no direct physical link with the actor in his acting, yet none the less contribute to the film the power and richness that make it a truly cinematic work of art.

In my view the discovery of the correct methods for the rehearsal period will only be attained by keeping clearly and exclusively to our main purpose. The purpose is, of course, the actor's work on his acting image. All the rest, the demonstration of the whole film to the executives, the learning by rote of set-ups in advance (which latter is, in fact, never completely possible unless the film limits the canvas it shoots to the space within the studio walls), must be subordinated to the maximum fostering of conditions aiding the actor to solve his main technical problem—embodiment in the image.

What, then, are the main postulates of the methodology of the rehearsal period? First let us consider the editing structure set out in the sheets of the shooting script. The sheets of the shooting script list a series of short pieces. Nearly every element of the actor's behavior linked to the inner order of the action is interspersed with numerous pieces showing the audience either parallel action by other actors at quite a different location, or epically developed elements of events into which the actor is incorporated by developments of the general action, or both.

Suppose such a scene: a person in a room is talking to a man who excitedly awaits a meeting with his brother. The brother is expected by air. The excited wait is interrupted by the ring of a telephone bell. Information is given that the aeroplane is about to land. On the screen the action changes to an aerodrome where we see the plane and a sudden crash that causes the death of the brother arriving. The next piece to follow portrays the waiting brother receiving the terrible news.

Should one in the rehearsal period strive to work out separately the two pieces of the state of the waiting man, separated as they will be on the screen by the conventionalized plane crash?

For work with the actor this would not only be unnecessary, but wrong and harmful. The only correct course is to rehearse both pieces in conjunction, thus enabling the actor to stay in the acting image without interruption, and to replace the specifically cinematic element of the portrayal of the crash by a single telephone call announcing the disaster.

Suppose on the screen an actor, fleeing from pursuit, swims a river, and meets on the opposite bank a man whom he was seeking in order to deliver to him some message, it would, of course, be futile and stupid to waste time and energy by staging an actual swim across a river during the rehearsal period. What is important for the actor during rehearsal is the presence somewhere in his role of a serious obstacle in his feeling during his conversation with the person met beyond the river. In rehearsal conditions, any physical obstacle could serve as equivalent for the river, a window, for example, through which he might have to climb, or a door he might break down, before entering the room.

I choose obvious examples of this kind in order to make clear the simple point that the separate shots (or editing pieces) of the shooting script, divided into its multitudinous incidents, an abundance of which cannot be reproduced on the stage, should properly be transmuted into some other form for the actor to facilitate his concentration in rehearsal on the absorption of the unity of the acting image.

This new form of script might be termed an "actor's script." In an actor's script the separate pieces concerning him would be approximated to one another for the paramount purpose of preserving for him as far as possible a longer duration and less interruption in his acting. The whole material of the director's editing or shooting script would be preserved. Only it would be rearranged in a new sequence, enabling nearer approximation of the shots in the actor's role, thus giving him larger pieces of united inner movement.

Of course, such a linking up of the separate pieces in a role will in some cases entail the replacement of certain pieces by equivalents, as in the just instanced case of the telephone ring instead of the plane crash.

The actual task of translating a shooting script into actors' scripts is certainly one which requires considerable practical experience for its proper performance. But its purpose is clear and simple.

Stage practice, particularly the practice of the Stanislavsky school in the matter of "interval" or "hiatus" pieces in rehearsal alluded to by us before, can be particularly fruitful for film rehearsals.

Kozintzev has stated that during rehearsal work with the actors on his latest film, *The Youth of Maxim,* he concentrated solely on those parts of the role outside the actual action of the film.

The point of his observation is, once again, the fact that the main problem of director and actor invariably boil down to the establishment in rehearsal of the inner unity of any given piece with the role as a whole.

So as not to confuse the actor with theatrical conventions alien to the cinema, the director must surround him at rehearsal with real equivalents practical within the limits of a stage or rehearsal room. So as not to force the actor to waste energy in imagining such things as rivers that he will meet in the actual story, the director and actors in rehearsal add equivalent pieces, enabling the inner content of the actor's behavior to remain unchanged, the river he will have to swim being replaced by some analogous obstacle such as those I have already suggested.

Let me once again emphasize the extreme danger of introducing into cinema rehearsal work specifically theatrical conventions unconnected with actual problems of shooting.

Kuleshov's method of solving the rehearsal problem by having the whole future film played over on the floor involves such a danger.

I repeat once more, also with emphasis, that an "actor's script" such as I describe requires careful, meticulous, and profound modification to replace real-life conditions set out in the editing script with equivalent real conditions practicable for the rehearsal stage. And this process can no doubt best be effected in actual concert with the actor.

The beginning and end of the old system was its orientation around the reduction of the actor's work to an almost mechanical performance of a "task" allotted him by the director. We shall never escape from the old system of treating the actor as a prop, as a type, if we do not set the question of creative inter-influence of actor and director right at the forefront of work on the film, already at the stage preceding shooting.

Hitherto the actor, encountering only the complexly constructed shooting script of the director, able to envisage his own future work only abstractly, has been deprived of the possibility of determining clearly and concretely any possible disagreement he might have with the directorial conception of the part. I suggest that an "acting script" and rehearsal work with it will provide that now missing concrete basis for a creative mutual influencing of actor and director.

The director's will and effort are devoted to maximal expression of the whole of the film, and his work on the editing or shooting script is oriented from this angle, exploiting in this script all the wealth of the specific methods provided him by the technique of the cinema. But subsequently he should compress the shots in this shooting script into an acting script. This new acting or rehearsal script would not merely represent the solution of the given shooting problem as set out in the shooting script, but also the concrete fulfillment of the requirements postulated by the actor's need for aid in maintaining unity and vividness in his image. From this script, in the process of rehearsal, new data would doubtless be forthcoming, justifying a second edition of the shooting script, inevitably, quite properly and to creative advantage replacing the first. And only in this last form would the script actually go forward for shooting.

This is a means whereby might be achieved a real linking of the actor to the unity of the work of the whole shooting collective.

THE EDITING IMAGE

We now come to the shaping of the editing image. This concept, the subject of the most acrimonious controversy, is in fact the crux of the novel and different nature of the cinema, distinguishing it from the theatre.

When the stage actor works on his inward embodiment into the acting image, his work is bound inextricably with two tasks: firstly, the search for its external form of expression—voice, gesture, grimace—and secondly, the clear consideration of that general ideological tendency of his role that links his work with the performance as a whole and with each of its details separately.

Let us analyze the first task. In working on his external expressiveness, the stage actor naturally moulds the whole process of his acting into a rhythmic form. His speech receives in delivery intonational emphasis or weakening according to whether he wishes at any given movement to seize and hold the audience by the "content" or the "emotional" side of his speech. In his pattern of movements and gesture he also creates moments of rise and fall, of vividness and restraint, of strength and weakness. But an actor moving and speaking on the stage always remains at relatively the same constant distance from the spectators, in a position in space more or less constant in respect to them. For the spectators to see his hand, he must show it to them; for the spectators to hear his whisper, he must raise it to the level of loudness.

The cinema has to create its analogous rhythm of externally expressive form in a different manner. I have already described how the camera and microphone can move to approach or recede from the actor, how they can espy the finest movements of his body, eavesdrop the most delicate intonations of his voice. By this means the acting of the actors, treated in long shot and in close shot, angled from various set-ups, is rendered especially vivid and expressive.

If the stage actor, in the course of working out the maximum external expressiveness of his role, wishes, at some given moment of the performance, to centre the whole attention of the audience on, let us suppose, his smile following the word "No," then he knows perfectly well that not only must his word be spoken well and his smile smiled well, but that the audience must listen to the word and watch the smile especially attentively.

For this purpose, the actor uses in support of the stage delivery of his role all the complex mechanism of theatre technique. He can use sets, or composition of the action in them, leading the attention of the audience away from his colleagues and fixing it precisely at the crucial moment, on himself. He can use a pause immediately following, spot-lights concentrating their light on him alone.

In the cinema all this complicated system of methods can be re-duced to a single close-up. The close-up in the cinema is an integral part of the rhythm of external expression of the actor.

The editing of separate camera angles in the cinema is the more vivid and expressive equivalent of the technique that obliges a stage actor, who has inwardly absorbed his acting image, to "theatricalize" its outer form.

The film actor must clearly understand that the moving of the camera from place to place is not simply a means of realizing purely directorial methods. The understanding and feel of the possibilities of the shooting of shots from various angles must be organically included in the process of the actor's own work on the external shaping of his role.

The film actor must feel the urge and the necessity for a given camera position for the shooting of any given piece of his role in pre-cisely the same way as a stage actor feels the necessity, at a given point in the course of his role, for making an especially emphasized gesture, or for advancing to the footlights, or for ascending two steps of a scenery stairs.

The actor must appreciate that it is in this very movement of the camera that lies latent that essential sensitivity that removes work in the field of art from the sphere of shapeless naturalism.

However profoundly the stage actor embodies himself into his role in the course of his work on the image, he must not, and in fact does not, forget the need always to consider also the objective content and value of the final result—his behaviour in acting on the stage during the actual performance portrayed to the audience. The image, how-ever deeply absorbed by the actor, does not exist in the performance as a separate entity. Linked by the course of the action, it is subject to the complex interplay and mutual influence of all the forces comprising the performance as a whole.

The supremely important social class significance of the actor's performance is determined by the performance as a whole. There is not an element in the performance, be it the acting of a colleague or the material composition of a scene, but must be linked to the final form of the whole and therefore of the remaining parts. Even during the very first moments of work on the image, when the actor is mainly seeking and feeling for ways òf embodying himself as a given individual in the image he intends to play, he is yet clearly conscious of and sets before himself as his aim the figure sketched out by the libretto of the play, which figure eventually will move and speak upon the boards. He appreciates what the future stage image is and how it is embedded in the entirety of the performance. But on the stage the actor who sought and shaped the role yet remains in the finally discovered and shaped performance a live person. The image he finally finds and fixes in himself and in the performance, he never separates from himself as from a living, feeling, and speaking person.

In the film it is quite otherwise. The culminating achievement of the actor's work—in the theatre the stage image—is in the cinema something of a quite different order. As a final result appears the edited image—a screen image of the actor, recorded and fixed once and for all upon the film, a final and optimum version of his work's achievement, which, quite apart from any other distinction, has in the course of its expression been subjected to a technical finishing process quite impossible of application to a living being.

Just as in the unity of the stage show the image of the actor is "produced" in the fullness of its content by the complex interaction of all the forces comprised in the performance, so in the cinema the separate pieces of shot acting of the actor are moulded into a unified image the unity and orientation of which are determined not merely by the unity found by the actor within himself, but also by the exceedingly complex interaction of those many pieces containing alien phenomena, situated exterior to the actor.

The most comprehensive, the profoundest lines determining the content of the image, are discernible, of course, only when the whole composition of the film is available.

We have already noted that the wealth of events of the world of reality which the cinema can embrace is much wider than that accessible to the theatre. While the relationship between a given actor and the whole performance is on the stage determined principally in the conflict between the actor and his colleague, an actor using dialogue like himself, in the cinema the actor encounters not only man. In the completed film the acting actor is brought into relationship with the whole tremendous complexity of objective reality, and in this respect therefore is placed in a position nearer to that of a part of a literary work than to that of a *dramatis persona* in a play.

Thus the concept of the edited image by no means implies (as some have sought to declare) a negation of the necessity for unified work by the actor on his role. The concept of the edited image is by no means an affirmation of the doctrine that the film actor is merely a type actor providing piecemeal material for mechanical composition into a psuedo-whole in the process of editing.

On the contrary, this concept, analogous to that of the stage image, demands from the film actor firstly a knowledge of how consciously to exploit the possibilities of vari-angled shooting for the purposes of his work on the external shaping of his role, and, secondly, clear consideration of its creative place in the edited composition of the whole film, in order that he may understand and bring out the most comprehensive and profound bases of his acting.

In stage work there exists a clear and precise concept, the ensemble; in the creation of the ensemble participates not only the producer, but also each separate actor, building his work in direct connection with the whole of the performance. In the cinema, the equivalent concept has reached in its shaping almost the limit of technical precision. A film, a work the material of which includes the acting of actors, can attain, in the exactitude and precision of its rhythmic construction, the exactitude of the rhythmic construction of a musical compositon. Hence the especal strictness and rigidity of the requirements to which film actors must subordinate their work in the course of its external shaping, those film actors, that is, who value not only their own roles, but the film as a whole.

The stage actor knows well that an unhappily chosen or badly played tune preceding his speech can not only damage but distort the role he is trying to create. The film actor must understand that a piece of landscape or some other phenomenon, either preceding or following the piece with his acting in it, will indubitably enter as a component into the line of his image as it will be apprehended by the audience.

The edited image is that final and definite form that enters into interaction with the third element comprising the work of art—the spectator. In distinction from the stage image, it is divorced from the living actor, and for this very reason, in order not to lose realistic unity, must be conceived by the actor and thought out carefully from the very first stages of his work on himself and his role.

While on the stage the actor can more exactly adjust his place in the whole during the actual course of the second performance to the audience, the film does not give him this opportunity. Further, the work of the actor in endeavouring to reach sharpest apprehension of the film as a whole is more complex and difficult. Therefore it must be regarded as particularly paradoxical that this side of his work, the study of his relation to the film as a whole, is far more deeply provided for in the theatre than in the cinema.

Here we should mention still another difficulty characteristic of the work of the film actor. In the theatre exists the so-called "living link" between an actor and his emotionalised audience. It s a well-known fact that performances of a show differ, and that this difference depends on and is caused by differences of audience composition. There exists an abundance of stories concerning notable actors and how the living reaction of audiences has forced them at various times to find new business for their roles, or to discard business they had previously found and used.

All stage actors declare that they derive the real high-pressure tension and inspiration necessary for full value in their acting only from the feeling of the audience being moved.

In the cinema we are in the presence of an entirely new phenomenon: never, not even during the most important moment of his acting, when the actor is face to face with the camera recording his final achievement, has he the chance to feel directly the reaction of a single spectator. He can imagine his spectator only as a future spectator.

In the "living link" between actor and spectator should be distinguished two elements, which we shall analyze separately in their relation to the cinema.

The two elements are these: first, the general excitement and inspiration felt by the stage actor aware of thousands of eyes centered upon him, conscious of a thousand-fold concentration of attention upon his acting, and second, the presence of the living reaction of the audience, as it were itself taking part in the creative process of the development of the role, and thereby helping the actor.

The first element, direct consciousness in the actor of the multiple spectator, is completely absent in the cinema. At the moment of shooting, the actor sees in front of him only the dumb mechanisms of the camera and sound-recording apparatus. The system used for lighting, which entails the surrounding of the actor with lamps, seems also as though deliberately engaged in isolating him into the space allotted for the taking of the scene, a space so small that sometimes the actor is even cut off from seeing the whole of the room in which the action takes place.

But does it follow that the feeling of an audience and the creative excitement and inspiration deriving from the audience are thereby necessarily excluded from the work of the film actor. I hold that it does not. True, this feeling of the audience can come into existence only in a new and peculiar manner.

I remember a conversation with the now late V. V. Mayakovski. He told me once about the feeling he experienced when, during the years of revolution, he declaimed his verses to an enormous crowd that had collected in front of the balcony of the building of the Moscow Soviet.

V. V. complained that nowadays he never felt that tremendous inspiration he did then. "Only in one circumstance," he said, "do I feel the same excitement, if not an even greater than in those days, and that is when I make a speech on the radio."

I maintain that Mayakovski was completely and utterly sincere. It is interesting that to a man like him, who undoubtedly had organically lived and nourished his creative process on the reaction of the mass audience, the broadcasting studio did not feel like a solitary confinement cell isolating him from his listeners. That creative imagination which is part and parcel of every great artist, which makes him one with and related to all the world of reality, enabled him not only to appreciate intellectually, but to feel directly, that the words spoken into the microphone spread immediately over a gigantic area and became received by millions of attentive listeners.

Let us be clear that Mayakovski was not referring to an intellectual understanding of the importance of radio, but to a direct excitement and inspiration caused in him by work before the microphone. Once more I repeat that Mayakovski likened this excitement to that which he had felt when directly before him he had seen listening a crowd thousands strong.

I consider that for a film actor who really and truly lives in his art the possibility of such an excitement is not excluded. On the stage an actor plays before hundreds of persons, in the film actually before millions. Here is a dialectical instance of quantity increasing over the boundary into quality to give rise to a new kind of excitement, not less real and, of course, not less significant.

Let us turn to the second element. The collaboration in creation on the part of the spectator, his living reaction to the acting, his acceptance and applause of the right and felicitous, his cold repudiation of anything mistaken—none of this, also, can be present in the taking of a film.

Hence, I urge, upon the director, who is the one and only witness of the acting during the shooting of a film, reposes an especial responsibility, in no way corresponding to any equivalent in the theatre. The solitude of the actor during the taking of the scenes weighs upon him. The director, of course, if he desire to give the actor the maximum of help, if he wish to create for him the optimum conditions for free, easy, and sincere acting, can so react to the work of the actor as to become for him a fine, responsive, and friendly—if sole—spectator.

I put forward this point in all seriousness, the possibility for the director to make the actor believe in him not merely as a theoretician, as a thinker and mentor, but also as a directly affected, either admiring or disappointed, spectator.

The finding of this inner contact between director and actor, the establishment of a profound mutual trust and respect, is one of the most paramountly important of all the problems in the technique of the work of a film collective.

My own practice in working with actors, which I must confess myself quite unable up to date to codify into coherent or unified form that might in any degree be called a system is based entirely on this contention, that all the most important moments of an actor's work are based absolutely on this trust in me on the part of the actor.

I recall how, taking full advantage of the silence of the cinema in the old days, I used literally to be unable to restrain myself from uttering words of excited praise that reached and encouraged the actor in the middle of his acting by reason of their obvious and complete sincerity.

It is of interest to mention here that Baranovskaia in *Mother* categorically declared to me (we were then about half-way through the film) that she could not act unless I were in my accustomed place beside the camera. I cite this declaration as further confirmation of the fact that the presence of the director responsively reacting to the actor's acting is an organic necessity for the latter. I recall that I have invariably tried to establish the most intimate personal relationship possible with all the actors playing principal roles in my films before the actual work of shooting began. I have always regarded it as important to win in advance the deep-seated trust of the acting ensemble, so that later the actors could fall back on this trust and not feel solitary.

Many speak of the inevitability of a duality in the actor during his acting, when with one side of himself he lives and plays in the acting image, and with the other as though controls this play objectively. In my view this second, controlling side, is not at all a kind of imaginary spectator dwelling within the actor. This second side must, inevitably, be rooted in the living spectator existing external to the actor; it takes into account and bases itself on the former's reaction, fulfilling its essential purpose in doing so, for otherwise the actor would be locking himself within his own subjective circle and becoming a coldly abstract phantom.

I believe that the coldness and externally mechanical formalisation of acting often encountered in the cinema can usually be explained by the coldness and mechanical formalisation in the director's method of work with the actor in shooting.

I emphasize that the decisive importance of the work of the director on the actor in shooting is characteristic for the cinema, and no equivalent obtains with anything like equal sharpness in the theatre.

In the theatre the actor must not only find the image, absorb it, approximate himself to the external forms of its expression, sense the necessary rhythmic forms of its playing and its link with the show as a whole, but he must during the repeated rehearsals fix all this and "can" it in a definite shape. Although it is not disputed that at each subsequent performance the actor will continue to a degree to develop his role, yet the element of learning by rote, fixing and "canning" his acting is inevitably present in the theatre to a considerable degree. Thus the stage producer at a given point cedes his place to the spectator, and the show reaches its perfect form without his direct participation.

In the cinema the burden of the element of "canning" and memorising is removed from the minds of actor and director by the mechanism of the visual and sound cameras and by the laboratory, which indefinitely multiplies copies from a single negative. In fact, until the very last, the culminating moment of their joint creative work, the actor and the director in the cinema march in the liveliest and most direct contact.

Principles

of Directing

By B. E. ZAKHAVA

In order to fully clarify the relationship between actor and director it is necessary to understand two particular qualities of theatre art. The first is the collective basis of theatrical production, and the second is that the basis of production is the actor, a human being who, though he may be the material with which a director practises his art, is in his own right a creator.

The staging of a play calls for the use not of a single artistic medium as in other arts but for the combination of many art forms. The playwright, director, the scenic designer, the musicians, the costumer, and the actors each invests his share of artistic energy in the whole production. Hence theatre art emerges not as the expression of an individual but of a collective; the collective is the author of the finished dramatic result, the production itself.

If any one of the many components engaged in production allocated to itself the function of "author" it would be to the detriment of the initiative of other components and the play would lose in smoothness, flexibility and freedom. Closely bound up with this would be a loss in the force of conviction—an irreplaceable factor in any major artistic achievement. The play will assume a harmonious unity of construction only when each participant in the artistic process freely and without constraint creates within the specifications required by the laws of theatrical art, and with the active co-operation of the other craftsmen. No one individual, not any particular craft but rather all together should appear in the theatre as a single collective artist who sustains the truth of the play throughout the intricacies of production.

In the history of the theatre we are very familiar with periods in which one or another of the specialized arts of the theatre has usurped a position all out of proportion to the collective nature of theatrical production.

Thus, famous in his time, was Sologub who believed that the theatre was the playwright's exclusive property. In 1908 he wrote as follows, "The first nuisance which must be eliminated is the actor. . . . The more talented the actor the greater is his tyranny over the playwright and the worse is it for the drama he enacts." According to Sologub the performance should proceed in this manner, "The actor should be substituted by a reader, or preferably be the reader himself, and the reader should sit quietly and patiently in some remote corner near the stage. He might have a table upon which to rest the script of the play about to be presented. Everything being in order he would begin. He would first read the title of the play, the name of the author, the cast of the characters, the stage directions of the playwright. He would then read the play including all stage directions no matter how trivial. During all this the curtain would rise and reveal the actors going through the motions called for by the reading of the script."

In this manner the actor is turned into a marionette. But this in no way dismays the creator of the theatre of a "single will." "After all what difference does it make if the actor is a marionette," asks Sologub.

To what does this sort of usurpation by one art lead save the lowering of standards for production, and for the theatre in general. A script read clearly and distinctly is far from being a dramatic production. Only its literary values are realized in a reading. In order to realize its dramatic values it must be *acted*. Analogous ventures to further the principle of the "single will" may be found outside the field of playwriting. Too often we find a similar opportunism among directors. There is, for example, the case of Gordon Craig, well-known in Russia for his presentation of *Hamlet* with the Moscow Art Theatre. He contended, at the time of this production, that the theatre needed neither a playwright nor actors. Craig's stand against the playwright was an esthetic reaction against the tendency of playwrights to literarize the theatre. But Craig also came out against the actor. He wrote at that time that acting is not art and he concluded by saying that the actor must go, and in his place a lifeless figure, called a super-marionette be substituted.

So we often see the playwright and director each firm in his pet conviction of a "single will." Each of the cases cited above dreams of the substitution of the living actor by a lifeless doll. Each in this manner tries to nullify some existing form of artistic endeavor in the hopes of creating alone and to his own individual credit.

Often the actor is the offender against collective work. The "star" monopolizes the play, ruthlessly marring passages where his or her own peculiar talents are not best displayed. Such stars never really characterize a type, only themselves. Such a star usually surrounds himself by any kind of cast at all. His needs emerge as the "single will" that activates the production. The result is that the audience will miss in the production the *whole* play of, say, *Hamlet* or *Othello*. At such productions the public watches the star and ignores the rest of the cast. For this one factor in production many others are sacrificed and as a result the audience can not really understand such a distorted presentation. It is impossible to understand Hamlet if the characterizations of Polonius, Rosencrantz, and all other so-called secondary roles are poorly prepared

In every instance of the usurpation of creative rights by one craft or another the production is ruined whether it is because the play is mechanically adapted to the one-track mind of the director, or because the actors' development is interfered with to gratify the ego of the playwright, who in turn is unwilling to accept the planned calculation of the director. The results in these cases are that human beings are turned into automatons and living art into drudgery. Besides this, the nature of the theatre requires that every thread in its fabric be woven in the spirit of vibrant life. This must impregnate every word, every movement of the actor, every stage effect. All these combine into a presentation of life in its completeness, an organic harmony of human emotion out of which will be born the creative will of the theatre collective.

The harmful tendencies which we have described above are off-springs of the "rugged individualism" existing in bourgeois society at the decline of the capitalist system. Could either Sologub or Craig understand how the development of an art could be carried to the highest point of unity by the collective energy of a group of creative artists? No, such possibilities are forbidden to them. For them nothing on earth

exists except the inflated, sanctimonious "I." It seems to them that
without the "I" there would be a vacuum—and death of the universe
and all humanity. Such are the illusions of the professors of subjective
individualism. The permanent quality of theatre art as we conceive
it does not permit of such illusions.

A production of serious importance in the theatre cannot be born
as a result of the subjective desire of a single creative personality. Nor
can it be *ruled* by the single will of any one artist. The creative artist
participating in a production should have no will but the united will
of the collective.

It follows then that every worthwhile production requires the presence of a collective possessed by a single creative will. This is possible
only if the group is closely bound together in general outlook, in the
political and social convictions of its members, and if it creates for itself
a common method of artistic procedure. The very basis of collectivism
lies in interdependence and co-operation. Honest freedom of expression
is a pre-accepted right and duty. Creative freedom of the participants
in the constructive process of staging a play is the result of the realization by the collective of the need for such a relationship. In this manner
each one fulfills his own particular function. His creative freedom is
restricted only by that which separates his specialty from that of the
others—the actor acts, the director directs, etc.

Out of the close co-ordination of the theatre collective, as it begins
to function, we observe a new and specific quality about theatre—*its
synthesizing nature*. In the theatre there are not only many artists but
also many arts intermingling with one another. There is literature,
the art of acting, the graphic arts, music, dancing, etc. In considering
these we notice that only one, the art of acting, is peculiar to the theatre
and that the others exist outside of the theatre as well. So the problem
arises of organizing these arts so that their synthesis achieves *one theatrical result* rather than the overbalanced display of any single art. Every
art must be converted into theatrical terms and perform a dramatic
function. And in the fulfillment of this function each of these arts will
take on a new character, a character with a theatric purpose. Theatre
music is no more like other music than graphic art for the theatre is like
other graphic art, and so with the others.

To what end are these specialized tasks distributed among the
participants of a dramatic creation? What gives them this theatric

quality? First of all, let us determine the focal point upon which the entire collective must be fixed. It is soon obvious to all that the position of the actor is the focal point.

The art of acting exists only in the theatre. The actor can project himself only in the theatre whereas the playwright can write for publication, the artist can paint murals, and so on.

Let me put it this way: an actor can step upon a platform and relate an incident to a friend much in the same manner as he works in the theatre. But then what is the theatre anyway? Is it the building where a show is given? Can't you see that the source of theatre is wherever the actor reveals himself *acting*? A written but unacted play is not theatre; a room decorated with pictures—that surely is not theatre. But even a simple anecdote cleverly told and demonstrated with the help of the actor's tricks, gestures, inflections, and improvisations which reveal an artist conscious of his influence upon his audience—this is theatre or, at least, the embryo of theatre. The actor cannot function outside of the theatre because he, so to speak, carries the theatre with him or, better still, in him. He is theatre and he can not be separated from the theatre nor the theatre from him. Therefore we say that the actor is the most important, the basic element, in theatre.

We may check this by a methodic elimination of the various components of the theatre. We see that, while the elimination of any one of them would lessen interest in the theatre, the exclusion of the actor would spell its destruction.

Let us ask whether in the final analysis the theatre can survive without the playwright. It can because there does exist the theatric form, pantomime, and because the actor can assume the dramatist's function of writing the dialogue just as the construction of the production plan can be made by the entire collective as well as by the director. Such a procedure would of necessity lack polish, but it has been and can be very effective. The actor does not ask the playwright for help because he can not do without him, but because he is willing, good-naturedly, to relinquish one of his original functions in order to specialize on others, speech, movement, etc. In the sensation of this freedom he sacrifices his possibilities as a dramatist and seeks new depths for his acting talents.

This is all confirmed by a historical approach to the question. The theatre grew not out of playwriting but playwriting was a product of theatre. Theatre grew out of the festivals of the people—their social and religious celebrations and ceremonials. At a certain stage in the development of theatre there arose a division of labor; the function of the playwright appeared and fell into the hands of specialists. These first playwrights were not literary men in the abstract sense; they were active theatre workers and a production had to them a theatrical, not a literary, significance. It is only in recent times, with the decline of the theatre, that plays began to be published as literary works. In this manner playwrights were separated from the theatre.

Such a state of affairs could not but call forth protests from the ranks of theatrical workers. The first playwrights were children of the theatre, the present are not, grieved Gordon Craig. And his grief was quite in order. However, he wanted not merely to urge the dramatist into his true theatrical place, but to eliminate him entirely. He wanted to turn back the progress of the theatre. It is not hard to see that his pining for the dead glory of the past in the theatre is like that of many theoreticians who speak for the bourgeois system in the period of its decline. To turn back the wheels of history and return to the "happy bliss" of primitive barbarism is a vain dream.

We react differently. Controversy within the theatre among specialized theatrical workers performing assigned functions is not at all a sign of sickness as Craig maintained. It is a sign of progress, and is a result of esthetic development, of dramatic culture. Only through specialization is it possible to attain the requisite degree of technical excellence on the part of each participant in the creative process. But specialization in the theatre, like anywhere else, may of its own momentum turn negative and show inverse results. Specialization with the individualist approach would ruin the theatre. *Specialization in terms of our socialist culture, with further penetration into the spirit of the collective, will build it.* Thus by our logic it is absolutely useless to turn the theatre back to a primitive stage, or to deny those realities which are problems of its historical development.

Playwriting and playwrights must obviously not be banished. But the playwright must realize the fact that the actor is the most important element in the theatre. In the theatre the dramatist, director, scenic designer, musician, etc., each speak to the public, not directly, but through the actor. The actor then is not only the basic element in the theatre; he is the *central figure* in theatre art. He alone steps out into the nouse to establish that vital communion between the audience and the artists. They can talk only through him. Each craft must bring to him its ideas so that he may realize them; otherwise these ideas will be forever inert. The actor accepts what is offered him, evaluates it, separates the wheat from the chaff and, having allowed it to permeate his artistic being, he can then project these spiritual treasures across the footlights. Those words of the playwright which the actor does not endow with life, which he does not make his own, will remain dead; a beautiful prop or a beautiful piece of scenery placed on the stage, but never touched by the actor either physically or sensually, will also remain dead and should be removed from the stage. The dramatic significance of every theatric idea on the stage is communicated by the actor. All those factors or ideas which in turn depend on their translation into life on the stage are theatric. Everything which lays pretension to a self-sufficient significance is non-theatric. By this standard we distinguish a play from a poem or a story, a scene design from a picture, a stage-set from an architectural construction.

The contributions that go to make up the art of the theatre are essential only so long as they furnish the material for the creative activity of the actor. That which is negative to the actor is negative to the theatre because the actor is the focal point and foundation of the theatre. And since this basic foundation is a human being with a human relationship to the audience this latter appears to be a distinctive factor of the theatre, separating it from all other arts.

THE ACTOR AS MATERIAL FOR THE DIRECTOR

Thus far we have worked on the following premises: that, primarily, the art of the theatre is a collective art; that the basic material of the art is the actor; and that the director should appear as the co-ordinator of the unity of the whole production, and that he should be the spokesman of the collective's sentiment.

But since we have proven the actor to be the basic material of the art, and the director the mechanic of its expression, the actor appears in a new light in relation to the director.

The actor is a human being. In him are involved mind, body, feelings, preceptions. In short, he is not merely material for the director's creative powers; he is himself a creator. He is simultaneously (for himself and the director) both the subject and object of creativeness. What in the actor, shall we say, is the instument for the director's creative powers—his body, his soul, or his personality?

Which of the preceding qualities of the actor are the basic instruments for the director's exploitation? The answer to this question is essential.

Many directors consider the actor's body as their sole instrument to play upon. They see the disposition of the physical activities of the actors as their chief problem. They force the actors into a purely mechanical pattern which seldom permits any latitude for creative expression.

What is their method of work? We see an example of this in their carefully plotted floor plans. The more closely the actors carry it out, the more neatly they copy what has been demonstrated by the director, the better he likes it. It is easy to see that such methods lead to the mechanization of the actor. Under such treatment the actor ceases to be a creative talent and becomes a Craigian marionette.

But there is another no less mistaken answer to the problem of sources for the director's material. It exists in that method of directorial work where the chief object of the director's attention is not the body but the soul of the actor. The director is then no longer concerned about what position the actor's body shall assume at any given moment, but rather how he shall *feel* at that particular moment. The director is convinced that if only the actor will feel the correct emotions his body will fall in line with a corresponding position. And so he proceeds to instill those emotions which according to him, the director, are called for by the specific role. In this case also, the actor behaves as an object of a director's manipulation, not as a creative force; he is a more vital, inspired marionette this time, it is true, but still a marionette in the hands of the director. In one case the director plays his harmonies by utilizing as his instrument the body of the actor; in the other case he plays upon his soul. In neither case is any creative talent called into being.

But a third method of directorial work is possible. This method denies the theory that either the body or the "psyche" of the actor is the sole material for the director, but rather the actor's creativeness. *The material of the director's creativeness is the creativeness of the actor.* Not only the body, or the ability to call forth on demand a variety of emotions, but the intimate thoughts and dreams of the actor, his artistic conceptions and principles, his sensations and feelings, his imagination, his social and personal experiences in life, his education, his tastes, his temperament, his sense of humor are all material for the director's art.

This material is neither fixed nor static. Acting is a process—and process implies change. Having accepted this factor about the process—in order to supervise and guide it—the director will try to overcome all obstacles to its growth, and to cherish it and nurse it along as a gardener nurses a baby plant. Fluidity, rapidly-shifting currents, continuous movement—these are things to which the director must accustom himself.

ART AND REALITY

When it has been discovered that the director's productivity is closely bound up with the actor's creativeness, one fully appreciates the importance of awakening all the potentialities of the actor. If the director does not draw out this self-sufficient creativeness on the part of the actor his hands will be empty of the only material out of which any worthwhile theatrical production can be shaped. Or, his material will be second-rate and, instead of the living vitality of the actor, the director will have the easily influenced, subservient will, the mere body of the actor lacking in all creative energy, a soulless doll, a Craigian marionette.

What must the director do, then, to put the actor on the right track of self-sufficient creativeness?

To answer this question it is absolutely necessary to define for our purpose the term "creativeness," and also in what respect artistic creativeness differs from craftsmanship.

Various theoreticians in the field of art, various teachers of esthetics often refuse to recognize the theatre as an art. They insist that the work of scene designer, director, actor does not fit into the definition of artistic endeavor, and therefore the theatre is not an art. So, for instance, a literary critic, famous in his time, U. Eichenwald, in a thesis (in the collection, *Controversies in the theatre*, 1913) maintained that since all that acting consists of is standing on a platform and spouting forth words written for someone else and totally strange to the person who delivers them, it could not properly be called creative work and hence was not art. Eichénwald also said, that to a cultured person, theatre was superfluous, since a well-loved play could best be enjoyed in the seclusion of one's home rather than in the loud vulgarity of the theatre, where any possibility of meditation was destroyed. The imagination of the cultured reader, he felt, was far richer than any interpretation put upon a play by the theatre with its false tinsel and its coarse materialism. If the theatre was useful, it was because it pandered to the tastes of the illiterate and semi-literate elements in the audiences. Very well. Let this audience, which cannot read the play, see it in the theatre; as for the cultured person, within his imagination he can enact a far more remarkable version than could possibly be presented by the most talented company

We should recognize the logic of Eichenwald's arguments. However these arguments hold good only for that theatre which is considered such by the process of mechanically transposing a play onto the stage. It is true of a theatre in which the play is a substitute for life, and is offered as an escape from life. Such a theatre hardly has the right to class itself as art. Theatre which is merely photographic, and which is a re-production of literary work is truly superfluous to the cultured audience.

By what standards then does the work of the actor and director become creative work? The director and actor work on the basis of the material given them by the dramatist; this latter in itself does not in any sense or degree lessen their right to create. There is no art where the artist creates out of thin air. Every artist utilizes that cultural heritage which has accumulated in his particular field. He must inevitably profit by this accumulation in his art. More than this we know that, in the history of art, great artists have created their finest masterpieces by using the work of their predecessors. For instance, it is well known that Shakespeare wrote *Hamlet* on the framework of a Scandinavian saga preserved in the vaults of the Danish scholar Saxo Grammaticus and revised before Shakespeare by Belleforest and Thomas Kyd. It is also no news that Ostrovsky often borrowed plots from Frecnh comedies. This does not in any degree lessen our admiration for Shakespeare or Ostrovsky. It is not at all important whether the artist made use of the work of others for his creative purpose or not. However, something else is. It is important to know what use the playwright has made of this material. He may have used it mechanically or he may have used it creatively. To use *creatively* means to use any given material as an ex-pression of one's own reaction to life. This cannot be done if the artist is ignorant of life. An understanding of life is a presumed qualification of any genuine artist in any field. Nothing is lost if to fulfill his own work he incorporates in it material from another artist. If he understands the phenomena of life more deeply and truly his product will always be more valuable, more meaningful than the original borrowed material on which he elaborated.

The name of Shakespeare linked to *Hamlet* is familiar to literate humanity the world over while the names of Saxo Grammaticus, Belleforest, and Kyd are known only to a few pedants and students of letters.

Hence, simply because the director and actor utilize the product of the playwright we cannot, for that reason, discount them as noncreative elements.

True, if the director and actor are entirely passive toward life and reality, if they persist in looking at the play through the eyes of the playwright without feeling the slightest obligation to observe and absorb life (independently of the playwright's version of it) they do not have the right to call themselves creative artists—they are merely technicians. But if the basis for their work lies in a well-grounded and serious understanding of life they are real artists—genuine creators.

If a theatre collective mechanically accepts the idea of a play and all the experiences and solutions of a playwright as if they were truly its own then that theatre is resting upon false laurels. Here there is no question that the theatre fails to be creative. In regard to such a theatre Eichenwald is right. In such a theatre the director and actors are in bondage to the playwright, and the artistry of such a theatre can never rise above the mediocrity of better or worse photographic illustration.

The case would be entirely altered, however, if the workers in the theatre—the director, actors, etc.—independently of the playwright arrive at those same realities which they are called upon to portray. If they have gone through similar experiences, have made similar observations, have had similar training, such a theatre would have the right to extend a hand to the playwright and invite him (or accept the latter's invitation) to collaborate, for then only would there be the possibility for joint work of playwright and theatre.

Our problem at present is not the relationship between playwright and theatre, but those of actor and director. Nevertheless, an understanding of the basic principles of the former relationship helps us to understand those factors upon which rest the artistic standards of the actor and director, and all other creative activity in the theatre.

Therefore we explained that certain axioms must be established for honest creativeness for the director as well as the actor, and of course what will follow is a happy harmony for creative reciprocity between them. Without this agreement both the actor and director will fall into the tentacles of the playwright and become craftsmen for whom the theatrical cliché will be the only means of identifying themselves with the theatre.

CREATIVE RECIPROCITY

Now let us determine possible variations in the relations between actor and director.

1. If the director is a person of wide social and individual experience with a fine cultural and academic background, with opinions and convictions on those phases of life which are the activating influences in the play about to be rehearsed, and the actor, on the other hand, has negligible experience, limited background, and education insufficient for the particular presentation, what will be the result of this collaboration of actor and director?

The contribution of the director will here be of a creative character. In the work of the actor there will be no creative element whatsoever. This makes it obvious that creative reciprocity between actor and director is impossible. Such collaboration is top-heavy.

The actor can by no means influence the director in such a set-up. (That is if we discount as "influence" the usual difficulties presented by his material to any artist, whatever his medium). In this case it is not the actor's creative ability that is exploited by the director but rather his body, which is made the vehicle for the expression of the ideas and experiences of the playwright and director. In other words, the director's purpose is achieved by superimposing upon the actor a complete nervous-and-skeletal system which will respond to its master in a wholly mechanical manner.

2. Now let us imagine another situation. The actor, in this case, has a great fund of experience, scholarship and judgment needed for the vital interpretation of the problem at hand. The director, on the

other hand, is lacking in insight into the particular phase of life offered by the dramatist. What happens? By his creative energy the actor will dominate the director. The actor will be constantly conscious of the director's weakness and will feel that the director does not know his subject, and hence can't talk about it; in short, he doesn't know the life he is trying to portray. Without knowing or having studied life one cannot create, because life is the source of all creative art. If the actor's personal and human experience is richer than the director's, the latter will, in the natural course of events, lose his creative privileges and hence his guiding influence over the actors. If the actors get no instructions from the director, or if the instructions are unclear or vacillating or inconsistent, the actors instinctively tend to behave as they choose in order to express their individual ideas. The production invariably suffers from lack of unity both from the point of view of substance and of form and stylization.

The director need not of necessity be familiar with every stage trick. He need be an actor himself no more than he need be a playwright, an artist or a musician. But he must have a more penetrating and comprehensive knowledge of those manifestations of life underlying dramatic construction than that possessed by any member of the acting company. Unless he possess these qualities, the loss of his leading position is inevitable. He will be trailing along somewhere among the other components, under pressure not only from the playwright but also from the actors.

We have already mentioned the negative consequences which result from the suppression of the creative personality of the director by some of the other components; no less sad are the consequences to the production of the director's loss of his leading position—in both cases the final result is the same: the basic organizational function of the director —the binding of all parts into a harmonious unity—remains unfulfilled.

3. Finally, there is possible a third, no less important variation in the relation between the actors and the director. Needless to say this occurs when a true understanding of the realities involved is present in both the director and the actors. Out of such a creative relationship there develops true collaboration.

Let us examine this collaborative process in more detail.

The director starts work on a script. He determines its theme. In terms of the theme offered him by the script he begins to study. To do this he rallies all his senses, his memory, his personal and social experience; he utilizes every source of material, literature, the press, the motion pictures. He tries to absorb as great a store of observations as possible and is always on the lookout for new concrete impressions from actual life. All this wealth of gathered material he subjects to a careful analysis to establish the differences between appearances and unchanging facts of living reality. As a result of this research he arrives at what is *his* conception of the theme. This conception or idea lives in his consciousness surrounded by the wealth of factual data he has acquired. Now he once again approaches the script. He returns to the author's ideas, armed this time with his own idea of the given reality, and he enters into creative cooperation with the author—he is beginning to formulate his production plans.

When this production plan is ready the director presents it to the actors. He demands that each actor understand his role in terms of the whole play and also in terms of his central idea.

But the actor, if he is an honest creator, having received the script given him by the director, will, before starting work on it, mobilize his own personal experiences, observations, and conceptions; he will begin to enrich these experiences by watching those phases of life that interest him at the moment and consider them in the light of the script. Correlating his ideas with the director's, and on comparison finding himself in general agreement with the director, he is eventually ready to start work on his role, building his own creative interpretation in collaboration with the director.

But, you ask, what if this accord between actors and director does not materialize? Suppose they do not see eye to eye on the same subject? There is only one answer: team work is then impossible. The only two courses open are: either the differences will have to be settled through a collective discussion of the director's exposition, or an individual actor must resign his role to someone else. We have already established the premise that the theatre is a collective art and hence each participant must abide by the will of the working collective. And so all these individual differences between actor and director must be disposed of to insure the unity and strength of the single will of the collective.

Let us assume then that there are no outstanding differences or that they have been eliminated by mutual persuasion, and the actor and director aim in the same direction as far as the social and ideological interpretation of the play and the characterizations are concerned. Rehearsals begin. The director gives the actor a concrete instruction pertaining to a particular movement or a given moment, or a certain phrase or intonation. This order may take the form of an explanation or a demonstration—this is for the present unimportant. The actor receiving this direction and considers it in terms of his understanding of reality. This direction, if the actor is at all familiar with life, cannot but arouse in him a whole series of associations from his observations of actual life, his reading, his conversation with people, with the result that the direction given him and this experience fuse, synthesize, and a complete interpenetration takes place. In fulfilling the task set by the director, the actor realizes the essence of this synthesis. He has done more than mechanically carry out a directorial request; he has demonstrated to himself his creative personality. Having given the actor his formulation the director has it returned with interest, so to speak, in the form of the actor's stage technique. For while its meaning was being digested in the creative personality of the actor it became enriched with all the added resources of the actor and not only those of the director who conceived it. The director, in this fashion, gets in return from the actor somewhat more than he gives. It follows that in fulfilling the director's instructions the actor influences the director. This will be an incentive to the director not to repeat himself in giving further instructions. In this way there will always be a quality of freshness about these instructions which would be lacking should the actor fail to give of his own creativeness and merely execute mechanically the task as required by the director. New directions will go through the same cycle within the actor's consciousness and again serve to stimulate the director. In other words, each new phase of the progress is dependent upon the preceding one. Thus and only thus is there true inter-influence between actor and director. In this manner the director's creativeness is rooted in the actor's, and is not merely a rigid control over the actor's physical being. At one of his rehearsals Vakhtangov reproached his students for lacking in creative response to his directions. He said, "You'd like to get by with only the material I give you. It's not enough. If you continue in this way, anybody who'll see the production will say, 'There is no individuality in the actors.' "

What then did Vakhtangov recommend to his students to help them gain a creative approach to their roles? He demanded first of all that they work on their role at home and bring the result of this work to rehearsal. "Make it a habit to reflect on your role," says Vakhtangov. By "reflect" he meant to allow the imagination free play. It was of this that the preparation of the role at home was to consist.

But whether the human imagination is sufficient source material for work as a substitute for living experience is a question. An understanding of life is the true prerequisite for the productivity of the imagination. Let us take, for example, even such a highly fantastic thing as a mermaid. What is a mermaid anyhow? A creature with a female human face and the tail of a fish. Such creatures do not exist in real life, of course. But the elements out of which a mermaid is made are real enough. A female face and the tail of a fish are sufficiently familiar to all of us. But if you try to create with the help of your imagination a single thing which is outside of human experience you will soon find that to do so is quite an impossibility.

The work of the imagination, then, is based wholly on experience, on knowledge of life. Poverty and sterility of the imagination is, for the most part, associated closely with the absence of a well-rounded human background and poorly developed observation.

If the artist is familiar with many phases of life he then has food for the imagination. All that remains for him is to learn to correlate this knowledge for a self-set purpose and towards a harmonious solution of an artistic problem. Which brings us back to the argument that in order to be able to "reflect" on his role the actor must be familiar with the realities which are its prime ingredients. And only by this same method can a director guarantee a creative and not a mechanical production. . . .

PRINCIPLES
OF DIRECTING

PART II

IN ANY ARTISTIC EFFORT OR PRESENTATION, we must feel the artist's complete command over all its composite details, both concrete and abstract. How, then, can we achieve the proper union of concrete and abstract elements unless both have been clarified in the artist's mind?

Suppose a specific difference arises between myself and the actor. How shall we arrive at a single conception of a character if our points of view toward this character are, for many reasons, at great variance?

During work on the production of Gorki's *Dostigaev and Others,* this situation arose. The young actors, having been born after the era of the Tsar's cadets, could not conceive of the characters as living people but saw them rather as mummified remnants of the dead past. In order to familiarize the actors with the period, and the people who lived in it, I urged them to read the pre-war literature and poetry, the contemporary magazines and newspapers of the time; to study photographs of the people, and to poke around in other similar channels of history. As a result of the persistent study of these materials each actor began to feel that he too might have lived in this period. The script began to take on meaning through an endless chain of associations. Having enriched himself in new capacities, the actor could not but reflect these changes. There was a new sparkle to his eyes, a new vigor to his movements; he acquired poise and conviction. The final result of such an approach is the development of greater independence and initiative on the part of the actor. He no longer takes orders mechanically from the director—he has entered into a creative partnership with the director just as he has with the playwright.

These points cannot be stressed too strongly. The importance of the director's function in the theatre has been increasingly recognized in recent years. Undoubtedly this is significant. But this constructive factor can easily be nullified should the actor surrender to the director his own invaluable creative rights. In that case not only the actor suffers but the director and the theatre as a whole. The actor then hangs like a deadweight from the neck of the director, who is forced to coddle him and guide him around.

I have often observed the pitiful condition of an actor who permitted himself to assume such a relationship to the director. Let us assume, for example, that the director has explained to the actor some phase of his role. Not satisfied with merely a verbal explanation, the director then mounts the stage and demonstrates his point with every detail of position, movement, inflection. The actor carries out all these instructions. He is docile and willing. But what happens when he reaches the point where the directorial explanation and demonstration comes to an abrupt stop? What then? The actor, his hands slack at his sides, looks bland and says, "What shall I do now?" He resembles a mechanical toy which has run the gamut of its accomplishments and needs rewinding. And such an actor dares to call himself an artist, a creator, a craftsman!

The strengthening of the director's position in the theatre will be accomplished only in those cases where cooperation exists between the actor and the director, founded on the principle of creative reciprocity. It does not imply the subjection of the actor to the individual will of the director, and would indeed become impossible if the actor were compelled to relinquish his artistic prerogatives.

THE CREATIVE ROLE OF THE ACTOR

Thus the first problem of the director in relation to the actor involves his full exploitation of the actor's creative resources. The correct channeling of the actor's energy will determine the entire course of the production. It is the director's job to see that his instructions are always within the grasp of the actor. The actor should be asked to take nothing for granted. He must maintain complete creative flexibility throughout the course of his work. The director must not merely avoid mechanical domination of the actor, he must constantly strive to preserve the actor's creative freedom and to see that nothing disturbs it during the course of the production.

What is the creative status of the actor? *The creative status of the actor exists where his response to an expected stimulus is as spontaneous and true as his response to an unexpected stimulus.*

Let us analyze this. The creative role of the actor involves complete freedom of reaction. This means simply the expression of the free associations of the actor without hampering or conditioning by any outside force. It lies in his spontaneous, characteristic manner of speaking. He does not do a thing just so because the director has told him to or because he has gone over it in his own mind. A response slips out unpremeditated; totally unihibited. If the actor, in rehearsals, feels constant pressure upon him from the director, his free initiative is bound to be cramped. However, in our definition of the creative status we demanded not only freedom but also truth. The actor will readily comprehend given stage directions if he feels them to be logical in the given situation and in the whole production. This specific gesture, that specific tone, this specific piece of business will then appear inevitable, and he will not grope about for any other.

But to put this principle into practice is very difficult. The director may say to the actor; "This is how you should react," the actor agrees, since he sees the logic of this proposed reaction in the light of his own analysis of the role. However, when he tries to realize this reaction it appears artificial, studied, forced. The director will then say, "I free you of all responsibilities, do what you want to do in this instance." The actor does what he wants to do, but it turns sour and does not fit the situation or the general scheme of the play. It is only when the correct thing is done with perfect freedom that the logic of it and the freedom of its execution combine to make it right.

The actor must respond to every stimulus he receives in the stage environment in such a manner that it is fresh and totally effortless, which means that he reacts in this specific manner because *he cannot react otherwise.* At the same time this reaction must coincide with a consciously set plan (either the director's or the actor's). This demand is very severe but absolutely necessary.

How shall the actor fulfill this premeditated plan as an organic necessity? Suppose an actor has to perform a certain passage requested by the director. He has to perform this passage each time at rehearsal and eventually at each performance. He must execute it because its presence is by no means accidental, but has a premeditated effect; it fits neatly into the rest of the play, helps to characterize the persons of the play, or gives a glimpse of their activities. All of which proves that only a premeditated interpretation can be given by the actor if we are to honestly say that the actor creates. He does not create if he uses his freedom as a means for his personal, subjective expression instead of in the search for the inevitable form, or if he mechanically goes through a series of stage tricks previously invented by him or the director. In neither case is there any true creativeness.

What then is the practical solution? The director should use all his weapons to convince the actor of the correctness of his directives. We have analyzed our demand for freedom of association and reaction on the part of the actor in the stage environment. The director must also clarify the logic of these reactions.

But still a third necessity exists, and this is that the actor's reaction to an expected stimulus shall be similar to his reaction to an unexpected one. This means that even though the actor knows in advance every line and bit of business in the play, he must nevertheless receive each new bit as a complete surprise. It is only when he can thus receive them and thus react that he can give the freshness of ever-renewed creativeness.

What factors develop the creative status of the actor and which ones hinder it?

THE DIRECTOR'S EXPLANATION

The arbitrary demand for immediate results from the actor at the very beginning of work on a production is the most harmful of all directorial dictums. Unfortunately, this occurs very often.

By "results," we mean particularly the actor's "emoting" as expressed in terms of stage patterns, voices and movements. If the director, in the course of early rehearsals, demands of the actor a finished product, (a specific emotion to be registered in a specific form), he demands of the actor something which cannot be done. "Here you should laugh a little," the director says, and the actor, embarrassed, makes an effort to laugh. Inevitably the product is artificial, strained, insincere. "Here you should cry," and the actor musters all his resources to simulate a measure of grief. But it is obviously false and melodramatic. Feeling, and the genuine form by which it is expressed, is the product of a long chain of processes. To express an inner state the actor must follow a systematic process. There are no short cuts, but if led along this route, the actor will reach his true destination.

How shall this process be developed? Every emotion, together with the true forms it assumes, is a result of the individual's conflict with his environment. Any human want leads to an attempt to satisfy that want. Should the individual satisfy this want, a pleasant sensation results. If, on the other hand, difficulties lie in the way of the satisfaction of this want, suffering may ensue. Besides, hand in hand with the activity attempting the satisfaction of these wants go all the sensations of pleasant anticipation or fear of possible failure.

Thus we can see that each sensation depends on the satisfaction or lack of satisfaction of an individual desire. First we have the will or desire, then the activity of the individual is directed toward the satisfaction of this desire. In the course of this process emotions arise as a result of circumstance and often in spite of the individual (I don't want to cry but I can't help it).

The actor must first of all consider what he (as the character in the play), wants, and then what he is going to do about it. His feelings, and the methods of their expression, are conceived involuntarily in the course of his attempt to satisfy one or another of his specific desires.

"You can't act out emotions," says Stanislavski — "The actor should not worry about emotion. Emotion will come of itself." An actor's attempt to portray emotion inevitably makes him a rubber stamp, and gives the spectator a false and mediocre substitute for real emotion. This leads us to the conclusion that an actor does not go behind the footlights to *feel* but to *do*. Only then can he come alive and feel. "Don't wait for emotion, start functioning right away," again says Stanislavski. "The actor is not an ornament on the stage, he is a functionary." If the director immediately demands emotion from the actor, he is pushing him into a swamp and shutting him off from the path toward creative initiative. This is the glaring fault of the majority of directors.

The director should not exact the imitation of emotions from the actor but the execution of specific actions. He must tell the actor what to do, and not how to feel.

Doing differs from feeling chiefly in the element of will which is present in it; to persuade, to quiet, to beg, to mock, to bid farewell, to wait, to drive away, to hold back the tears, to hide one's joy or suffering; these are all verbs inferring a will-power (I wish to persuade and I do persuade, I wish to quiet and I do quiet). The actor can undertake to execute such action at any given time provided he understands the motives behind them. These verbs may and should be used by the director to guide the actor in his work on a role. Other verbs: to get excited, to pity, to laugh, to get angry, to be impatient, to despise, to love, and so on; all express feeling (I don't want to get excited, but I do; I don't want to pity but I do), and therefore should not be used as stage directions.

The ham-actor usually does exactly the opposite of what is natural. With his "bare hands," so to speak, he tears into an emotion, and "gives it all he's got." "He always begins at the end, that is, from the sum total of all his art," says Stanislavski. The director must know how to present a production problem to the actor, hinting, at the same time, the answers to two basic questions concerning the situation and the character:

1. What is the character doing, and
2. For whom, or why, is he doing it? (In other words, what does he want at the given moment?)

Let us answer the second question first. How does the character expect to get what he wants? The solution to this problem must be worked out by the actor himself in cooperation with the rest of the company.

We see then, the problems of staging in the light of three factors.

1. Activity (What I do).
2. Desire (What I want, or why).
3. The solution (How I do it).

The first two become quite clear at the outset after a discussion and analysis of the role. The third (the solution), like emotion, is the product of reciprocity and inter-activity between the members of the acting company. Let us take an example. Suppose the actor has to portray a man who has just been imprisoned in a small dark cell, in solitary confinement. After having studied the state of mind of the man, the director comes to the conclusion that it is one of utter despair. However, the director would be making a colossal error if he immediately asked the actor to register despair. Despair is an emotion and we have agreed that we are not going to try to enact emotions. We have to act a stage problem, the emotion will follow. If the director immediately poses the problem of despair, the actor will inevitably seek the path of least resistance and becomes a rubber stamp. He'll grab his head, pull his hair, groan, etc. All this will be unconvincing. Instead of a vital and fresh artistic solution the spectator will be given vulgarized and trite samples of the actor's stock-in-trade.

To avoid this the director must point the way by which the actor can evoke a true feeling of despair. He has to present two questions to the actor: What is this character doing in the present situation? Why is he doing it?

If the director will say to the actor, "You are looking for an escape from this prison. You will examine the strength of the bars, the possible loose stones in the floor, etc." The actor will have a chance to get busy immediately. In the course of all this business, the director will warn the actor that the walls of the prison are very solid, the bars very strong, the stone floor impossible to undermine. Thus the actor, having fulfilled all these suggested instructions with sincerity, involuntarily begins to feel his confinement, the hopelessness of his position. If now the director will tell the actor to find something to occupy his attention, to help him forget his sad plight, the actor will realize, in carrying out these directives, the impossibility of any kind of escape and will feel despair in his heart. By posing a series of closely connected improvisations the director can, unknown to the actor, raise the latter to almost any emotional state. The attention of the actor will be constantly occupied by the things he is doing. He won't be thinking of how he should be feeling or of what forms his feelings should assume. Thus the artistic result, the emotion and its expression, will be a by-product of the process of activity.

We observe this in the later relationship of characters on the stage. For example: the script calls for a quarrel between two of the characters. One of them is the attacker, the other is on the defensive. The director wants the actor who plays the part of the attacker to display rage and the victim to be helpless to the point of tears. If the director keeps repeating to one, "You are angry, show rage," and to the other one, "You are ashamed and should be crying," nothing tangible will be achieved. However, if the director will carefully study the script he will be able to grasp the motives behind the feud and clarify them for the actors, if the director makes himself clear, the desired emotions will result, from the inter-activity between the actors.

The director may demand outright the display of emotion only when he is certain that the actor will be able to translate the directives into terms of stage technique, and then only if the director sees that the actor is already in the creative mood and can absorb the directives with great flexibility no matter in what terms they are couched.

THE DIRECTOR'S DEMONSTRATION

The director's order may be given in two forms: as an explanation or as a demonstration. The first of these is superior since no matter how the director phrases his explanation it demands the active participation of the actor. Therefore whenever it is necessary for the director to resort to demonstration, he should not attempt to show any particular inner state but rather a specific stage problem.

If we accept the demonstration as a form of directorial technique we must examine its values, and the circumstances in which it can be used to best advantage. In the method there are certain dangers. It may make the actor a mere carbon copy of the director's personality, completely subjecting him to the director's will. It is not at all strange that this method prevails in practically all theatres suffering from mechanization and formalism. However, we cannot utterly ignore the method. Such an evasion would rob the director of one of the best ways to stimulate the creative resources of the actor. It is often only by the help of a demonstration that a director can put his ideas over dynamically, since only through demonstration can he show the organic unity between word and movement. The method often has the effect of inspiring and exciting the actor when long explanations have proven barren. Last, but not least, it is a great time-saver. Where an explanation may take effect only after an hour or two, a demonstration will do the trick in a couple of minutes. Clearly the method of demonstration possesses usefulness for the director. Since we do not dismiss it, we must lay down some principles to guide us in the use of this valuable but dangerous instrument.

What are these principles?

Before we set these down it should be absolutely clear that this method cannot be considered basic in the director's work. The basic method is not demonstration, but explanation, elucidation. The demonstrative method should be a last resort used only under certain conditions.

One condition essential to its success is the developed creative status of the actor. This will insure the actor against copying mechanically the details of the director's demonstration. If this creative status is present all the director's energies may be used in calling it forth and this may be done by demonstration as competently as by explanation. It is only when he sees the actor already independently creative that the director has a right to enrich and widen the scope of the actor through demonstration. If the actor is in a passive state, demonstration will not only fail to help him, but will do untold damage. This works in inverse proportion: the more brilliant and penetrating the director's demonstration, the more shocking it will be to the actor who will either creep back into his shell at the comparison between the scintillating talent displayed by the director and his own puny efforts, or he will try to mechanically imitate the director's exhibition. Both reactions are equally bad.

But even when the director uses this method he must suit his demonstration to the peculiar situation. It is important, for instance, that the demonstration cover a *general* situation to describe a *specific* one, and a *specific* incident to throw light on a *general* state. This means that the director is not to show the exact tone and gesture to be used on a specific line, but should merely give an idea of varied approaches. It is wiser for the director not to use the script but rather to improvise lines, similar in meaning; not to apply special movements to the bit of characterization under discussion but to use other patterns which might generally characterize and vitalize the person. The most appalling of all faults in a director is the pedantic insistence upon a particular inflection and particular movement in a particular bit in the role.

Unusually apt in the use of demonstration was the late Vakhtangov. His demonstration had a generosity. He never attempted to lay down an arbitrary method of speech or movement, rather he improvised so richly upon the text that he gave the actor a choice of interpretations. By the actor's reaction he could tell which was the most suitable and he then gave the actor the greatest degree of encouragement to expand upon it.

The director must show the *general,* never the *specific.* But even that is a loose interpretation. The director should never, in demonstrating a bit of acting, give a finished product, a little masterpiece of acting. He should only suggest to the actor, give him a friendly shove in the right direction, hint to him the potentialities of a part. Having made these hints in the demonstration he should permit the actor to find the needed artistic materials to give them polish. The actor will develop and complete for himself what he has received from the director in a sketchy form. The creative initiative used to do this will come from his personal experience and observation of life.

We know that very often the director is a former actor. Having been talented in his work he now demonstrates to the actor he is directing how he would himself act the part were he cast in it. This is a serious mistake. The director, showing how he might have acted the part, inevitably makes use of his individual peculiarities, his temperament, his physical make-up, the mobility of his face, voice, etc. This is exactly what an actor should do in attacking a role. But this is not the case with a director demonstrating it. The director should not only forget about *his own personal acting materials, but also of those of the actor whom he is directing.*

Before entering a working relationship with an actor the director should place himself in the actor's position and be able to adjust himself to the actor's degree of expressive power. He should keep that degree of expressive power as a measuring rod in any demonstration he gives to the actor. Only then can the director safely say, not only how *he* would act a certain role but how the actor in point should perform it. An honest director never gives exactly the same instructions to any two actors even through they are rehearsing the same role. Only through an appraisal of his capacities can the director establish a true reciprocity between himself and the actor.

A director worthy of the name always seeks to develop the creative individuality of the actor. He discovers these individual assets, guards and expands them. And on the other hand, a director who ignores this creative material present within the actor and chokes this individuality vitiates his most productive source of creativeness. He uses actors arbitrarily and opportunistically. No matter how great and fine, such a director may be and no matter into what raptures he sends the exclusive audiences who watch his demonstrations, the majority of his actors remain mediocrities, uninspired, stereotyped. Their work appears as a pale shadow of the brilliant directorial rendition, and leads to fond reminiscences of that original perfection. With such a director actors don't grow creatively; they stagnate, and at parting they will remain what they have been made, helpless parasites feeding on the pap of the director's vitality.

If the director does not wish to establish creative reciprocity between himself and the actors he should at least be willing to set the actor's creative initiative at play. He must be able to discover in a mass of unrealistic and chaotic material the worthwhile and appropriate bits in order that he may guide the actor forward from step to step. Then the valuable details will not be lost, but will be conserved to help in the evolution of the whole. In such a case the actor would himself discover the business and the director would act in the capacity of a critic recommending to him just what to keep and what to discard.

But this is insufficient. The director should be able to help in the labor pains of those unborn ideas in the actor which are blindly searching for an outlet and expression. These ideas come to the very threshold of his mind pleading to be allowed in, but he cannot crystallize them and lift them from obscurity. Here is where the director must help the actor perceive what already exists in himself, but which has been unable to find a true artistic outlet. The director must have his tentacles sunk deep into the psychologic mold of the actor. He must be able to put himself in the actor's place constantly. Only then will he be able to regulate and organize the actor's creativeness without coercion or imposition.

Again I can't help remembering Vakhtangov. I know of no director who penetrated more closely into the inner life of the actor I often watched some performance or rehearsal, where Vakhtangov having watched the actor, then amazed and shocked him by relating in detail every experience which the actor, as a human being, had passed through in the course of his appearance on the stage. He'd say ·

"In such and such a spot you got frightened, then gathered your

B . E . ZAKHAVA

forces and improved. Then, pleased at how well things were going, you wanted to be still better, and so over-acted and became disgusted with yourself and acted passively, just 'any old way' from then on."

Vakhtangov made observations such as these about more than one of his students and often about all those in the scene at once. It is difficult to realize how anyone could remain so objective at so many points of concentration. It is a faculty every director should strive to achieve.

In his diary Vakhtangov wrote, "Stanislavski has the perfect comprehension of the actor. He knows him from head to foot, from his guts to his skin, from his thoughts to his spirit." It was this science Vakhtangov absorbed from Stanislavski and it is a science which should be acquired by every director. Without it a true reciprocity between actor and director can never be realized.

Up to now, in discussing the director's demonstration, we have established the responsibilities, which fall upon the shoulders of the director. However, there are obligations not only for the director but also for the actor, who must know exactly how to utilize the director's demonstration.

If the actor approaches each directorial exhibition with the intention of mechanically copying it, then all the efforts of the director to rouse his creative potentialities are wasted. The actor must approach the problem posed by the director and handle it in a resourceful manner. He must be able to seize the *inner meaning,* the *essence,* inherent in the particular demonstration and independently translate the idea into terms of stage technique. It is even desirable that the actor analyze the director's demonstration in terms of activity. What is he doing? What does he want? Why? Having answered these questions the actor, by activity, without consciously worrying how he must look, or sound, will invariably fulfill the task to the satisfaction of the director. A good director is not a stickler for externals, the only important consideration is the realism and meaning of the work. Moreover, an honest director will never accept from the actor a shallow, mechanical, even if polished, presentation. An inflection or movement that has been too readily copied by the actor becomes repulsive to the honest director and he makes every effort to change it for a fresher one. He is willing to change over and over to rid the actor of any glib or superficial stage tricks.

In conclusion, we may say that the demonstration, like any other method of work, is only one of many means toward an end which is the correct channeling of the creative energies of the actor. Only with this approach to the demonstration on the part of the director and actor will it lead to a rewarding artistic cooperation between them.

THE IMPASSE

Now it is time to examine some of the obstacles that face the director in solving the problem of his relation to the actor. Often it appears that the director has taken all the steps necessary to set the actor on the track of independent creativeness: he has always tried to develop the creative imagination of the actor, he has clarified the actor on his inter-relationship with other members of the company, he has carefully avoided anything arbitrary in the stage directions but still nothing happens. The actor still does not reach a creative status. In this case what shall the director do? Take the actor out of the role? Not so good. The actor, we shall assume, is talented and suited for the part. Then what?

First of all, the director must find, or guess, the condition in the inner state of the actor which restricts his creative expression. He must find the cause of the sterility. Once its cause is discovered, it will be easy enough to eliminate it.

Before assuming that the obstacle to creative work lies in the actor it would be useful for the director to thoroughly check himself to see if the impasse may not be his own fault.

Errors in the approach may have one of two sources: one stems from the psychology of the actor, the other from that of the director. It often happens that the director torments the actor, expecting the impossible. A disciplined actor good naturedly fulfills the stage directions but logically enough nothing results if these directions are not intrinsically fruitful. Sometimes neither the actor nor the director notices this failure and they press deeper into the artistic vacuum. Let us say the director incorrectly stated the problem he gave the actor. Perhaps it has no logical tie with what comes before or after and does not flow into the general pattern at all. Obviously the actor cannot fulfill these instructions, much as he would like, since the problem is a total misfit in the organic life being depicted.

Or perhaps the director has demanded of the actor an unrealistic point of view toward another character or situation in the play. Try as he may he cannot realize the director's request. It is an impasse. Finally, the director presents the actor with a problem beyond his experience and understanding. It stands to reason that the actor cannot produce the desired results if the problem is foreign to his background and present comprehension.

Therefore, before laying the blame for the creative impasse upon the actor, the director should check and recheck his stage directions for possible errors. This is the way experienced directors work. They are careful. They try over and over, carefully feeling their way. Incidentally, young and inexperienced directors, especially those inflated by self-importance, often evade the responsibility they have toward the actor. It is painful to see the perseverance, worthy of a better cause, with which such a director hangs on to the actor to demand a precise bit of business or a phrase. Every bright idea that pops into his head he regards as an inspiration and he sticks to it to the bitter end.

But is it not possible that the reason he so prizes all his ideas is because in actuality they are so few and far between? A typical characteristic of such a director is lack of faith in the actor. To him each actor seems lacking in talent. He expects nothing of the actor, he is impatient and demanding. He does not understand that creativeness is a coordinated process, that the production as a whole, and each individual component separately, is like an embryo which one must safeguard. Such a director demands results in the very first rehearsals, and if he does not get them superimposes his own arbitrary directives of doubtful quality and sulks if the actor refuses to accept them or if their execution is unsuccessful. In each case, such a director blames the actor but never himself.

A director, who understands the nature of acting and of the actor, (the clay of his art), behaves very differently toward the actor whom he loves and values. Such a director, before blaming the actor, always seeks the reason for failure in his own mistakes. He is his own severest critic. He tries to make all his instructions to the actor not only true but also clear, simple and easily understood. He knows that a direction given in vague diffused ideas is not effective. He tries in simple words and expressions to clarify the meaning of a particular relationship, a particular stage problem. He does not fatigue the actor with excess theorizing. He talks little but encourages the actors to discuss their roles at great length. He is attentive to the actor. He is severe when necessary and also, when necessary, he is gentle and kind. He adapts himself to each actor as the demand is made upon him. He never forgets that the material of his art (the actor), is the most delicate, most perishable, most temperamental, most sensitive, most complicated mechanism in the world; *a human being.*

Now let us assume that the director has carefully examined all the demands he has made on the actor. After a duly serious and extensive research, he has found no errors which can be traced to himself so that it becomes necessary for him to seek the reason for the impasse within the actor himself. How shall he remove this impediment?

Let us first consider what common impediments exist for the actor.

1. *Lack of attention.* One of the primary rules for stage behaviour is that during every minute he spends on the stage, the actor must have his attention fixed upon some object. First of all, he must see the person with whom he is playing, not pretend to see but actually *see;* he must also hear all that is said by his partner; not pretend to hear, but actually *hear;* and not only listen, but understand what is said to him. Only by absorbing what is actually given to him will the actor be able to behave properly toward his fellow actors.

There are often actors who hear and see nothing that is happening on the stage. It is as if such an actor were in a trance, like a sleep-walker. Creative fulfillment of a stage assignment becomes impossible. He cannot induce human emotions. His acting becomes highly stilted. A creative impasse sets in.

"If the actor on leaving the stage," says Stanislavski, "remembers only how well he played, it means he played badly. On the other hand, if he does not recall how he himself acted but remembers only how beautifully his colleague acted, then he acted well."

This is easy to understand. If the actor remembers how his colleague performed, it means the latter was the constant object of his attention. He watched and listened, observed his face, his gesticulations, his mimicry, his intonations. Having observed his colleague, the actor was able to better adapt himself to the latter, to influence and be influenced by him. He lived and functioned not for himself, nor for the spectators, but for his colleague. He was *creating.*

Concentration is one of the prime factors in the creative status of the actor. Its absence results in serious harm to creativeness. It is often possible through concentration to eliminate the difficulty and leave no sign whatever of the creative impasse. It is sometimes sufficient for the director to merely remind the actor constantly to listen, *actively* listen, not passively; or actively to see an object which he handles on the stage. By doing this the actor can bring to life a stage problem which previously he could not master. Many inhibited creative impulses now finally find expression through a systematic method of concentrating the attention.

The actor rehearses part of his role. He squeezes out of himself all the emotion he can; blows the roof off his head; overplays pitifully; feeling all the while the inadequacy and falsity of his acting. He becomes enraged at himself and at the director, quits in disgust, and then begins the whole agonizing process over again. Stop such an actor at a pathetic spot in the scene and suggest that he minutely examine the button on his colleague's jacket. Have him note its color and shape. Then have him observe the way the man has combed his hair. When the actor is completely engrossed in these observations say to him, "You may now resume playing at exactly the point where we stopped." You will marvel at the instant change in the actor. He'll come to life, gain in color, and sensitive, genuine emotion will appear as from nowhere. This is one method of eliminating an impasse but it does not always work. Obstacles to free creativeness do not always arise from lack of concentration. Apparently there is another handicap which inhibits the actor.

2. *Muscular Tension*. One of the very basic requisites for the creative task of the actor is the free flexibility of his muscular system. This means that for each movement and position of his body, he must use a precise amount of energy; no more and no less.

This proper distribution of the energy throughout the body, which is unconsciously done in his daily life, often manages to disappear when the actor goes on stage. He finds himself full of muscular tensions. Since the nervous and muscular systems are in such close coordination this tension causes much of the nervous agitation which often plagues the actor at openings or troubles him in the course of performance. The resulting effect is woodenness in the actor and the loss of all rhythm or plasticity of movement through nervous constriction of the muscles.

If the actor concentrates his attention on various objects and persons he loses a good deal of his initial nervousness and fear. This gradually loosens up the muscular tension.

However, the inverse process is also possible. If the actor frees himself from the muscular tension it will be easier for him to overcome his nervousness, which in turn will help his concentration on the whole stage problem. The director should immediately point out to the actor the danger of wasted motions and whenever the existence of muscular tensions becomes noticeable the director should warn the actor, "Relax your face, your forehead, or your neck," so that the actor, freeing himself from pressure, will at the same time feel free of oppressive barriers to creative work.

3. *The absence of justification.* The creative activity of the actor is possible only if all his stage environment, including the play and its development, has reality for him. Everything on the stage must have an established significance; every passage, the time element, every prop, every bit of the set, every minor and major characterization, every word, every movement, every sound, every fact, every incident, every trifling detail, must have its *raison d'etre.*

What is this stage truth and how is it known? This quality is primarily based on clarification, motivation. Every action on the stage must spring from a logical motive. This motivation must be in complete accord with the character and situation. A given motive must "feed" the actor; must give him the opportunity of arriving at newer and more distinctive creative images. Different actors playing the same role arrive at this theatric significance by varied routes. One actor playing *Hamlet* will explain his love for Ophelia by one reason; another by another. All of the justifications may be inherent in the Shakespearean script but the tendency is for the actor to select the one closest to his own personality and temperament. In terms of his own ideas he can convert the stage activity into personal conviction. This conviction is the essential quality demanded by his audience.

If, therefore, there is anything at all in the stage business which remains obscure to the actor, as, for instance, why he must say so-and-so to his colleague; why he must assume such-and-such a position; this piece of business must be motivated or the actor cannot create. The lack of conviction in the slightest detail throws the actor off-balance and dangerously threatens his creative functioning. That is why it is so necessary for the director to be sure that nothing remains obscure to the actor, even though it may seem like a thoroughly trivial matter.

4. *The lack of creative "food" may also be the cause of an impasse.* It often appears that the accumulated mass of observations and facts pertinent to the stage problem have been exhausted in past rehearsals. The work has not yet been finished but the raw materials appear to have been consumed. Repetition of yesterday's ideas won't do. The words and ideas have no longer any freshness or stimulus. The rehearsal is at a standstill. The actor has reached an impasse. It is obvious that if the actor ceases to move forward he falls behind rapidly, losing even the ground he has won.

What is the director to do? The best thing is to stop rehearsals completely and look about in search of new "nutritive" material for the actors. To do this he must again encourage the actors to do research in the particular sphere of life pertinent to their characters. It is impossible that the actor should fail to find something new and genuine in the honest pursuit of information concerning his character's background. Then, together with the actors, the director should discuss and reflect upon this new-found information. The newly resulting ideas, in terms of stage technique, will supply the material for continued rehearsals.

5. *The attempts of the actor to enact emotions.* The first suspicion a director has of the attempt on the part of an actor to give an imitation of self-styled, superimposed emotion should be a warning to him to stop this actor immediately. The best way is to give him a specific task to perform.

6. *When falsehood creeps in.* Often the creative impasse arises in the actor as a result of seemingly unimportant falsehoods which creep in unnoticed by the director. Let a falsehood reveal itself in some trivial detail, such as a physical bit of business, and a lot of disastrous results will follow. One falsehood drags many in its wake. The existence of even a slight untruth is symptomatic of the fact that a true feeling of conviction is not present in the actor. And if this conviction is lacking he cannot create.

This is why we stress the need for the director to remove every possible shred of doubt from the mind of the actor. This is why

Stanislavski attaches such significance to the execution of the slightest physical task. It is actually through the fulfillment of these simple tasks that the feeling of conviction is best fortified. Having established a command over these simple tasks the actor is in a position to grasp complicated psychological problems. A contempt on the part of a director for these simple tasks is, to say the least, very harmful.

Sometimes the actor fakes in some small detail. The director hesitates to stop him, thinking, "I'll remind him of it later." He knows that they will soon come to a scene on which they will need a good workout. He is saving the time for this precious scene! This is incorrect. The very artistic truth he wants to preserve in the future scenes is being choked in the present one. He will find it necessary, when he has reached this future scene, to go back and correct the initial error, to remove the cause of the dishonesty.

This is a basic principle for directors. *It is never worth-while to proceed until unquestionable honesty of execution has been attained in a given bit.* It should not irk the director that he may have to spend one or two rehearsals on some elusive phrase. The loss of time will be more than compensated. Having spent two rehearsals on seemingly trivial details, the director will be surprised at the facility with which the actor will go through the subsequent scenes. Having understood this particular artistic necessity the actors will quickly grasp every new instruction and execute it with truth and vigor.

Always avoid a procedure in which the director runs through the script "any old way" allowing many falsehoods to creep into the interpretations, hoping to undo present mistakes on some vague future occasion. What a pitiful delusion! The point remains that a falsehood will entrench itself just as firmly as a truth. It is particularly hard to root out a falsehood which has sprung from a questionable source in the actor's consciousness and gained strength by repetition. Repeat only what is true, at all times. It may not yet be entirely clear and sharp but that is no cause for worry. Expressiveness, brilliance, and polish can be cultivated at rehearsals if the basic actions are true.

Now we have arrived at certain basic principles concerning the creative status of the actor, the violation of which will result in an intellectual and artistic impasse. Consistent concentration on the part of the actor; muscular relaxation; examination of motives; the knowledge of actual life and the flexibility of the actor's imagination in terms of this knowledge; the execution of actual stage problems and the harmonious relationship with his fellow-actors which flows out of these; the need for artistic conviction. All these, together, are the corollary to the creative status of the actor. The absence of even one factor will soon mean the loss of most of the others. They are all closely related. Without concentrated attention there is no muscular freedom; no feeling of conviction. The admission of even a slight untruth detracts from the ability to concentrate and hence from the fulfillment of the stage tasks to follow.

The director must determine, in each specific instance, exactly what stress is needed to preserve the actor's creative status. He must hammer away at that weakness which is most dangerous to the whole plan. It is sometimes necessary to keep reminding the actor of the object of his concentration; sometimes to warn him of possible muscular tension; sometimes to further clarify the dramatic motivation; to prevent the actor from trying to simulate an emotion and to set him at work, instead, on a stage problem. Sometimes it is necessary to work hard in eliminating misconceptions and falsehoods that somehow find their way into the actor's subconscious. The director must, in each case, give the correct diagnosis. He must find the glaring mistake, the basic cause of the creative impasse. He must be able to put his finger on the weak link if he expects to mend the chain.

From all this it is clear how carefully the director must treasure the actor as the material of his art; what understanding, what keenness and discernment he must apply to him. All these qualities will evolve naturally if the director loves and values the actor; if he forces nothing mechanically onto the scene; if he remains unsatisfied up to the perfection point where the expression of the actor attains inner and artistic truth.

STANISLAVSKI
TO HIS PLAYERS

At the first rehearsal of THE BLUE BIRD

I AM HAPPY THAT you received *The Blue Bird* so enthusiastically when you read it today. In a few days we will begin to study the play in preparation for rehearsal, and will produce it at the beginning of next season, that is in October or November. Not only Moscow will watch us but our beloved and gifted author, Mr. Maeterlinck, may perhaps honor us by attending the first performance. We must justify the confidence which he has placed in us. Could anyone think of greater encouragement for the work before us? We know how great and responsible a work this is.

There are three main difficulties to be overcome. First of all, we must express on the stage the inexpressible; Maeterlinck's thoughts and feelings are so elusive and subtle that they can be transmitted across the footlights only if we, artists, regisseurs, painters, musicians, decorators, machinists, electricians, penetrate as deeply as possible into the author's mysticism, and create on the stage a suitable atmosphere irresistible to the public. Second, the sensibilities of the public are not ready to receive and comprehend abstract thoughts and feelings. Third, we have to personify sleep, a dream, a presentiment, a fairy tale. This is lace work, woven of fine threads like a cobweb, while the scenic means of modern stage technique are coarse and clumsy.

I shall let my imagination play with the impression made by this poetic creation, and with its different themes: what the author himself means, with what impressions the public will leave the theatre, and how to get those impressions.

To begin with the main theme, the author's idea. Man is surrounded by the mysterious, the awful, the beautiful, the unintelligible. These mysterious intangible things fall upon something young and vital and frail and quivering, or cover with snow the hopelessly blind, or astonish and dazzle us with their beauty. We are drawn toward the mysterious, we have forebodings, but we do not comprehend. At times, in exalted moments, our eyes perceive barely visible contours beyond the clouds of reality.

Man by his animal nature is coarse, cruel, and conceited. He kills his own kind, he devours animals, he destroys nature, and believes that everything was created for his caprice. He reigns on the earth and hence thinks he understands the mystery of the universe. In reality he knows very little. The most important things are hidden from man. Thus he lives absorbed in material blessings, getting farther and farther from spiritual, contemplative life.

Spiritual happiness is given to only a few of the elect. They strain to hear the rustling of the blade of grass in its growth and to see the phantom-like outlines of worlds invisible to us. Having caught a glimpse and a sound of the world mysteries, they are greeted with the wide open eyes and distrustful smile with which men look upon geniuses. Thus centuries go by and the rumbling of cities deadens the sound of the growing blade. The smoke of the factories hides the beauty of the world from us; manufactured luxury blinds us; plastered ceilings separate us from the sky and the stars. We are stifled and look for happiness in the stench and smoke of the life we have created for ourselves. Sometimes we attain real happiness, out in the open fields in the sunshine. But this happiness, like the blue bird, becomes black as soon as we enter the shadow of the ill-smelling town.

Children are nearer to nature, from which they came not so long ago. They love contemplation. They are able to love toys and cry on parting with them. They enter into the life of an ant, a birch tree, a little dog, or a kitten. They are capable of great joys and pure dreams. That is why Maeterlinck, in *The Blue Bird,* has surrounded himself with children to undertake the journey through mysterious worlds. He succeeded perfectly in this world of children's fantasies, horrors and dreams. Let us, too, attempt to turn back to youth.

The production of *The Blue Bird* must be made with the purity of fantasy of a ten-year-old child. It must be naive, simple, light, full of the joy of life, cheerful and imaginative like the sleep of a child; as beautiful as a child's dream and at the same time majestic as the ideal of a poetic genius and thinker.

Let *The Blue Bird* in our theatre thrill the grandchildren and arouse serious thoughts and deep feelings in their grandparents. Let the grandchildren on coming home from the theatre feel the joy of existence with which Tyltyl and Mytyl are possessed in the last act of the play. At the same time let their grandparents once more before their impending death become inspired with the natural desire of man: to enjoy God's world and be glad that it is beautiful. Let the old people scrape off from their souls the scum that has befogged them, and look attentively into a dog's eyes and caress it as a sign of gratitude for its dog-fidelity to man. Over there in the quiet of the sleeping town, perhaps, they will feel in their souls the distant land of memory in which they will soon be slumbering.

If man were always able to love, to understand, to delight in nature! If he contemplated more often, if he reflected on the mysteries of the world, and took thought of the eternal! Then perhaps the blue bird would be flying freely among us.

I believe the author will be gratified if we convey a hundredth part of this impression to our audience, but how can we do this with a thousand-fold public? The Moscow theatre public is usually late for the performance, enters the hall noisily, looks for a seat for some time and settles itself gradually amid a rustling of clothes and programs. Such a crowd will frighten away the mood of Maeterlinck's phantoms, deaden the fluttering spirit of the mysterious, and disturb the dream of the beautiful child's sleep. People will not be carried away at once and quiet down. First of all they will have to shake off the daily worries which they bring with them to the theatre in their minds and their tired nerves. Thus will the first act pass.

Yet not a single word of Maeterlinck's play must be lost. It is necessary to get the attention of the public at once without waiting for the development of the play to draw them away from their cares.

Formerly this was attained by simple means. In the days of our grandfathers they did not quiet the audience, they produced an artificial cheerfulness with an orchestra which played a deafening march or a polka with castanets. Then the play and the actors were different, and the decorations and costumes bright and loud. Everything acted sharply on the sight, the hearing, and the primitive imagination of the spectator. Now both the purpose and the manner of seizing hold of the spectator have changed, and the old theatrical manner no longer satisfies. The theatre does not wish to amuse the public under the guise of diversion, it has more important aims.

The author and the artist use the theatre as a means of conveying noble pictures and thoughts. Through it the poet Maeterlinck sings his liturgy and Ibsen the thinker preaches the freedom of the human spirit.

Everything abstract is less intelligible to the middle class public and therefore our task is more complicated, but happily we have new means of expression more effective than the old methods. The theatre has become strong through the cooperation of representatives of all the arts and crafts of the stage, and their creation is irresistible. We do not need striking decorations or costumes; exquisite paintings and materials in subdued tones take their place. Old, straight-laced actors with wheezing voices are replaced by modest people of culture and quiet manner. They do not need to go to the extreme of what they feel, for it is only to the stupid that you have to explain everything in words. The regisseurs have learned to bring into common harmony all the creative elements of the performance, and in this harmony lies the strength of the theatre. Therefore we shall attempt to win the audience at the rise of the curtain.

The leading role in the ensemble belongs to you artists. In order to make the public listen to the fine shades of your feelings you have to experience them intensely yourself. To live through definite intelligible feelings is easier than to live through the subtle soul vibrations of a poetic nature. To reach them it is necessary to dig deep into the material which is handed to you for creation. To the study of the play we shall devote jointly a great deal of work and attention and love. But that is little. In addition you have to prepare yourselves independently.

I speak of your personal life, observation which will broaden your imagination and sensitiveness. Make friends of children. Enter into their world. Watch nature and her manifestations surrounding us. Make friends of dogs and cats and look oftener into their eyes to see their souls. You will be doing the same as Maeterlinck did before writing the play, and you will come closer to the author.

Just now I cannot stop longer on this most important point, the work of the artists, to which we shall devote many sittings and rehearsals. I must hurry on to that part of the production the realization of which does not permit of delay. I mean the decorative, the musical, the electro-technical and other phases of the work for which the craftsmen are waiting.

More than anything else, we must avoid theatricalism in the external presentation of *The Blue Bird* as well as in the spiritual interpretation, for it might change the fairy dream of the poet into an ordinary extravaganza. In this regard, the play is all the time balancing on the edge of a knife. The text pulls the play in one direction and the author's remarks in another. We must look at these remarks with particular attention and understand in them the hidden plot and intention of the author. The ordinary conventional approach to executing these remarks will inevitably bring theatricalness which will convert the play into extravaganza.

In every extravaganza the walls assume fantastic contours, and the public knows perfectly well that this is accomplished by transparencies and gauzes. In each ballet the dancers spring out from the parting scenery. Their gauze costumes have a similarity just like soldiers' uniforms. A hundred times we have seen the transformation of Faust and we know that his costume is pulled down from him through a hole in the floor. We are weary of transparent halls with running children. What can be more horrible than a child as theatrical supernumerary?

All these effects carried out literally according to the remarks of the author will kill the seriousness and the mystic solemnity of the work of the poet and thinker. All the given directions are important for the substance of the play and they should be carried out—not by old theatrical means, but by new ones, by better ones which the latest technique of the stage has invented.

The same applies to the costumes. On this question I am undecided. To be sure I understand the poet's purpose. Here, too, he is looking for the primitive imagination of a child. But he is unquestionably mistaken. On the stage before the footlights such costumes will become vulgar and offensive. Instead of wandering souls we shall get costumed masqueraders and again the serious and graceful performance will be changed into extravaganza.

Will it not be better if these souls fly like constellations around the wandering children? This may be attained by very simple means and the illusion made complete. The human figure can be given ingenious forms. The actors will be seen in full light and walk on their own legs although neither feet nor body, up to the chest, will be seen by the audience. They will be souls in the shape of heads with the arms flying in the air.

Every surprise on the stage, applied at the right time and place, rouses the audience from its usual attitude and gives an illusion of reality. To avoid theatricalness, surprises are necessary in setting as well as in scenic tricks. The so-called luxurious *mise-en-scène* of an extravaganza consists in its motley and complex character; therefore let us look for something less complex in character and more simple and interesting to the artistic imagination.

222

For instance one of our artists is interested in children's work in the field of painting. He has gathered together a whole collection of drawings, showing how simply and how effectively children invent clouds and other natural phenomena. Let these drawings serve us as material for sketching the settings. I think our imagination will become younger through the influence of the child's creative spirit. The decorations must be naive, simple, light and unexpected, just like children's imaginations. Above all, there must be no suggestion of the theatrical.

It is impossible to get along without music in Maeterlinck's play. The music serves an unusual purpose; otherwise it would bring discord in the ensemble. We have tried several times to apply music to drama on our stage, and find that this domain, too, has a conventionality and theatricalness of its own. I shall not attempt to judge the use of music elsewhere but our own experiments in this regard have been sufficiently convincing.

Symphonic music with a fine orchestra in which an accustomed ear can distinguish the familiar sound of the violin, oboe, etc. tends to weaken rather than to increase the illusion of drama. It pulls the drama toward opera and concert or recital. Our musician and composer has invented other combinations of sounds, beautiful and unexpected to the ear. In *The Blue Bird* his imagination has an unlimited field. It is a pity that we are obliged to give him definite directions regarding those parts of the play which will require a musical accompaniment. The very substance of the performance will make these indications clear.

But our first step in this great work is to live in the play. Hence, to work!

This translation of an informal address delivered by Stanislavski in 1908, is arranged by Lucie R. Sayler.